C000218215

Royal
Champion

Queen Elizabeth, the Queen Mother presents the Queen's Vase to the Queen at Royal Ascot, 1979.

Royal Champion

The Story of Steeplechasing's First Lady

Bill Curling

LONDON
MICHAEL JOSEPH

Also by Bill Curling

BRITISH RACECOURSES

THE CAPTAIN: A BIOGRAPHY OF
CAPTAIN SIR CECIL BOYD-ROCHFORT

THE GRAND NATIONAL (WITH CLIVE GRAHAM)

DERBY DOUBLE: THE UNIQUE STORY OF
RACEHORSE TRAINER ARTHUR BUDGETT

ALL THE QUEEN'S HORSES

First published in Great Britain by
Michael Joseph Limited
44 Bedford Square, London WC1
1980

© 1980 by Bill Curling

All Rights Reserved. No part of this publication may
be reproduced, stored in a retrieval system, or
transmitted, in any form or by any means, electronic,
mechanical, photocopying, recording or otherwise,
without the prior permission of the Copyright owner

ISBN 0 7181 1930 4

Filmset and printed in Great Britain by
BAS Printers Limited, Over Wallop, Hampshire
and bound by Dorstel Press, Harlow.

Contents

List of Colour Plates

Acknowledgements

I wish to thank Her Majesty Queen Elizabeth the Queen Mother most sincerely for her encouragement in writing this book and for allowing the reproduction of pictures from Clarence House of her steeplechasers.

I must also thank, in particular, Colonel Sir Martin Gilliat, Private Secretary to Queen Elizabeth, who has kept records of the racing careers of Queen Elizabeth's steeplechasers and has been a fount of information on racing matters. I am most grateful to Peter Biegel who has generously allowed me to reproduce his sketch of Laffy, which so beautifully compliments the paintings in Clarence House. I must also thank Lord Abergavenny, Queen Elizabeth's former Racing Manager; Edward Cazalet, eldest son of Peter Cazalet, Queen Elizabeth's principal trainer for nearly a quarter of a century; Michael Oswald, Manager of the Royal Studs; Brigadier A. D. R. Wingfield, a former Manager of the Royal Studs; Fulke Walwyn, Queen Elizabeth's present principal trainer; Jack O'Donoghue; Mr and Mrs Ken Oliver, William Hastings-Bass and Captain Richard Head, who have also trained some of Queen Elizabeth's horses.

The men who have ridden Queen Elizabeth's horses over a period of thirty years have all been most helpful and have added greatly to the book. They include T. W. Biddlecombe, A. Branford, R. J. Dennard, D. V. Dick, D. B. Evatt, R. Francis, A. Freeman, N. Gaselee, A. Grantham, E. F. Kelly, R. McCreery, B. Marshall, D. Mould, D. Nicholson, Lord Oaksey, G. W. Robinson, M. Scudamore, W. Smith and C. Tinkler. I have also had great help from Jim Fairgrieve, an accomplished versifier and headman to Peter Cazalet throughout the post-war period, and other members of the Fairlawne staff, members of Walwyn's staff at Saxon House, Lambourn, and of the Royal Studs at Sandringham and Wolferton.

I have found Ivor Herbert's book *The Queen Mother's Horses* and Dick Francis's book *The Sport of Queens* most helpful. I also wish to thank a large number of people who have helped me, including: R. Aird, I. A. Balding, Captain E. N. C. Beaumont, G. H. Beeby, Miss R. Bennett, W. A. Benson, Captain H. Birkbeck, Sir Cecil Boyd-Rochfort, Lord Cadogan, Mrs P. Cazalet, T. G. R. Cook, Captain R. H. Conrage, Captain W. Crosbie Dawson, Mrs G. Digby Whitehead, A. Gaselee, Lord Glentoran, N. R. H. Graham, Major W. R. Hern, Captain P. M. L. Hibbert-Foy, J. Irwin, Sir David Llewellyn, Captain J. M. G. Lumsden, M. J. Masson, Mrs J. Mildmay-White, Lady Mount Charles, M. Parkhill, Major C. Price, K. Rose, R. Scott, Major R. Seymour, Mrs G. H. Smith, Sir Charles Strong, Miss M. Tinniswood, H. E. Whiteman, R. S. Wilkins, B. E. Wilkinson, Major E. W. O. Wilson and N. C. Wright.

I wish to thank the Editor-in-Chief of *The Daily Telegraph* for permission to quote from the outstanding reports of John Oaksey on steeplechasing battles of the past and the Library staff of *The Daily Telegraph* for their help with research. I am indebted to The Editor of the *Sporting Life* for permission to quote from his contributors John Bliss and Jack Logan, and the Editor of *The Times* for permission to quote from the leader on Lord Mildmay.

Finally I wish to thank my wife who has been through the text, noticed mistakes, and made suggestions.

Black and white illustrations— Photographers' credits

The author and publishers are most grateful to Queen Elizabeth for the loan of many of her photographs, including No. 55 which was taken by Princess Margaret; to Mr Edward Cazalet for the loan of his set of the Fairlawne training records for Queen Elizabeth's horses from which many of the early photographs have been taken, and to those members of the Fairlawne staff who have not already been thanked: Frank Chapman, John Hole, Alex King and Sam Manktelow.

George Selwyn: frontispiece, 93, 95, 102, 103, 107, 108, 109, 110, endpiece
Bernard Thorpe Ltd.: 2
Reuter: 3, 50
Fox Photos: 5, 40, 41
Associated Press: 6
Daily Mirror: 9
Sport & General Press Agency Ltd.: 10, 14, 22, 24, 27, 61, 64, 65, 67, 69, 73, 74, 82, 89, 98, 100
Central Press Agency Ltd.: 23, 34, 35, 42, 54, 71, 77, 85, 86, 87, 88
Primrose Productions Ltd.: 28
Lynn News and Advertiser: 38
Daily Express: 47
Ruck Press Services: 48
Keystone: 53
Geo. P. King: 68
Bernard Parkin: 75, 81, 94, 99, 104
Kendal Photographic Co.: 76
Bespix: 79, 80
Kenneth Bright: 83
Gerry Cranham: 84, 96, 97
Foto-Call: 90
Desmond O'Neill: 91
Reading Evening Post: 92
Provincial Press: 101
W. W. Rouch: 105
John Grant: 111

Introduction

THIS IS the story of the steeplechasers and the hurdlers of Her Majesty Queen Elizabeth, the Queen Mother, of the men who have ridden them, trained them, bred them and cared for them. Steeplechasing has gained enormously in popularity in the last thirty years, and if there is any one person responsible for this immense increase in prestige, it is Queen Elizabeth, who has championed steeplechasing steadfastly throughout the period. Not only has Her Majesty been an owner since 1949 and won over three hundred and thirty races, but she has taken a close interest in the breeding side and has herself bred a couple of top class chasers; she has supported strongly the Injured Jockeys Fund from its early beginnings, she has come to many of the big meetings, opened stands, presented cups to winning owners—and has sometimes received cups herself for the successes of her own horses. She has even encouraged the National Hunt jockeys to play cricket, and the colours of their cricket XI, by Her Majesty's gracious permission, are her own racing colours.

The Kings and Queens of Great Britain have usually supported flat racing from before the days of Queen Elizabeth I. Steeplechasing as an organised sport is much younger in origin. 1830 is the date of the first St Albans Steeplechase, and it can be said that steeplechasing has taken place regularly now for a century and a half with the exception of certain years of war. In that one hundred and fifty years, no other member of the Royal Family has given such devoted support to steeplechasing as Queen Elizabeth. It is true that King Edward VII, first as Prince of Wales and then as King, supported steeplechasing for a quarter of a century, having his first runner in the Grand National in 1884 and his last in 1908, but from 1886, when, as Prince of Wales, he founded the Sandringham Stud, his heart was principally in flat racing. Steeplechasing, therefore, has had no other Royal champion like Queen Elizabeth, and nowhere else in the world is steeplechasing supported so strongly now as it is in Britain.

Whereas most Derby winners have been bred in the studs of rich men, many of the best steeplechasers come from the homes of those who can perhaps only afford a couple of brood-mares and send those mares to stallions standing at very modest fees. One of the best of Queen Elizabeth's steeplechasers was bred by a Norfolk publican out of a mare he bought to hunt, another by the wife of a Northumberland farmer from a mare she saved from the kennels and a third from a mare which a recently retired soldier had bought to hunt and point-to-point.

The steeplechasers of Queen Elizabeth's own breeding have clearly given their owner particular pleasure, for she has known them from their earliest days and, when based at Sandringham, has watched their progress keenly. As with flat racing, there is no comparison between a horse bought at auction with ability already clear to a home-bred one known and nurtured from its earliest days. With steeplechasing, however, there is a very long time between seed time and harvest, between the time the mare is safely in foal and the progeny runs in its first steeplechase perhaps six years later.

Queen Elizabeth as an owner of steeplechasers and hurdlers has had over sixty different horses which have won races for her. I have tried in this book to tell the stories of the best of them and to ignore some of those of small account. Queen Elizabeth on the whole has not had as much luck as she deserves in most of the big races, but she has had the thrill of seeing most of her favourite horses in action and has seen many of their triumphs. Steeplechasing is a dangerous sport for horse and rider, and Her Majesty, like all steeplechase owners, has had some very bad moments amongst the good ones. As one would expect, she has taken the bad moments in her stride.

I should like to place on record, having done research on this book amongst many people, that Queen Elizabeth has always seemed to find time to show herself considerate alike to trainer, rider, head lad, stableman, blacksmith, stud groom, stud hand, and all connected with her horses. Perhaps because Her Majesty is always so giving of herself, everyone in racing loves her for it. As a humble racing scribe, I hope I am allowed to say that I am among the many who are full of admiration.

I

Early Days at Fairlawne

QUEEN ELIZABETH'S active interest in steeplechasing stems from Ascot week in 1949, when among the guests staying at Windsor Castle for the Royal Ascot meeting was the 2nd Lord Mildmay of Flete, the leading amateur rider of the day, who had twice come near to winning the Grand National and was then the most popular figure in the world of steeplechasing. His horses were trained with much success at Fairlawne near Sevenoaks in Kent by his close friend Peter Cazalet.

As the Second World War ended, the Royal Stud was beginning to flourish again after a lean spell and King George VI won the One Thousand Guineas of 1946 with his home-bred filly Hypericum, watched by his elder daughter, the then Princess Elizabeth. The whole house party at Windsor in June 1949 were thrilled to see another top class Royal filly, Avila, win the Coronation Stakes at Ascot from a big field. The King had recovered well from an operation to the circulation in his right leg two months before and, seated in the Royal Box, was able to see Avila win. With a successful stud, it was natural that the King should concentrate on flat racing, but would it not be rather fun, suggested Lord Mildmay, after Avila's success, for the Queen to branch out on her own and have a horse in training for jumping? Anthony Mildmay was an enthusiast and a man of great charm and his words did not fall on barren ground. Her Majesty decided that she and Princess Elizabeth would like to have a jumper in training between them. She asked Lord Mildmay to act as her racing manager and to look out for a suitable horse, and she readily agreed that it should be trained, like all Mildmay's horses, by Cazalet at Fairlawne.

The choice of Cazalet as a trainer was a natural one for the Queen, for apart from the Royal Family's friendship with Lord Mildmay, Her Majesty had known the Cazalet family since girlhood days when she had been to stay at Fairlawne with her contemporary, Thelma Cazalet. Cazalet and the King's principal flat racing trainer, Captain Sir Cecil Boyd-Rochfort, were also friends and Cazalet, in fact, had already trained a winner of the King's breeding in Billposter, a very difficult customer with whom Boyd-Rochfort could no nothing and who, as a last resort, had been sent to Cazalet to see if he could make a hurdler of him. The King's flat racers

1   Queen Elizabeth (on right) on her first visit to Fairlawne in 1912 with Thelma Cazalet, now Mrs Cazalet-Keir.

were then all in training at Newmarket, a busy bustling racing town on the borders of Cambridgeshire and Suffolk. Fairlawne, a lovely William and Mary country house, built in part of grey Kentish ragstone and in part of brick, stood on its own, surrounded by lawns, borders, trees and parkland, a mile out of the Kentish village of Shipbourne. The stables, built by Peter Cazalet's grandfather Edward in the 1870s, were hidden from the house on lower ground. Below them were a lake and water gardens, and from nearby ran a secret underground passage to Ightham Mote, a beautiful moated house, partly dating to the fourteenth century. The contrast between Fairlawne and Boyd-Rochfort's yard on the main Bury St Edmunds Road could not have been more marked.

Fairlawne was an unexpected place in which to find a training stable. It was, in fact, the brain child of Peter Cazalet, who had caught the racing bug in his university days at Oxford at the end of the 1920s. Prior to university, Peter Cazalet had not been keen on horses. He happened to be a very good schoolboy cricketer, making a century for Eton in the Eton v Harrow match at Lord's. At Oxford he won blues for cricket, racquets, real tennis and squash. He played cricket regularly for Kent, and had reluctantly declined an invitation to captain the county side.

The Cazalets were a family of Basque origin who came to England originally as Huguenot refugees and to Fairlawne over a century ago in 1871. Peter Cazalet was the youngest of three brothers. The eldest, Edward, had been killed in the First World War, the second, Victor, was a

Conservative M.P. of independent mind and high ideals, whilst his only sister, Thelma Cazalet-Keir, has become in 1931 one of the first women M.P.s in the House of Commons just at the time her younger brother Peter was starting to train horses at Fairlawne.

William Cazalet, Peter's father, was horse-minded, too. He had started a thoroughbred stud at Puttenden on the outskirts of the Fairlawne estate before the First World War, and since the middle of that war had horses in training at Manton near Marlborough on the Wiltshire Downs, first with Alec Taylor, one of the outstanding trainers of his day, and then with his successor Joe Lawson. His colours had first come to the fore in 1918 when Prince Chimay had unexpectedly defeated the great Gainsborough in the Jockey Club Stakes and Air Raid had won the 1918 Cesarewitch. They were to the fore again in 1930 when Paradine was second in the Two Thousand Guineas and when Shell Transport won the Exeter Stakes at Newmarket.

The year of 1930 was one of decision for Peter Cazalet for, after showing little interest in horses until his university days, he had started to support the University Drag, encouraged by Henry Douglas-Home and like-minded friends, and had taken part in the university 'grinds'. In 1930, he rode his first winner under National Hunt rules.

The trainer to which amateur riders were often attracted in those days was 'Sonny' Hall whose stables were at Fenny Compton on the borders of Oxfordshire and Warwickshire. Hall, with his bow tie and the cigarette he was apt to suck stuck in his mouth, was easily identifiable on the racecourse. He was the selling-plate king of the chasing world and he used some of his considerable brains in placing his horses to great advantage. An Easter Monday with eight winners at different meetings was a Red Letter Day, and he was a man from whom any would-be trainer had much to learn. It was Hall who found for Cazalet a chaser called Youtell, on which, in 1930, the young man from Fairlawne defeated some of the leading professionals in a steeplechase at Manchester.

Harry Whiteman, whose father had trained for the Brocklehurst family and others near his Herefordshire home, was Sonny Hall's hard-working right-hand man and, in 1932, Peter Cazalet obtained permission from his father to forsake his business career and start a stable at Fairlawne with Harry Whiteman as the trainer of the horses owned by himself and his friends. William Cazalet, in fact, gave the scheme his clear blessing by removing his flat racers from famous Manton and bringing them back to Fairlawne for Whiteman to train.

Sadly, a few months later William Cazalet died suddenly of a heart attack, but by that time Fairlawne as a training stable was established. The stables formerly used for coaching horses and hunters, now held racehorses. Schooling fences had been built in the park below the house, a dirt track was made in fields below Shipbourne church where horses could exercise when the ground was hard and Chilhams on the opposite side of the road running past the Fairlawne gates was also laid out as an exercise ground.

A month before William Cazalet died on a September day in 1932, Peter Cazalet appropriately rode his own horse Youtell to victory at Colwall Park—the first Fairlawne winner with over 1200 to follow. Cazalet, in only his second season riding under rules, had ended up seventh in the amateur riders' list. Jack Fawcus from the north, Fred Thrackray, and George Owen from Cheshire had been the three leading amateurs that season, followed by Alec Marsh, the future Jockey Club starter, the soldier riders Sir Peter Grant-Lawson and Captain Cecil Brownhill, and then Peter Cazalet, Robin Mount, and Peter Payne-Gallwey. Fawcus, Owen and Payne-Gallwey, in addition to Cazalet, were all to make their marks as trainers after the Second World War.

In its first season as a training stable, Fairlawne had three runners in the 1933 Grand National—the stockbroker Edward Paget on Egremont, on whom he had been second the previous year, Cazalet on the 1932 winner Shaun Goilin on whom he completed the National course, and Anthony Mildmay on Youtell. For the next four years, there were always to be two or more Grand National runners from Fairlawne, Cazalet himself riding in the race on four occasions without luck, but Mildmay was very unlucky not to win the 1936 Grand National on Davy Jones. When Cazalet was forced to give up race-riding after smashing his left wrist in a fall at

Sandown, Fairlawne as a training centre was firmly established, and in the National Hunt season before the war Cazalet himself took over the stable from Whiteman. Mildmay, now based on his estate at Shoreham near Fairlawne, was well in the saddle as one of the leading amateur riders.

This, therefore, was the stable Queen Elizabeth decided to support in her first venture in steeplechasing. It had revived quickly after the Second World War though Peter Cazalet had suffered severly in it. His first wife Leonora, step-daughter of the novelist P. G. Wodehouse, had died after an operation, and his only remaining brother, Victor, was killed in an air-crash off Gibraltar in which General Sikorski, the Prime Minister of Poland and Commander-in-Chief of the Free Polish Forces, also died. Peter Cazalet and Anthony Mildmay, both serving in the Welsh Guards, had survived unharmed during the bitter fighting in Normandy, and when they came back lost no time in getting into racing harness again.

There had been no steeplechasing in Britain in the latter half of the Second World War but, as the Irish Free State had remained neutral throughout the war, steeplechasing had continued there and there were plenty of Irish horses to be bought to get steeplechasing going again in Britain. When the Queen and Princess Elizabeth decided to join forces,

3 Peter Cazalet (right) on Rideo and Anthony Mildmay on Cromwell riding work in the Park at Fairlawne in 1948.

Fairlawne had already taken its place amongst the leading half-dozen jumping stables in Britain with Anthony Mildmay, then Cazalet's principal owner, far ahead of his fellow amateur riders. Fairlawne's chief training rivals were then Fulke Walwyn's Saxon House stable at Lambourn on the Berkshire Downs, the stable of Major J. B. Powell at Aldbourne on the Wiltshire Downs between Lambourn and Marlborough, Fred Rimell at Kinnersley in Worcestershire, George Owen near Malpas in Cheshire, Major John Goldsmith and George Beeby on the Berkshire Downs north of Newbury, and the Yorkshire trainers Neville Crump, Bobby Renton, Jack Fawcus and Charlie Hall. Miss Dorothy Paget, training with Walwyn, had the biggest string of jumpers. Lord Bicester, who supported Beeby, Mrs L. Brotherton with Renton, Mr P. G. Thompsom with Goldsmith, Anthony Mildmay who had just succeeded his father to the title, and Mr Clifford Nicholson, who trained partly at home in Lincolnshire and partly with Hall, were all among the leading owners.

There were between thirty and forty horses in training at Fairlawne when the Queen and Princess Elizabeth joined Cazalet's other owners, who then included the present Lord Abergavenny and his father, Sir John Carew-Pole from the West Country, Mr C. S. Crawley, with whom Cazalet used to play racquets, Mr A. S. Gaselee, Master of the West Kent, who lived nearby at Hamptons, Mr Edward Paget, his earliest supporter, who also lived nearby, Mr F. C. Penney who came to be known as Mr Lucky Penney, the Holland-Martin brothers from Worcestershire, and Colonel G. R. Westmacott, a family friend and a contemporary of Victor Cazalet.

Tony Grantham, son of the well-known Sussex horse dealer Tommy Grantham, was stable jockey. Tony Grantham and Ryan Price were point-to-pointing rivals in the south shortly before the outbreak of the Second World War. Grantham had first made his mark at the end of 1946 as an amateur at a Plumpton meeting, where he nearly landed a hat-trick. He had then turned professional and, after seeing him ride again at Plumpton in the spring, Cazalet, encouraged by Lord Abergavenny, had rung him up to ask him to be the Fairlawne stable jockey. Cazalet had already saddled between thirty and forty winners that season so it did not take Grantham long to accept, and down in the West Country in May, riding for his new stable for the first time, he won three races in three weeks on Prince Paramount. The retainer was sealed.

In the same month that Grantham came to join Fairlawne, there arrived from Newmarket on April Fool's Day, 1947, the first Royal horse—Billposter. He was a big good-looking chestnut colt by William of Valence out of Canvas, a mare who traced back to King George V's 1928 One Thousand Guineas winner, Scuttle. He was therefore well-bred but a menace at Newmarket. Captain Charles Moore, Manager of the King's

Studs, thought that a course of jumping might make him mend his ways. At Newmarket, if he was prepared to work at all, he would stop in the middle of a gallop as if he had been shot, leaving his rider no chance of staying aboard.

When Billposter arrived at Fairlawne, he refused to cooperate. Jim Fairgrieve, a Scot from the Borders and Cazalet's head lad and right-hand man after the war, took on the horse. When Fairgrieve, an experienced nagsman who broke nearly all the Fairlawne horses when necessary, got on Billposter's back and tried to ride him, Billposter refused to budge and was wont to turn his head and grab Fairgrieve's foot. It was decided, therefore, that the only solution was to castrate Billposter and to treat him as an unbroken horse and start all over again. However, he was still sticky when ridden. He had his first school over the small hurdles in mid-July, had a set back and was seen by Captain Moore in another school over hurdles in mid August.

It was a dry autumn in 1947 and there were few runners from Fairlawne on the hard ground, but at the October meeting at Folkestone where Cazalet usually had several runners, Billposter made his first appearance on the racecourse. He had been leased to Cazalet in case he should disgrace the Royal colours, and he had only two opponents in the £102 Smeeth Hurdle, but Billposter refused to struggle after jumping the last flight of hurdles, and allowed himself to be beaten by John Goldsmith's London Casino, a very moderate performer.

The only chance seemed to be to try a hood, so to Fontwell Park in Sussex went Billposter nearly a fortnight later. The ground was still hard but the hood worked. Grantham rode a waiting race and Billposter turned Folkestone tables on London Casino. Cazalet took Billposter up to Cheltenham, hoping that he would be good enough to run in the King's name in future, but it was not to be. He went up to the December Sales, changed hands, refused to race for his new owner, and eventually went to the Borders and found his way to Mr W. Murray of Redden, Roxburghshire, who hunted him for several seasons with great success. Cazalet, Mildmay, Grantham, Fairgrieve and a hood had between them got one £102 hurdle race out of the first Royal horse at Fairlawne. Better things were to come in the future.

2

Monaveen

PETER CAZALET married for the second time on the eve of Royal Ascot in 1949. His second wife was Zara, daughter of Sir Harry Mainwaring. She had been married previously to the present Lord Belper who, as Mr R. Strutt, had won the 1934 National Hunt Chase at Cheltenham on Crown Prince. On getting back from their honeymoon, they were thrilled to hear from Lord Mildmay that Her Majesty the Queen and the then Princess Elizabeth together wished to have a jumper in training at Fairlawne.

Three months previously, Tony Grantham had had a chance ride at the last moment in the 1949 Grand National on Monaveen, who had carried him well for a long way in the race. He spoke strongly in favour of Cazalet buying Monaveen, who was then owned by Mr D. Hawkesley, at the time a leading trainer of greyhounds at the London track at West Ham. He was trained at Epsom by Peter Thrale, who had a great reputation as a good judge of a horse and trained many winners both on the flat and over fences. Monaveen's breeder in Ireland was a County Meath farmer, Mr George Flood, who tried to tame Monaveen's spirit by putting him in a milk float to deliver milk to the people of Navan before sending him up to sell at Goffs at the end of his three-year-old days in 1944. At the sale, he only got ninety guineas for Monaveen in spite of the fact that a full sister, Gun Hill, had won on the flat. Mr James Raferty, a County Galway man, bought him, thought highly of him and sent him over to England for Peter Thrale to train. Monaveen, however, would not settle at Epsom, went right off his food and did no good. Raferty lost faith in him and passed him on for a song as a six-year-old to Hawkesley.

It was only when Monaveen started to run in a hood that he began to show his merit. At the end of the 1947–48 season, when he fell three times on different courses, Thrale decided that a long rest and a change of scene were worth trying. When he came back into training in the early autumn of 1948 he began to show real ability. He won a three-mile handicap chase at Kempton Park and carried a ten pounds' penalty to victory a fortnight later in a similar race in heavy going at Lingfield Park.

After these victories, it was decided to enter him in the Grand National, and Thrale hoped that Martin Molony, younger brother of Tim Molony,

and a brilliant jockey, would ride him at Aintree. Unfortunately, in his preliminary race, the Leicester Grand National Trial Chase in February 1949, Monaveen fell two fences from home when leading. Molony broke his arm in a bad fall and put himself out of court for the Grand National. Thrale then engaged for the National the Epsom jockey Vincent Mooney, who had won on the horse at Kempton and Lingfield, but on the first day of Aintree Mooney was also hurt in a fall and Grantham took his place. In fact, Grantham had the leg up on Monaveen for the first time on the morning of Grand National day. In the race itself, the horse jumped brilliantly throughout the first circuit of the course, took the lead going

4 Monaveen (A. Grantham) at Fairlawne in October 1949.

away from the stands for the second time, but at the next open ditch pecked badly, giving Grantham no chance of staying in the saddle. The feel Monaveen had given him was, however, enough for Grantham to recommend Monaveen wholeheartedly to Cazalet.

In due course, Mildmay and Cazalet went over to see Monaveen at Thrale's Epsom yard. The Hawkesleys were not keen to part with him but were persuaded and on 22 July 1949 the Queen's first racehorse arrived at Cazalet's a fortnight before Her Majesty's forty-ninth birthday. 'It was a great day for Fairlawne,' Jim Fairgrieve noted in his diary later, 'as it was the beginning of a long and happy association with Her Majesty Queen Elizabeth the Queen Mother.'

Since running so well in the Grand National, Monaveen had won on firm ground at Folkestone in May and had run well again on firm ground at Fontwell in June. He had shown that he liked Fontwell and did not mind the top of the ground, so it was decided that he would appear quite early in the autumn wearing Princess Elizabeth's newly-registered colours of 'scarlet jacket, purple hooped sleeves and black cap' at the Fontwell October meeting. The Cazalet stable had got off to a flying start to the new season in the West Country and already had a dozen winners to its credit, when Monaveen reappeared, carrying top weight, in the Chichester Handicap Chase. There were only two to take him on on the firm ground—Random Knight from J. M. Gosden's Sussex stable at Lewes

5   Monaveen, led by his lad Frank Chapman, in the parade ring at Fontwell before his first race for his Royal owners on 10 October 1949.

and Martin M, owned by Colonel Walter Skrine, a gallant soldier who had undergone a difficult leg operation so that he could ride Martin M at Aintree, where he had won the Valentine Chase. Skrine could not ride at this October meeting and his place was taken by another soldier, Major 'Monkey' Blacker, now General Sir Cecil Blacker, who was to win the Grand Military Gold Cup a few years later on Pointsman. Princess Elizabeth, with Lord Mildmay and Cazalet beside her, saw Martin M attempting to make all the running, but Grantham was biding his time on Monaveen, who was in need of a race, and in the end he won easily, wearing the big open 'cup' blinkers which he always wore as an aid to concentration. Cazalet and Grantham had learnt early at Fairlawne of their necessity when schooling over fences. Monaveen in fact had given Grantham an ugly fall when schooling without them.

Monaveen, a medium-sized light-framed bright bay gelding with a star on his forehead and excellent bone, was by the sire Landscape Hill, a son of the Derby winner Spion Kop out of a Gainsborough mare. Landscape Hill was the sire of other good jumpers including Lord Mildmay's favourite Cromwell and another of his chasers, Hill Breeze.

The following month, Fairlawne's three sons of Landscape Hill all went up to Aintree to run at the autumn meeting—Cromwell in the Becher Chase, Monaveen in the chief race the Grand Sefton, and Hill Breeze in the Valentine Chase—all three ridden by Grantham. Princess Elizabeth and Princess Margaret both came up by train to Liverpool for the day to see Monaveen run, but he was beaten on merit by Freebooter, an outstanding Grand National winner, who had the size and scope to give away plenty of weight. Monaveen ran really well and led at the last fence but could not hold the relentless Freebooter in the long run-in. Nevertheless, he had again shown that Aintree had no terrors for him and he might well run with credit in the 1950 Grand National. Princess Elizabeth and Princess Margaret, accompanied by Lord Sefton and Lord Derby, stewards of the meeting, watched an exciting race from the roof of the grandstand.

Cazalet's policy once a horse was fit was, in normal circumstances, to keep running him regularly to give his owners fun and to earn his keep. He did not believe in keeping horses in cotton wool at Fairlawne. However, Monaveen showed his races. Nonetheless, after his good showing in the Grand Sefton, it was decided to run him again at Sandown Park near the end of November. Cazalet was laid low with pleurisy and Lord Mildmay was running the stable. Monaveen duly won Sandown's Walton Green Chase, but he was possibly lucky to do so for the chasing mare Salmiana II from Ivor Anthony's famous Wroughton stable had taken the lead from him approaching the last fence, only to fall at it, leaving Monaveen to win at his leisure. No doubt his victory was a better tonic for his stricken trainer than a load of pills!

6 Monaveen (A. Grantham) wearing the colours of Princess Elizabeth, leading Inchmore (R. Curran) at the water in the Grand Sefton Chase at Aintree on 10 November 1949.

By 1948, most jumping courses had been restored to normal after the war. Hurst Park near Hampton Court by the banks of the Thames was an exception. It was to resume jumping, after a lapse of ten years, on the last two days of 1949 and, to commemorate the occasion, Sir John Crocker Bulteel, the clerk of the course, and a relation of Lord Mildmay, instituted a new three-mile handicap chase, named the Queen Elizabeth Chase. It was natural with such a title that the Royal chaser Monaveen should be entered in it, and it attracted most of the best staying chasers in training— Lord Bicester's Roimond, Crump's Wot No Sun, winner of the Emblem Chase at Manchester, Walwyn's Rowland Roy, winner of Kempton's King George VI Chase, Klaxton and Salmiana II from Wroughton, Tom Masson's Cloncarrig, who was to come near to winning a National, and Rimell's Old Mortality, winner of the Great Yorkshire Chase at Doncaster. In such a field, Monaveen was at the foot of the handicap and not much fancied by the public. Princess Elizabeth was now based on Malta as Prince Philip was serving in the destroyer H.M.S. *Chequers* in the Mediterranean Fleet. She was, however, able to fly home to see Monaveen run and then go on to Sandringham to see in the New Year with the King and Queen and her year-old son Prince Charles, whom she had left temporarily with her parents whilst in Malta.

Hurst Park was a sharp right-handed course with the jumping circuit a bare mile in circumference. Monaveen was a bold jumper and a brave horse who was at his best when making running or disputing the lead. He went particularly well for Grantham. The change from Epsom to

Fairlawne seemed to have suited him, and Grantham believed that he was improving with every race. Cazalet, still convalescent, was just fit enough to come with Lord Mildmay to see Monaveen run. The Royal chaser was adorned with a new brow band which an anonymous well-wisher had sent to the Queen and Princess Elizabeth for luck. It was woven in the Royal colours with a tiny gold crown neatly embroidered on each side.

It was decided that Monaveen would go out in front and make the running, if that was possible. Indeed, such a pace did Monaveen and Wot No Sun set that Roimond and Freebooter were soon well behind. With two fences still to jump, Wot No Sun was tiring fast. Monaveen was clear at the last fence and went on to win comfortably from Freebooter. For the Queen and Princess Elizabeth to win the first running of the Queen Elizabeth Chase was the sort of result one usually only finds in fairy tales, but it did happen to be true on the last day of the Old Year. Princess Elizabeth went on to Sandringham thrilled to the core by Monaveen's brilliant victory. The only sadness was that neither the King nor the Queen nor Prince Philip had been with her to share the intense excitement of the race.

Lord Mildmay and Jim Fairgrieve had prepared Monaveen and had saddled eleven winners during Cazalet's illness. To commemorate their successes together, Lord Mildmay found in the family safe a silver horse which he presented to Fairgrieve as a memento. Needless to say it was a present which was greatly appreciated.

Meanwhile, Monaveen returned to Fairlawne apparently none the

7   The winner Monaveen (A. Grantham) and Wot No Sun (A. P. Thompson) at the open ditch in the Queen Elizabeth Chase at Hurst Park on 31 December 1949.

worse for his Hurst Park victory. A wiry horse, who did not carry much flesh when fit, Cazalet felt that he probably only needed one more race before the Grand National on the last Saturday in March. As Hurst Park clearly suited him, the race chosen was the George Williamson Handicap Chase at Hurst Park in the second week in February over the same course and distance as the Queen Elizabeth Chase. Since the King's leg operation the previous March, the Queen had had to take on a heavy load of public duties and had not been able to see Monaveen run. Princess Elizabeth was back in Malta but the Queen was able to come to Hurst Park for the George Williamson Chase, named in memory of the jockey who had won the 1899 Grand National on the great Manifesto in the colours of Sir John Crocker Bulteel's father, Mr J. G. Bulteel. Monaveen had won the Queen Elizabeth Chase with bottom weight—10 st. He now had to shoulder top weight in heavy going against four opponents, three of whom had recent winning form—Inverlochy, trained by the Scot Alec Kilpatrick on the Wiltshire Downs and a stable companion of Martin M, John Beary's Battling Pedulas, and Fortune Founded, trained at Reigate in Surrey by the Irishman Jack O'Donoghue, to whom the Queen was to send horses in the future. The outsider of the five was Lord Bicester's Parthenon, who was a horse well past his best.

Monaveen, as in the Queen Elizabeth Chase, led practically throughout but made a mistake at the second last fence and was hard pressed to give 19 lb. to Inverlochy, and the Queen, accompanied by Lord Mildmay, must have been relieved to go into the unsaddling enclosure and congratulate Grantham after the race. Grantham himself was about to go down with jaundice and he had done extremely well to win. Monaveen had now won three races off the reel, but it was clear that the handicapper had more or less got his measure. Nevertheless, he clearly had a great chance in the Grand National which was his next race. He was an improving horse, he had shown he could jump the feared Aintree course

8   Monaveen leading the string at Fairlawne: Peter Cazalet is on the grey.

and he stayed reasonably well. It was against him that he was a front runner, and front runners do not often win the Grand National. Though he was bold, he was also apt to make a mistake in a race. Horses may get away with it on a park course like Hurst Park but not often at Aintree.

Four days before the Grand National, the Queen went down to Fairlawne to see Monaveen. She had not been to stay there since girlhood days. Princess Elizabeth was to have accompanied her but had a heavy cold. She went round the racing stables for the first time and met Frank Chapman, the trim West Countryman who was looking after Monaveen. Chapman, a good horseman who was to win races in the future both on the flat and over fences, was to move shortly further west to Ken Cundell's stable on the Berkshire Downs, so as to be nearer his relations in Devon. 'A lovely striding horse who was at his best on top of the ground, but a horse who, being light framed, did not stand up to a lot of racing; a very good ten stone horse, but not a good twelve stone horse', was how Chapman summed up Monaveen.

The Queen also saw Lord Mildmay's Cromwell, who was making his third bid to win the National. Three of the horses Monaveen had beaten in the Queen Elizabeth Chase were now his most fancied Aintree opponents—Mrs Brotherton's Freebooter, Roimond and Wot No Sun. There were forty-nine runners and to the delight of the crowd the King was fit enough to make the journey north, and he came with the Queen, Princess Elizabeth, Princess Margaret and the Duchess of Kent, and they all watched the race from Lord Sefton's box on top of the Aintree grandstand.

9 King George VI and Queen Elizabeth with Lord Sefton at Aintree on the morning of the 1950 Grand National. Princess Elizabeth is in the centre of the group in the background, with Princess Marina, Duchess of Kent, on the right of the group.

Let Tony Grantham, relaxing in his home in Sussex within sight of the South Downs thirty years later, take up the story: 'When I won the Queen Elizabeth Chase on Monaveen, he made most of the running, out-jumping his opponents throughout. He was such a super jumper that he usually jumped his way to the front early in a race and it did not pay to disappoint him. In the National, Roimond and I were, I think, the two leaders at the first fence; Monaveen pecked a bit but got away with it, and Freebooter just led me over Becher's, which I hit fairly hard. After that Monaveen jumped really well to the fence before The Chair, where he stood off too far and hit the top. I lost both irons and was almost gone, and I was lucky to get my irons back before The Chair, but this mistake knocked all the stuffing out of Monaveen, and he was never going so well afterwards.' It was, indeed, a marvellous recovery on the part of Grantham. How he stayed in the saddle I do not know. At The Chair, Freebooter himself made a bad mistake and his jockey Jimmy Power likewise did well to 'stay put', and Power did not attempt to make up the ground on Freebooter until approaching the Canal Turn again, by which time Monaveen's winning chance seemed to have gone. With three fences to go, the race lay between Freebooter and Cloncarrig, owned in partnership by Sir Alan Gordon-Smith and Mr J. Olding. Cloncarrig, ridden by Bob Turnell, hit the second last hard and came down, leaving Freebooter to win from Wot No Sun, Acthon Major, Rowland Roy and Monaveen. Only seven of the forty-nine finished the course. Poor Cromwell was brought down at the fence after Valentine's first time round.

The Royal Family had very much enjoyed the race and in an enthusiastic letter to her trainer, the Queen wrote that they had all been very pleased with the way Monaveen had run. 'Of course I had steeled myself for anything,' said the Queen, 'falling at the first fence, being knocked down, almost any disaster, but I must say the race was far more thrilling than I could have imagined. . . . The next thing is to try to win the National again, if not next year, then the year after that. . . . I have great confidence in Monaveen. He must be a great-hearted horse.'

Cazalet was very pleased to get such an appreciative letter from the Queen and, in thanking Her Majesty, fully agreed that it had been a particularly thrilling National. 'Those first few minutes,' he wrote, 'when Monaveen was in the lead and jumping so beautifully, will certainly live for ever in my memory. I have no doubt that if he had not made that mistake at the fence before The Chair, he would have been very close to the winner at the finish. . . . Tony Grantham did magnificently to stay on. I am afraid Monaveen must have hit his leg at the same time as, although he seemed quite all right after the race, his off-fore leg had swollen up quite badly by the evening. The vet has seen it and does not think he has strained anything but that the swelling is due to a severe blow which

10 Monaveen (A. Grantham) taking the last fence in the 1950 Grand National in which he finished fifth to Freebooter.

should get quite well again in a few weeks. . . . The Grand National is without any doubt the greatest race in the world and I am so pleased that Your Majesty is determined to win it and, since to train the winner is my greatest ambition, I have every hope that before long we shall be leading in the winner together. I cannot tell Your Majesty how honoured and thrilled Zara and I were by your visit to Fairlawne. You cannot imagine what joy and happiness it gave to everyone who was fortunate enough to see you. . . .'

Monaveen was naturally finished for the season and so was Cromwell, but not Lord Mildmay nor the Fairlawne stable. Mildmay had two of the best novice chasers of the season in the French-bred Manicou and in Statecraft. Manicou, Mildmay up, had won his fifth race off the reel when taking Division I of the Broadway Novices Chase at the National Hunt meeting at Cheltenham, and it was decided to give him one more race in a handicap chase at Ludlow at the end of April, but again Lord Mildmay was attacked by the ghastly cramp in his neck which had probably cost him the 1948 Grand National on Cromwell. He had to throw himself off as, unsighted himself, Manicou came to the last fence. The injury had originally been caused by a bad fall on hard ground on the depressingly named Fatal Rock at Folkestone on the day on which the King's Billposter had made his hurdling début two and a half years before. It had clearly not come right.

Ten days after the Ludlow incident, Lord Mildmay went to Cazalet's local course at Wye where Fairlawne always had plenty of runners. He had his fifth victory of the season on his hunter chaser Prince Brownie, bringing his score for the season to thirty-eight, of which all but eight were on his own horses. Cazalet with seventy-five races won was the leading National Hunt trainer of the season for the first time, with Monaveen the stable's biggest winner in prize money. Mildmay had just bought Puttenden—where William Cazalet had his stud—on the edge of the Fairlawne estate, and was intending to move there shortly, although he already had a house and land at Shoreham a few miles away.

Anthony Mildmay went down to his home at Mothecombe in Devon for the weekend. He had guests staying and he was due to ride at a local meeting at Newton Abbot the following week. He went out for his usual early morning swim. He was a strong swimmer and he was apt to swim out to a small islet off shore. He was never seen again, but there is no doubt that he must have been attacked by cramp in his neck again and drowned. On the beach was a basin of fresh water in which he always washed the sand off his feet after bathing. Dr Bill Tucker, who dealt with a large number of injured jockeys and footballers at the time, including Mildmay, regretted bitterly after the tragedy that he had not warned him that his neck cramp might easily recur in cold water and that he should not swim out to sea.

His tragic death was an appalling blow to his only sister Helen Mildmay-White and to his greatest friend, Peter Cazalet. Mildmay and Cazalet had done so much together for over fifteen years. More than that, steeplechasing had lost a shining personality, a man the racing public really loved for his skill, courage, honesty and modesty, and the Queen had lost her racing manager all too early in her racing days.

A leader in *The Times* under the heading 'Amateur Rider' put Lord Mildmay's attributes in apt relief:

As a nation, the British have always owed their survival as such and the projection of their spirit into a wider sphere to a capacity for taking risks; and it is perhaps an almost tribal instinct among them to feel a peculiar affection for those who exhibit this capacity at its best. The man who plays for safety is only a little less revered by them than the man who does not play unless he feels confident of victory. By the dare-devil they are interested rather than impressed, for they distrust stunts; those whom in whatever field they honour most highly as sportsmen are generally men who combine the skill and authority of a professional with the pluck and insouciance of the amateur.

This partly explains why grief at the unlucky death of Lord Mildmay is shared so widely throughout the nation. He was only forty-one. He was not a public figure and he shunned the limelight which is nowadays so willing and so able to convert dear distinction into cheap celebrity. Yet all over the country thousands of people who had never even betted on a steeplechase let alone seen one run are vaguely aware that by his death the country has suffered a particular loss. The war, in which he served with distinction in the Foot Guards, made a big gap in his career as an amateur rider. He never achieved his ambition, cruelly denied him by a broken rein in 1936, of winning the Grand National, but he had a remarkable record of victories, and even if the list had been only half as long, he would have left his mark upon the sport for which he lived. Modest, gay, quizzically resolute, he was the exemplar of a brave and honourable tradition. There never was a harder rider, a better loser or a more popular winner; and although he always valued the race more than the victory, and the victory more than the prize, he would not, perhaps, have disdained the reward he has won—which is a kind of immortality among the English.

Three days after Lord Mildmay's death there arrived at Fairlawne the Queen's new horse Killarney whom Mildmay and Cazalet had found for her in Ireland. I do not know, but I suspect that if the Queen had not decided to go on supporting steeplechasing, Peter Cazalet would have given up training horses after a time. He was a rich man of great ability who could have made his mark in many walks of life. He loved steeplechasing and decided to go on training horses, and in the years ahead Queen Elizabeth was naturally the owner he wanted to succeed above all others. Her Majesty's sympathy and understanding at the time of Lord Mildmay's death made a great deal of difference.

3

Manicou

IN HIS will, Lord Mildmay left all his horses to Peter Cazalet including Cromwell, who was later leased to Anthony's only sister Helen Mildmay-White. Cazelet decided to sell some of the horses. Of Lord Mildmay's two good novices he offered Manicou to Her Majesty the Queen and Princess Elizabeth, and Statecraft to Helen Mildmay-White. Princess Elizabeth, with her husband in the Mediterranean and a second child about to appear in the world, decided not to take a share in Manicou. In early August, just after the Queen's fiftieth birthday and just before the birth of Princess Anne, the King and the Queen went down together to Fairlawne to see the Queen's new horses Manicou and Killarney, to see also at first hand how Monaveen had summered, and to see the Cazalets and their stable staff, still stricken by Lord Mildmay's death. Everyone at Fairlawne was greatly heartened by the Royal visit.

Killarney was a grey gelding by the 1937 Ulster Derby and Irish St Leger winner Owenstown, who was owned and bred by the Ulsterman Sir Thomas Dixon and trained by Matt Peacock at Middleham. Killarney's dam Desla's Star bred several good winners and, in fact, Killarney was a full brother (i.e. the same dam and the same sire) to Lord Fingall's future 1959 Cheltenham Gold Cup winner Roddy Owen. Unfortunately, this highly promising young horse developed ringbone and was never able to run and had eventually to be put down.

Manicou was a very good looking dark bay entire with a star and two white socks. He had come to England from France as the winner of one race on the flat as a two-year-old and four as a three-year-old and his first race in England had been on the flat as a four-year-old in the spring of 1949. He ran unplaced in a mile race at Alexandra Park behind the Two Thousand Guineas winner, My Babu. He was clearly a horse with plenty of speed and he showed it in the National Hunt season which followed when Lord Mildmay won two hurdle races and four novice chases on him. The Queen had certainly acquired a horse capable of doing great things, if all went well.

Meanwhile, Monaveen was not so forward in the autumn of 1950 as he had been the previous year, as was natural with a horse who had been let down after the Grand National. The race had undoubtedly taken a lot out

of him. When he reappeared in the middle of October he ran unplaced on his favourite course in Hurst Park's Grand Sefton Trial. He made the running for over half way but he had gone up a lot in the handicap and was giving weight to all except the winner Coloured School Boy from Rimell's stable, and his old rival Freebooter.

The present Lord Abergavenny had now succeeded Lord Mildmay as the Queen's racing manager. When Harry Whiteman first came to Fairlawne to train for Cazalet, the original four amateurs who usually rode out were Cazalet, Edward Paget, Mildmay and John Nevill, a neighbour from Eridge who was later to become Lord Abergavenny. So the Queen's choice of her new racing manager was much to the liking of her trainer.

Less than a fortnight after Monaveen had finished fifth at Hurst Park, Manicou appeared for the first time in the Queen's colours at the Fontwell November meeting. Her Majesty's colours had just been registered as 'blue, buff stripes, blue sleeves, black cap and gold tassel'—the colours of her great-uncle Lord Strathmore, one of the best amateur riders of his day, who rode in four successive Grand Nationals from 1847 to 1850. Cazalet's horses were striking form and on the first day of the Fontwell November

11 Manicou (A. Grantham), led by Alex King, going out for the Wimbledon Chase at Kempton on 24 November 1950.

meeting, Lord Mildmay's favourite Cromwell won in the name of Mrs Mildmay-White who had adopted her brother's colours.

Because of court mourning for King Gustav of Sweden, the Queen could not come to see Manicou run, but Princess Elizabeth was able to do so. On a rainy day, she saw a Cazalet double early in the afternoon, both winners ridden by Grantham. Another Delight, who had arrived at Fairlawne on the same day as the Queen's ill-fated Killarney, won the Middleton Novices Chase in the colours of the Queen's new racing manager, and Rhetorius won the Whitelaw Challenge Cup for Mr C. Winslow-Taylor, who had bought this entire the previous year from the former Polish cavalry soldier, Colonel W. J. Bobinski. In the future, Colonel Bobinski was to find a number of promising French horses for the Queen.

Manicou reappeared in the Petworth Handicap Hurdle, carrying top weight. A very robust and strong horse, who always carried plenty of muscle and flesh, he needed more work than most of his contemporaries. He was of exceptional temper for a colt and never got excited in his box. He was 'a Christian to do', as his lad put it. He was a horse who benefited

12 Manicou (A. Grantham) on right, wearing Queen Elizabeth's colours for the first time, racing with Sailor's Knot (T. Isaac) and Baire (A. Jarvis) in the Petworth Hurdle at Fontwell on 2 November 1950.

from a race and in the heavy ground at Fontwell he ran well for a long way and then weakened. For the rest of the season he was to run over fences.

The following week, Monaveen went up to Aintree again for the fourth time. On the previous day, Fairlawne's Prince Brownie, on whom Lord Mildmay had ridden his last winner before his death, won the Valentine Chase in the colours of Lady Carew-Pole, ridden by Grantham, but in the Grand Sefton Monaveen was opposed by most of the best three-mile chasers in training. At that time, before the days of sponsored races, the Grand Sefton was one of the few chases of much value before Christmas. Monaveen made the running to Valentines, jumping boldly and well, but he then weakened to finish fifth behind Mr J. V. Rank's top class mare Shagreen, Freebooter, Lord Bicester's Finnure, who had won the Champion Chase at Aintree the previous March, and the Grand National winner Russian Hero. The plain fact was that he was beaten by four better horses on the day. As Grantham said later, he had for the moment lost a bit of his dash.

The Queen was able to come racing for the first time in the new season a fortnight later to see Manicou have his first race over fences in her own colours, in the Wimbledon Handicap Chase at Kempton Park. The King had been well enough to act as host for the state visit of Queen Juliana and Prince Bernhard of the Netherlands which ended on the morning of Manicou's race at Kempton. After saying goodbye to the Royal guests, the Queen and Princess Elizabeth set out for Kempton Park. It was the first Royal visit to the course since Limelight had won the Duke of York Handicap for King George V in 1933. Being an entire and inclined to be stuffy, Manicou was all the better for his Fontwell race. The Duchess of Norfolk's Possible, a winner of the Molyneux Chase at Aintree, was fancied to beat Manicou and so was Printer's Pie in the colours of Colonel J. F. Harrison, father-in-law of Lord Abergavenny. Possible led most of the way but Grantham was biding his time, and Manicou won decisively. It was a grey day, made cheerful by Manicou's victory. Racing at Kempton the following day was wiped out by fog.

A week later Princess Elizabeth had departed for Malta but the Queen was able to come racing again to see Monaveen attempt to win the Queen Elizabeth Chase at Hurst Park for the second year in succession. In a field of nine Cazalet also ran Rhetorius, ridden by Bryan Marshall. Grantham thought Monaveen was back to form, was decidedly hopeful, and the horse started favourite. Monaveen, Printer's Pie and the mare Slender between them made the running. At the water second time round, going well, and disputing the lead, Monaveen took off too soon, as he was apt to do in a race, and just failed to clear the water. 'He did the same thing at Hurst Park as he had done at Aintree in the National and on one particular occasion when schooling at home, he stood off too far,' said Grantham later. 'In those days the landing side of the water was upright and you had to land on the far bank. If the landing side had been sloped as it is today, I think Monaveen would have got away with it. Monaveen broke a leg so badly that the vet had no alternative but to put him down straight away.' Fortunately the water jump at Hurst Park was to the left of the grandstand and not clearly visible from it, and no one in the stands realised immediately that Monaveen had broken a leg. It was only when the vet had done his unpleasant duty that the bad news spread, and Cazalet had the grievous task of reporting what had happened.

The Queen had flown from Sandringham for the day to see Monaveen run, and had a very sad flight back to Sandringham that evening. Members of the Royal family try not to show their grief in public. Perhaps in the quiet of the aeroplane, unseen, the Queen was able to shed a tear for her first steeplechaser, Monaveen. Fortunately the young Princess Elizabeth was far away with her husband and children. She would, I think, at that time, have found it harder to hide her grief. When one suddenly loses a lion-hearted horse who is giving his all, it is very, very upsetting. Though there has been no racing now at Hurst Park for nearly twenty years, a stone above his grave there still commemorates the date on which Monaveen ended his days at Hurst Park. Sir John Crocker Bulteel thoughtfully had it put up for the Queen.

Poor Grantham had a ghastly fall, was knocked out, broke ribs, and still has scars on his face to bear witness to it. He was unable to ride in races again for over two months and was missing, therefore, when Manicou reappeared nearly a fortnight later in the long-distance Ewell Chase at Sandown Park. Cazalet arranged for the Irishman Bryan Marshall, from County Limerick, to take his place. Bravely undeterred by Monaveen's loss, the Queen came to Sandown to watch her new horse. Manicou jumped well and won so impressively that it was decided afterwards that he would take on the cracks in the King George VI Chase at Kempton on Boxing Day, when he would be the only five-year-old in the field. It was a bold move, as Manicou had only run in three steeplechases since competing in novice chases and was therefore still short of jumping experience.

As usual there was a top class field for the King George VI Chase—two future winners of the Cheltenham Gold Cup in Lord Bicester's Silver Fame and Knock Hard; Coloured School Boy; Klaxton, who was to win three Grand Military Gold Cups in succession for his owner Major W. D. Gibson; Cobios, a promising young horse owned by Mr D. de Rougemont, and the Cazalet second string Rhetorius, who had no chance of beating Coloured School Boy on Hurst Park running.

Manicou was not a bold front runner like Monaveen. He had normally run in a hood when winning for Lord Mildmay the previous season and he needed a good deal of riding. 'I remember I went to a cocktail party given by John Goldsmith on Christmas Eve,' recalled Bryan Marshall, 'and Bill

OPPOSITE PAGE:
13 TOP: Manicou (B. Marshall) winning the Ewell Chase at Sandown, with ears pricked, on 14 December 1950.

14 BOTTOM: Manicou (B. Marshall) leading Silver Fame (R. Francis) at the last fence in the King George VI Chase at Kempton on 26 December 1950.

Payne, who had been champion jockey just before the First World War and was then training successfully at Seven Barrows, near Lambourn, told me he thought that if I really got hold of Manicou he would go close to winning. Bill Payne's words really put will-power into me and encouraged me, for my impression was that Manicou was inclined to be a sticky jumper. In the race itself, it was an average gallop the first time round, but after passing the stands they went on like hell. I always consider the Kempton fences amongst the best built in the country. They all have a slope on them. They are wide, big and fair, the width of the fences making them look small to the horse. Manicou jumped them well, took up the running at the open ditch going away from the stands and ran on very well to hold Silver Fame in the straight.'

It was an outstanding performance by a five-year-old against proven chasers and marvellous for the Queen to win the race named after the King. It looked as if Manicou was certain to go close in the Cheltenham Gold Cup and had a future of note ahead of him.

Manicou did not run again for a couple of months. He was badly kicked on the inside of the leg under the chest and was on the easy list. His reappearance was at Lingfield over two-and-a-half miles in holding going in the Jerry M. Stakes. Watched by the Queen and ridden by Grantham, Manicou was a disappointing third of four behind Lord Bicester's promising seven-year-old Bluff King. He made two or three mistakes and his rider reported that he 'gurgled' after the race.

It was a very wet spring and the National Hunt meeting at Cheltenham was abandoned after one day and the Cheltenham Gold Cup run instead on firm going in the last week of April. Manicou was started again at the end of March in the Walter Hyde Handicap Chase at Kempton over the same course and distance as his triumph on Boxing Day, but he began to tire at the fence after the water and finished a moderate fourth a long way behind his old rival Silver Fame who, in turn, was beaten by Crump's Lockerbie. The holding going clearly did not suit Manicou but it was a disappointing, listless performance.

In pre-war days during the season, horses from Fairlawne used to hack six miles to Knole Park, owned by Lord Sackville, and use the gallops in the park, which were in every way worthy of one of the great country houses of England. The old turf in Knole was superior to anything at Fairlawne and Cazalet continued to use Knole after the war but, owing to the increase in motor traffic, he had to box his horses to Knole and so did not go so often as in Whiteman's day. Nevertheless, he took Manicou two or three times up to Knole before the Cheltenham Gold Cup, hoping that the horse would recover his form.

The Queen, accompanied by Princess Elizabeth, flew from Sandringham to Cheltenham to watch Manicou run in the 1951 Gold Cup. The going was firm and Manicou ran well for a long way but made a bad

mistake in the final mile then, sadly, dropped back beaten, his old rival Silver Fame winning after a desperate duel with Mr J. V. Rank's Greenogue.

Manicou was sore after the race, and was to be dogged by leg trouble in the months ahead. The Queen suggested to her trainer that he might seek the advice of a well-known physiotherapist, Charles Strong, who had kept Lord Mountbatten's Royal Navy polo team fit in Malta before the Second World War and had then turned his attention to keeping the polo ponies sound, too. Strong had been serving in the naval hospital on Malta before the war and, encouraged by Mountbatten, had started to do considerable research into the cure of strains and sprains in horses through Faradism. After the war, he had continued his research and had produced a machine to give treatment to horses suffering from muscle and ligament damage in particular, with remarkably successful results in most cases. With tendons, Strong did not find that his treatment was equally effective, but the instrument he perfected had the additional advantage of pin-pointing, in most cases, the seat of the injury. In the years ahead, Strong was to treat a number of the horses at Fairlawne and then Jim Fairgrieve was to learn to

15 A group at Kempton on Easter Monday 1951 when Manicou was fourth in the Walter Hyde Chase. Left to right: Queen Elizabeth's Racing Manager Lord Abergavenny, Peter Cazalet, Queen Elizabeth, King George VI, Captain Charles Moore, Manager of the Royal Studs, and Sir Cecil Boyd-Rochfort, trainer of the King's home-bred flat race horses.

treat horses himself with much success, using the Strong equine equipment. The Queen's suggestion was to bear much fruit.

Manicou, however, never regained the brilliance he showed at Kempton Park as a five-year-old on Boxing Day. Towards the end of 1951, he was fired. He ran next a year later, in October 1952, in a handicap hurdle at Fontwell but broke down again. He then had two years off, spending most of the time convalescing at Sandringham. It was at this period in the spring of 1954 that he served a mare called Easy Virtue with highly beneficial results in the future for the Queen. With hindsight, Cazalet had probably run Manicou too soon after the initial firing. He now showed great restraint and did not produce the horse again until a month before the Christmas of 1954 at the end of Manicou's eight-year-old days, but sadly his perseverance was not to be rewarded, and Manicou finished a distant second of three in a steeplechase at Lingfield. He ran well for a long way in a steeplechase at Sandown before blundering three fences from home and being pulled up, and he had his final race at Kempton exactly three years after his triumph in the King George VI Chase when he again blundered badly and was not sound after the race.

Fortunately, however, he was an entire, and he was to make a considerable name for himself as a sire of jumpers in the years ahead at the Gables Stud Farm of Mr C. W. Godden at Rotherfield in Sussex. By the Tourbillon horse, Last Post, Manicou traced on his dam's side to Americus Girl, dam of Lady Josephine, who in turn was dam of the Aga Khan's flying filly Mumtaz Mahal. He had, in fact, the looks and the breeding to do well at stud, and the Queen was not to lose sight of him for many years to come.

4

Devon Loch

THE QUEEN had been exceedingly lucky to own at the start of her involvement in steeplechasing two horses of the merit of Monaveen and Manicou. With Killarney she had been unlucky. Her fourth steeplechaser to come to Fairlawne was Devon Loch, a name engraved on the hearts of all racing people of his time. He arrived at Fairlawne on the same February day in 1951 that Manicou had run so disappointingly in the mud at Lingfield.

Lord Abergavenny, Lord Mildmay, and Cazalet were all friends of a wise Irishman, Colonel Stephen Hill-Dillon, who had given good service to Britain in two world wars. He loved horses, was a fine judge of them, had good chasers to carry his colours in the 1930s and in his time showed much administrative ability as Senior Steward both of the Irish National Hunt Committee and of the Irish Turf Club. In the 1940s, he was living near Navan in a house called Hayes belonging to Sir Harry Legge-Bourke, who was to become a leading member of the Conservative party. Hill-Dillon made and broke his own horses there and trained a few for himself. It was Hill-Dillon who had recommended Cromwell, the first good chaser at Fairlawne after the Second World War and it was Hill-Dillon who had also found a succession of fine looking chasers to carry the colours of the 1st Lord Bicester—Silver Fame, Finnure and the Grand National second Roimond amongst them.

At Goff's Sales in Ireland in the autumn of 1947, Hill-Dillon was looking for a 'store'—a young horse to be stored away until mature enough to race. He bought a yearling colt by the Hyperion horse Devonian out of a mare called Coolaleen, bred by Mr Willie Moloney of the Shandnum Lodge Stud, Charlville, County Cork. Moloney's home, not far from the County Limerick border, is in the dairyland of Ireland, and Charlville is the home of one of Ireland's biggest cheese factories. Willie Moloney's father, also a horse breeder, bought Shandnum Lodge in 1906 and he bought Devon Loch's dam Coolaleen as a yearling at Goff's for 50 guineas in 1937. She had been bred by a sporting clergyman, the Reverend Charlie Daly, a neighbour of the Moloneys, at his home at Killaree. Coolaleen did not run until she was a four-year-old; she showed ability, but met with an accident in her second race and was kept for the

16   At Aintree, John
Hole leading out Devon
Loch (R. Francis) before
the 1956 Grand National.

stud. She was by the 1919 Irish Derby winner Loch Lomond out of the
staying mare Coup d'Essai, who showed exceptional stamina as a three-
year-old in Ireland and was the winner of four races. Coup d'Essai traced
to Penitent, dam of the 1893 Derby runner-up Ravensbury and full-sister
herself to the great race-mare Shotover, winner of the 1882 Derby. Coup
d'Essai's daughter, Coup d'Amour, was already the dam of a top class
chaser in Limestone Edward who finished sixth in the 1946 Grand
National and won many races in the north of England for his owner and
trainer, Mr Clifford Nicholson.

Moloney has always bred primarily for flat racing and he entered his
1946 Devonian-Coolaleen colt, who was a second foal, in a number of
valuable two-year-old races in Ireland. Hill-Dillon, rightly thinking that
the colt would grow into a big horse and looked a possible chaser in the
making, bought him for 550 guineas, took him back to Hayes, had him
cut, and determined to give him plenty of time to develop. Trained at
home, his head lad W. McCann holding the licence, Devon Loch's first

race was a flat race for maiden five-year-olds and above, at Leopardstown in January 1951. Ridden by a professional jockey, Devon Loch started second favourite but finished unplaced behind Prince Boudour and Rose Park, both of whom were to find their way to Fairlawne.

A fortnight later at Naas, in a two-mile bumper—a race for amateur riders only—Devon Loch won from two other future chasers who were to do well in England—Domata and Cardiff. The winner of an Irish bumper is automatically worth a lot of money as a potential chaser. Captain Charles Moore and Cazalet went over to Ireland to see Devon Loch, liked what they saw, and bought him on behalf of the Queen with a contingency of £1,000 if he should win the Cheltenham Gold Cup or £2,000 if he should win the Grand National. A dark bay with a pear-shaped star on his forehead, Devon Loch was a strongly-built horse, standing 16 hands 2″ with good bone, an intelligent and bold disposition, and what Cazalet described as an ideal conformation for steeplechasing.

Ten days after the arrival of Devon Loch at Fairlawne, the Queen and Princess Elizabeth both came down to see the new arrival and liked what they saw. They also learned of the narrow escape Devon Loch had had a couple of days after his arrival. Fairgrieve had put a saddle and bridle on him and taken him out in the park on a lungeing rein. He started to pull Devon Loch into him, when the buckle broke, and the horse was free to go where he would. He did not realise he was loose for a moment but when he did so, he took off across the park and disappeared. Fortunately he did not head for the road, and was eventually found in an adjoining field, having jumped the rails into it. There was not a mark on him and no harm had been done, but it was an unpleasant quarter of an hour for Fairgrieve.

In May 1951, the King declared the Festival of Britain open but by July he was feeling far from well and was not fit to go to Ulster on a four-day visit and the Queen had to go on her own. He went north to Balmoral but towards the end of September he had to return south to have a serious lung operation in Buckingham Palace. He had recovered sufficiently for the Queen to come to Kempton towards the end of November to see Devon Loch run for the second time over hurdles and finish second to the flat racer Rahshas. Six weeks later at Newbury, in the dying days of 1951, in another novices' hurdle, Devon Loch was second again to another flat racer Rodogat. He looked a chaser in build, and it was decided to turn him from hurdling to chasing and to run him at Hurst Park in a novices' chase in the middle of January. The King seemed to be better and the Queen and Pricess Elizabeth flew from Sandringham to see Devon Loch run.

Devon Loch's race was the £204 Mortlake Novices Chase, in which he was opposed by two brilliant novices—Filon d'Or who had already finished first in three novice chases, trained by Goldsmith and ridden by Winter, and Miss Dorothy Paget's Mont Tremblant, who was destined to

17 Devon Loch (B. Marshall) and Miss Dorothy Paget's Mont Tremblant (D. Dick) jump together in the Mortlake Chase at Hurst Park in January 1952 — Devon Loch's first steeplechase.

win the Cheltenham Gold Cup as a six-year-old two months later. With Grantham injured, Bryan Marshall rode Devon Loch. For a newcomer, Devon Loch jumped really well, made some of the running, but in the end was beaten on merit by Mont Tremblant. The Queen, elated, went back to Sandringham feeling that she had another good horse to carry her colours.

A fortnight later, the King and the Queen came down to London to see Princess Elizabeth and Prince Philip off on their projected East African and Australian tour. The King and the Queen went to London Airport to say goodbye to them. Then the King and the Queen went back to Sandringham. Less than a week later the King passed peacefully away in his sleep, leaving his widow very lonely and very bereft.

It so happened that for the rest of the year the three horses of Queen Elizabeth, now the Queen Mother, were all under a cloud. Killarney was about to be put down, Manicou had been fired, and Devon Loch unfortunately also developed leg trouble and was fired. There was outwardly little to report on the racing front for two years but, in fact, behind the scenes Queen Elizabeth was hoping to be able to continue to have horses in training, and Lord Abergavenny, as Queen Elizabeth's racing manager, had produced a scheme whereby, with Hill-Dillon's help, they would buy stores cheaply in Ireland, bring them over to Sandringham after a spell with Hill-Dillon, and then send them to Major Eldred Wilson, a tenant of the Royal Family, who farmed a few miles from Sandringham at Harpley Dams, a mile or so out of the neighbouring village of Hillington.

Eldred Wilson was himself a good amateur rider and had ridden at

Aintree and had nearly a hundred successes to his credit in hunter chases and point-to-points; he had a great reputation for making and breaking young horses and was keen to help with the scheme which Queen Elizabeth had discussed with the King before his sudden death. The first two of the stores, in fact, arrived at Sandringham from Ireland shortly after the King's death and in the next four years, nine more were to follow. None of them was to have the ability of Devon Loch, but then horses of Devon Loch's ability are rare. The stores bought by Hill-Dillon in Ireland, however, were a source of great interest to Queen Elizabeth as she watched their progress on her visits to Sandringham.

With Devon Loch on the sidelines throughout the 1953–54 jumping season, Queen Elizabeth made a new purchase. She bought the experienced French-bred chaser M'as-tu-vu. He had belonged previously to Colonel Bobinski and to another Pole, Mr B. Lubecki, who trained and rode him himself. With Queen Elizabeth in mind, Cazalet bought M'as-tu-vu as a seven-year-old in the spring of 1953, ran him without success in a long-distance hurdle race and put him by until the following season. Queen Elizabeth had been down to Fairlawne to see him work with other Cazalet horses before his outing at Lingfield.

The talented Welshman, Dick Francis, had been appointed stable jockey to Fairlawne before the start of the 1953–54 season. Before the war, Francis had made his name in showing and show-jumping but after service in the R.A.F. during the war, he had come into racing, starting as an amateur with George Owen and making a name for himself on Lord Bicester's horses. A beautiful horseman, he was to be an immediate success as stable jockey to Cazalet and come out as champion jockey in his first season with the stable.

At the end of October, M'as-tu-vu appeared in the Cazalet colours in a handicap steeplechase at Nottingham. The stable was in form and won hurdle races with Mrs Mildmay-White's Lochroe and Devon Loch's contemporary Rose Park, owned in partnership by Mr G. Lawrence and Mr R. S. Wilkins, then newcomers to the stable, but strong supporters in the future. M'as-tu-vu ran well to finish second and ten days later at Fontwell, ridden by Francis, he won the Whitelaw Challenge Cup. Queen Elizabeth bought M'as-tu-vu after the race and three weeks later saw him run for the first time in her colours at Kempton. She had not been racing for over a year. M'as-tu-vu was at the top of the handicap and had to give considerable weight to two recent winners—Nautical Print, trained by the ex-champion jockey Gerry Wilson, a great favourite with everybody, and Dry Martini, trained by another ex-champion jockey 'Frenchie' Nicholson, who was to become as well-known as a trainer of jockeys as of horses. Although M'as-tu-vu did not jump too well, Francis rode him patiently and brought him from behind to win his race—Queen Elizabeth's first victory for nearly three years and Francis's first Royal victory.

18 M'as-tu-vu (R. Francis), the winner, jumping the last fence in the Wimbledon Chase at Kempton Park on 27 November 1953.

With M'as-tu-vu in good heart, it was decided to run him again ten days later in the Blindley Heath Chase at Lingfield—a handicap chase over three miles in which Cazalet often had a runner. Blue Envoy, the ewe lamb of a crippled Hampshire owner-breeder Mrs E. M. Halahan, made most of the running and hung on well, but at the final fence M'as-tu-vu had his race won. Although it was an ordinary run-of-the-mill chase, it was a race Dick Francis was not to forget. Cazalet had appointed Francis as stable jockey earlier in the year and in the changing room at the Devon course of Newton Abbot on the first day of the new season at the beginning of August, he had come and sat down beside Francis and had told him there were two things he wished to say to him: 'First,' said Cazalet, 'all my horses are doing their best, and second, you will never look round during the closing stages of a race. I want you to remember that in my view many races are lost through jockeys looking round and getting their horses unbalanced.'

'I remember,' said Francis, 'that in this Lingfield race, after jumping the last fence clear of Blue Envoy, I thought that there was no more to worry about, and then I heard the crowd roaring, and thinking, Good Heavens alive, I'm being tackled. I did not dare to look round after Cazalet's instructions and rode out M'as-tu-vu for all I was worth. Only when I passed the post did I dare look over my shoulder and saw that there was nothing within striking distance! Everyone was so pleased and excited at Queen Elizabeth winning, that the crowd was merely cheering her horse home—and I was not used to such a reception.'

By the time M'as-tu-vu was in the winner's enclosure again, Devon Loch was back in action after an absence of over two years. Queen Elizabeth and Cazalet had been very patient with Deven Loch and their patience was going to be rewarded. Soon after Queen Elizabeth had returned from her highly successful tour of the United States and Canada, M'as-tu-vu and Devon Loch both ran at the Newbury December meeting. M'as-tu-vu was second in a handicap chase and Devon Loch ran respectably after his long lay-off in a novices' hurdle. Afterwards, Francis reported to Cazalet that Devon Loch had given him 'the hell of a feel' and he would like to ride him one day in the Grand National—very prophetic words.

It was then decided that Devon Loch would be aimed at the New Century Chase at Hurst Park. This was the course over which he had run so well behind Mont Tremblant three years before. At the time, this race brought out many of the best novices of the season and the 1958 season was no exception. Cazalet had three runners in different ownership—Mrs Mildmay-White's Lochroe, on whom Francis had already won four novice chases that season, including the competitive Henry VIII Chase, At Bay, a recent winner at Newbury in the colours of Mrs M. Beckwith-Smith, whose father's family founded Lingfield Park, and Queen

19   Devon Loch (B. Marshall) going well in the New Century Chase at Hurst Park in February 1955—his first victory for Queen Elizabeth.

Elizabeth's Devon Loch. Francis rode Lochroe, Arthur Freeman, now riding as second jockey to Cazalet, rode At Bay, and Bryan Marshall rode Devon Loch, on whom he had so nearly won before. Others in the field included Miss Dorothy Paget's Pelopidas, the Sandown winner Ballymore, Major H. S. Cayzer's Kempton winner Rendezvous III, Game Field from Jack Fawcus's Middleham yard and the Kempton winners Solar City, Marston Magna and Kind Answer. In fact, nine of the field of thirteen were recent winners over fences.

The Queen and Queen Elizabeth had been down together to Fairlawne in the autumn to see the Cazalet horses and they both were able to come to Hurst Park for the New Century Chase. Cazalet's orders to Bryan Marshall were: 'Look after yourselves and get him round. I hope you finish in the first three.' The Hurst Park steeplechase course was a sharp one and not an easy course on which to steer clear of trouble in a big field and Marshall was content to lie well back for the first part of the two-mile race. Rounding the final bend into the straight, Devon Loch was in touch with the leaders, but not, thought Marshall, in a winning position. 'Once one turned into the Hurst Park straight, one edged over to the left,' recalled Marshall. 'I took stock of my position at the second last and saw there was at least one in front of me going badly. As we approached the last, Devon Loch started to stagger with me, and I said to myself, take a hold of yourself, Marshall, let's get over the last fence before we have a real go. So I took a tight hold of his head, he jumped the last well, and he finished very strongly.' Devon Loch won by two lengths from Ballymore with the favourite Pelopidas, who made a mistake at the last, third. At Bay fell, and Lochroe could not act in the deep going.

The Queen and Queen Elizabeth hurried to Hurst Park's small unsaddling enclosure to greet Devon Loch and there was considerable merriment when Bryan Marshall confessed that he had taken his dentures out for the race as is normal custom on safety grounds, and had forgotten in the excitement of victory to retrieve them from Devon Loch's lad and

20   In the unsaddling enclosure afterwards. Left to right: The Queen, Lady Abergavenny, Lord Abergavenny, Queen Elizabeth, Bryan Marshall, Peter Cazalet, travelling head lad Bill Braddon, and Alex King.

put them back. The 'toothless wonder' went to weigh in with praise heaped upon him for his unexpected victory. A top class jockey with a great capacity to get the best out of horses, Marshall had won the two previous runnings of the Grand National on the Vincent O'Brien-trained pair, Early Mist and Royal Tan, and was at the height of his powers.

Devon Loch was sound after the race but did not run again till March at the National Hunt meeting at Cheltenham where he was started in the two-mile Cotswold Chase in preference to the more exacting three-mile Broadway Novices Chase. For his victory in the New Century Chase, he carried the maximum penalty and failed to give the weight to Manuscrit and Bob Tailed 'Un. A week later, again over two miles, he was started in the Beech Open Chase at Sandown and gave twelve pounds and a beating to the future Cheltenham Gold Cup winner, Linwell. Two years later when Linwell won the Cheltenham Gold Cup for Ivor Herbert's well-run stable, the form looked highly impressive. A week later Cazalet called on Devon Loch for his third race in three weeks and sent him up to Aintree for the Mildmay Chase, run over the Mildmay course with smaller fences than the National fences and a circuit of about ten furlongs. In Marshall's view, this sharp left-handed course did not suit Devon Loch and he fell at the eighth fence. This was his final run of the season.

The following day, M'as-tu-vu ran in the Grand National, ridden by Arthur Freeman who was already making his mark in his first season for Fairlawne. Son of Will Freeman, huntsman to the Eridge Foxhounds when Lord Abergavenny's father, the 4th Marquess, was master, Arthur Freeman had been born and brought up at the Eridge Hunt kennels and had therefore been known by the Queen's racing manager since he was a small boy and, as 'Little Treasure', was the apple of his father's eye!

21 In the 1955 Grand National, M'as-tu-vu (A. Freeman) No. 16, jumping the fence before The Chair with the winner, Quare Times No. 10, on his right and the third, Carey's Cottage No. 12, beyond.

Freeman was a strong fearless rider for whom Aintree had no terrors. M'as-tu-vu was a thoroughly exposed handicap chaser, not in the top class, and a 22-1 outsider in the Grand National. The race was run in deep going after heavy rain, and as a result the stewards decided to cut out the water jump. M'as-tu-vu had not the best of feet. He had thin soles, wore very broad racing plates and liked the going soft. The rain, in fact, had come at the right time for him. He was up with the leaders throughout the first circuit, but as the field came to The Chair—the biggest fence on the course—Freeman realised that M'as-tu-vu was going to meet it wrong. He thought he was 'for it' when Queen Elizabeth's chaser took off yards away but M'as-tu-vu had a strong sense of self-preservation and somehow got over the fence intact without taking too much out of himself. In fact, he took up the running soon after the field started on the second circuit, and was well placed until he made another mistake at Becher's second time round. He had no chance when he fell at the open ditch two fences after Valentine's. It was Quare Time's year, and he won easily.

The following season was to belong in a special way to Devon Loch. Dick Francis had not yet ridden Devon Loch in a steeplechase. He did so for the first time at Lingfield towards the end of November 1955, in the Blindley Heath Chase, the race Francis had won on M'as-tu-vu two years before. It was the first time Devon Loch had run over three miles. He made a mistake at the first fence but finished very strongly like a real stayer to give weight and a beating to Red Trump, a thoroughly fit, exposed handicapper from the yard of Tom Yates, who had taken over the stable of Cazalet's old friend, 'Sonny' Hall.

Devon Loch took on stiffer opponents three weeks later in the Sandown Handicap Chase, carrying a seven pounds' penalty for his Lingfield victory. He won but he was lucky to defeat the fast finishing Cottage Lace who lost narrowly after making a bad mistake at the last fence. Devon Loch was getting nearly a stone from the third horse, Mariner's Log, but instead of keeping Queen Elizabeth's horse to handicaps for the time being, Cazalet recommended running him against the cracks in the King George VI Chase at Kempton on Boxing Day. Devon Loch had only to run reasonably well at Kempton to go up a long way in the handicap. The Cazalet first string for the race was Lochroe, on whom Francis had already won three chases that autumn, so Marshall was reunited with Devon Loch, who ran in snatches to finish fifth, but sufficiently well to put him up a few pounds in the handicap.

Cazalet nearly always had a fancied runner in Sandown's Mildmay Memorial Chase, which he naturally wanted to win. He had won the second running of the race for Mrs Mildmay-White with Cromwell, and in 1954 he very much hoped to win it for Queen Elizabeth with Devon Loch. Francis was *hors de combat* after a bad fall at Newbury earlier in the week, so

Bryan Marshall again rode Devon Loch. After a tremendously exciting race, the weight told and Linwell, getting 23 lbs from Devon Loch, drew clear to win. Wise Child from the north, finishing fast, took second place from Devon Loch on the line. As the race was over three miles five furlongs—and therefore a thorough test of stamina—Devon Loch had acquitted himself really well. Both in the King George VI Chase and in the Mildmay Memorial, Bryan Marshall felt Devon Loch falter suddenly during the race but then to appear to get his second wind and run on strongly again. He reported it on each occasion to Cazalet; he felt the horse had some weakness but could not explain it.

There was a lot of snow at Fairlawne in the following month, and Devon Loch was thought by Cazalet to be short of work as a result when he appeared in the first week of March in the National Hunt Handicap Chase at Cheltenham. He warned Queen Elizabeth not to be too hopeful. Cazalet's orders to Francis for the Cheltenham race were: 'Give him a nice race. Do not murder him. Remember his next race is the Grand National.' Queen Elizabeth added: 'Of course, it would be very nice to pick this one up on the way!' In fact Devon Loch ran really well, finishing very strongly up the hill to take third place behind Bewicke's Kerstin, to whom he was giving a stone. Kerstin was to win the Cheltenham Gold Cup two years later. Afterwards, Francis was able to report to Queen Elizabeth: 'I had a terrific ride. Devon Loch was staying on really well, and I feel we have a great chance at Aintree.'

I was racing correspondent to *The Daily Telegraph* at the time and I remember to this day being enormously impressed by the way Devon Loch ran at Cheltenham, and choosing him to win the Grand National.

22   Peter Cazalet about to give a leg up to Dick Francis in the parade ring at Cheltenham before Devon Loch runs in the National Hunt Handicap Chase on 7 March 1956, whilst the Queen, Queen Elizabeth and Lord Abergavenny look on.

That Dick Francis was to ride him was in my eyes greatly in his favour, for he had already shone at Aintree on several occasions. The National field was smaller than usual with twenty-nine runners. Early Mist and Royal Tan, previous winners, were to do battle again. Quare Times was *hors de combat*. Mrs W. L. Pilkington's proven stayer Must was favourite, the second favourite was Sundew, who was to win the 1957 National, and Carey's Cottage, who had already run well in the race, E.S.B., Devon Loch and the mare Gentle Moya were well fancied. Queen Elizabeth's second string, M'as-tu-vu, again ridden by Freeman, was now a 40-1 outsider.

The Royal party came up to Aintree by special train from London overnight for the race and the train was put in a siding beside the course. They got up early and went on to the course to see the horses at exercise. Devon Loch was in charge of John Hole, who had come to Fairlawne as a nineteen-year-old lad in 1932 and was one of the original six stablemen when Whiteman started the stable. After breakfast, most of the party went round the course, and then went to lunch with Lord Derby before racing. In the race at Cheltenham, Devon Loch had been outpaced in the first mile, and Dick Francis, considering his strategy for the National, had come to the conclusion that Devon Loch would have to take things steadily in the mad rush over the first few fences and the hope was that he would not be brought down by a faller early on.

23   In the parade ring at Aintree before the 1956 Grand National. Left to right: Bill Braddon, Squadron Leader Christopher Blount, Lord Abergavenny talking to Peter Cazalet, Queen Elizabeth, Princess Margaret, Dick Francis, the Queen talking to Arthur Freeman (hidden), and Lord Sefton.

Let Dick Francis describe it, as he put it on paper* shortly after the race, now nearly a quarter of a century ago:

M'as-tu-vu went off in front, and Devon Loch jumped the first two in the middle of the field. But I soon found that he was not going to go slowly for the first mile, for he was striding out comfortably, and his leap at each fence gained him lengths. I have never ridden another horse like him. He cleared the formidable Aintree fences as easily as if they had been hurdles. He put himself right before every one of them, and he was so intelligent at the job that all I had to do was to ride him quietly and let him jump without fussing him.

Usually the National is more of a worry than a pleasure to anyone riding in it: Devon Loch made it a delight. Usually one is kicking one's horse along and taking risks to keep one's place: Devon Loch was going so easily that he had time to think what he was doing. Over Becher's we went, round the Canal Turn, and over Valentine's, and two fences later had our only anxious moment. Domata, ridden by Derek Ancil, was just ahead of us on the inside, and as he came up to the open ditch he dived at it, and I could see he was going to fall. As he landed, he rolled over on to the patch of ground where Devon Loch would have landed, but the great horse literally changed his direction in mid-air, side-stepped the sprawling Domata and raced on without hesitation.

From then on I had the sort of run one dreams about. Horses which fell did so at a convenient distance, loose horses did not bother us, and Devon Loch's jumping got better and better. He cleared the Chair fence and the water-jump in front of the stands, and went out into the country again lying sixth or seventh in a fairly closely bunched field. M'as-tu-vu was just behind us then, but three fences later he miscalculated the open ditch, and went no further. During the next mile Devon Loch was gradually passing horse after horse by out-jumping them, and as we approached the Canal Turn we were lying second. Armorial III was in front but Devon Loch was going so splendidly that there was no need to hurry. Never before in the National had I held back a horse and said 'Steady, boy.' Never had I felt such power in reserve, such confidence in my mount, such calm in my mind.

Armorial III fell at the fence after Valentine's, and Eagle Lodge took his place, but Devon Loch went past him a fence later and, with three to jump, he put his nose in front. Amazingly, I was still holding Devon Loch back, and when I saw beside me that E.S.B., Ontray, and Gentle Moya were being ridden hard, I was sure we were going to win. Twenty yards from the last fence I could see that Devon Loch was meeting it perfectly, and he jumped it as stylishly as if it had been the first of thirty,

* *The Sport of Queens:* Dick Francis (Michael Joseph 1957, revised 1968, revised 1974).

24 The 1956 Grand National at Becher's Brook second time round. Left to right: Devon Loch (R. Francis), E.S.B. (D. Dick) a neck in front, and Sundew (F. Winter) about to fall.

instead of the last. He landed cleanly. Behind him lay more than four miles and the thirty fences of the Grand National Steeplechase, and in front only a few hundred yards stretched to the winning post. In all my life I have never experienced a greater joy than the knowledge that I was about to win the National.

As we drew away from E.S.B., the cheers of the crowds greeting Her Majesty Queen Elizabeth the Queen Mother's great horse seemed to echo my own exhilaration. I had no anxieties. Deven Loch was galloping fast, incredibly fresh after the long race, and I had only to keep him going collectedly in the easy rhythm he had established. The winning post drew rapidly nearer, the cheers were coming to a buffeting crescendo, and I was rejoicing that I was being a partner in

fulfilling the dream of the horse's Royal owner. There were less than fifty yards of flat green grass to cover, and in about ten more strides we would have been home.

The calamity which overtook us was sudden, terrible, and completely without warning to either the horse or me. In one stride he was bounding smoothly along, a poem of controlled motion; in the next, his hind legs stiffened and refused to function. He fell flat on his belly, his limbs splayed out sideways and backwards in unnatural angles, and when he stood up he could hardly move. Even then, if he could have got going again he might still have had a chance, because we were a long way clear of E.S.B.: but the rhythm was shattered, the dream was over, and the race was lost.

25 At the last fence, Devon Loch leading E.S.B. and going much the better.

26 The collapse of Devon Loch fifty yards from the winning post.

We all have moments we remember in racing. Fortunately nearly all of them are the good ones. My most vivid memories of the Royal Family in racing are the victories of King George VI's Hypericum in the One Thousand Guineas after she had bolted before the start and all seemed lost, of the thrill of Aureole winning the King George VI and Queen Elizabeth Stakes at Ascot, and of Dunfermline coming from behind from a hopeless position to win the Oaks in Silver Jubilee Year and Queen Elizabeth beside her in the unsaddling enclosure.

My worst moment—and there is no shadow of doubt about it—was the completely unexpected and sudden collapse of Devon Loch fifty yards from the post in the Grand National of 1956, with the race at his mercy and everybody cheering wildly. It was absolutely shattering. A million to one on a Royal victory in the most famous steeplechase in the world, and the sudden collapse within sight of everyone in the stands. Dick Francis, now a great writer of racing thrillers, has described the race eloquently from the back of Devon Loch, but he could not see what we all saw from the stands and that was that after Devon Loch and E.S.B. had jumped the last fence almost together and Devon Loch had begun to draw steadily ahead in the long run in, Dave Dick had completely accepted defeat on the dead-tired E.S.B. and had stopped riding him long before Devon Loch collapsed. When Devon Loch struggled to his feet again after falling, there was still time for Francis to get him going again for Francis miraculously had stayed in the saddle, but sadly the hind legs were apparently immobile and just did not react. The wild cheering of the crowd was suddenly hushed, as people saw what had happened— expressions of horror on the faces of some, incredulity and misery on the faces of others.

The official verdict was E.S.B. the winner of the 1956 Grand National by ten lengths from the mare Gentle Moya with Royal Tan ten lengths further away third and Eagle Lodge fourth. Ontray, who had been in the hunt coming on to the racecourse, fell two fences from home.

When Devon Loch struggled to his feet and seemed unable to move, the only thing was for Francis to dismount, his misery and anguish clear to all. Bill Braddon, Fairlawne's travelling head lad, ran out on to the course, and loosened the girths on Devon Loch and soon afterwards he was led away to the racecourse stables. Francis was looking forlornly for his whip when an ambulance man came to his rescue, beckoned to him, and took him straight to the first-aid room. From here he was able to go to the weighing room and avoid the milling crowd.

A few minutes later, Peter Cazalet came down and together they went up to the Royal Box. It was very quiet. Everybody naturally was very sad and very upset and the Royal Family still had the nagging anxiety that there might be something seriously wrong with Devon Loch, though he had appeared to walk away sound. The Queen and Queen Elizabeth tried to

27 Devon Loch being led away after the race by John Hole, apparently sound. Dick Francis on his way back to the weighing-room.

comfort Francis, and then Queen Elizabeth with Cazalet went over to see Devon Loch. He naturally looked like a horse who had had a hard race but, apart from that, there was no heat nor swelling in his legs, and a vet who examined him found nothing wrong with his heart.

What caused Devon Loch to pancake in the way he did? Dick Francis emphatically rules out two theories which were advanced after the race. The first was that he tried to jump the water jump which he saw out of the corner of his eye. A ghost jump, it was called in the newspaper at the time, and the pictures did seem to suggest something of the sort was possible. A close look at the pictures revealed, however, that if Devon Loch had been going to jump a ghost water jump, as was suggested, he would certainly have taken off later—that is, nearer to the jump than he did. He was a horse of great intelligence and a brilliant jumper, and in Francis's view he would never have taken off so early had the ghost jump theory been correct.

Secondly, Francis is convinced that Devon Loch's collapse was nothing to do with heart trouble. He jumped the last fence full of running and was, in fact, sprinting home, unextended, when he fell. Surely a horse does not have a heart attack unless the horse is on the point of exhaustion and collapse, and Devon Loch clearly was not in that condition. 'I have ridden a lot of tired horses,' said Francis, 'and I know the feel of them. He was not going like a tired horse, rolling and staggering with effort.'*

Another theory is that the horse's hind legs just went away from him on false going and he came down. Several years after the race, Frederick Walmsley, a police officer on duty at Aintree on the day of the race, wrote as follows to Queen Elizabeth: 'My posting on this Grand National day was on top of the County Stand directly overlooking the water jump. During the morning before spectators arrived, I was looking down on the Aintree course, when I noticed what appeared to be an unusual darker patch of green turf by the inside rail of the flat course, directly opposite the water jump on the steeplechase course. I went down onto the course with a colleague and we found, on examination, that this particular patch was extremely saturated and absolutely sodden in comparison to the rest of the flat course. After investigation, I concluded that this was caused by a faulty stop cock nearly under the rail and used for filling the water jump. The stop cock was allowing water to seep into the adjoining ground. . . . I am not a professional racing man but may I suggest that Devon Loch struck this totally different going to the rest of the course and his feet skidded from under him?' Is this another simpler, explanation? Personally I think not, because it does not explain why Devon Loch pricked his ears, nor, I think, would there have been false going from the leaking stop cock several yards before the water jump—but false going perhaps could have been a contributory factor.

Two theories remain, one propounded by several people to do with the horse, and one by Dick Francis himself. The first of these two theories was that Devon Loch was suddenly attacked by some sort of muscular cramp or spasm in his hindquarters, which caused him suddenly to lose the use of his hind legs. Mr Denys Danby, for many years a leading vet, who treated Devon Loch, thought that red worm infestation in early life might have been responsible for some unseen damage to the horse, affecting his circulation. Bryan Marshall, in three of the races in which he rode him, noticed that he faltered unexpectedly during a race, suggesting the horse had some weakness. Alex King, then a member of the Fairlawne staff and now a stud manager, who was at Aintree on the day looking after M'as-tu-vu, was of the opinion that it might have been the result of giving too much glucose to Devon Loch in a certain form. Cazalet was a great believer in glucose and I believe it was thought that glucose as then given could cause cramp. But if it was cramp or a spasm, why did Devon Loch prick his ears before his hind legs went from under him?

I have left Dick Francis's theory to the last because I think myself now that it is the most probable explanation of Devon Loch's collapse, and I put it in Francis's own words.*

Devon Loch was galloping easily, he pricked his ears, and he fell for no visible reason in a peculiar way not seen before or since on the racecourse. If that was the only fall of its kind, it is worth asking

* From: *The Sport of Queens*.

whether on this one occasion there was anything else which had never happened before. There was. It was the only time that a reigning sovereign had been at Liverpool cheering home a Royal winner of the Grand National. [When Edward VII, as Prince of Wales, had won with Ambush, Queen Victoria had not been present.] Could there possibly be any connection of cause and effect in these two unique events? Sad and ironic though it may be, it is conceivable that it was simply and solely because Devon Loch belonged to the Queen Mother that Devon Loch fell where and how he did.

From the last fence onwards the cheers which greeted us were tremendous and growing louder with every yard we went, and although I knew the reason for them, they may have been puzzling and confusing to my mount, who could not know that his owner was a Queen. In order to hear better what was going on, he would make a horse's instinctive movement to do so, and into those newly pricked and sensitive ears fell a wave of sound of shattering intensity. The noise that to me was uplifting and magnificent may have been exceedingly frightening to Devon Loch. He may have tried to throw himself backwards away from it; he may have reacted to it in the same

28 On top of the stand at Aintree as Devon Loch starts to 'pancake' with the race at his mercy, some not yet realising the impending tragedy. Front row, left to right: Princess Margaret, the Queen, the Princess Royal, Mrs Cazalet, Peter Cazalet, Queen Elizabeth. Second row, left to right: Lady Paynter, Sir Martin Gilliat, 'Frenchie' Nicholson, Mrs Roddy Armytage, Peter Hastings-Bass, who later trained for the Queen, Lord Abergavenny and Jack Clayton, who trained for the Princess Royal.

convulsive way as a human being jumps at a sudden loud noise, and a severe nervous jerk at such a stage in the race could certainly have been enough to smash the rhythm of his stride and bring him down. The cheering was incredible . . . I have never heard in my life such a noise. It rolled and lapped around us, buffeting and glorious, the enthusiastic expression of love for the Royal family and delight in seeing the Royal horse win. The tremendous noise was growing in volume with every second, and was being almost funnelled down from the stands on to the course. The weather records show that there was a light breeze blowing that day from behind the stands, and this must have carried the huge sound with it.

I remember how startled I was when I first heard the cheers for M'as-tu-vu at Lingfield, and they were a whisper compared with the enveloping roar at Liverpool; so I think one must seriously consider whether Devon Loch may not have been struck down by joy.

Or to put it differently: was Devon Loch scared so stiff that he fell?

I do not suppose there was a comparable volume of cheering at Aintree again until Red Rum won his third Grand National twenty-one years later in 1977, and Tommy Stack, who rode him, was in no doubt afterwards that Red Rum had flinched and faltered, giving him the feeling of being terrified at the volume of noise as he approached the finishing post in that long run-in. The difference between Devon Loch and Red Rum, of course, was that Red Rum was fighting out the finish of the National for the fifth time, and so knew that the mass of people facing him as he neared the winning post was nothing to worry about as the course was to bear sharp left before he reached them. Devon Loch, taking part in the National for the first time, knew no such thing, only a deafening volume of noise and a crowd of faces facing him less than a hundred yards ahead.

Dick Francis has a growing number of friends who now support his theory of noise. He remembers Frank Pullen, who devoted his life to horses, telling him how he was standing next to his father on the grandstand watching the race and, as Devon Loch neared the finish, saying to his father that the crescendo of noise would surely terrify the horse—and no sooner had he said it than down went Devon Loch. Richard Pitman on Pendil, when just beaten in the 1973 Cheltenham Gold Cup, always felt that Pendil faltered suddenly in the run-in through fear of the cheering from the stands and that made the difference between victory and defeat. No doubt there are many more examples. The effect of noise on humans is unpredictable; the effect of noise on animals is unpredictable, too.

The following Monday, a B.B.C. camera team went down to Fairlawne to take pictures of Devon Loch. All went well until the leader of the team asked Peter Cazalet if he would kindly arrange for Devon Loch to 'pancake' to the ground as he had done at Aintree. Cazalet had not slept for two nights worrying about the reason for the horse's fall and the B.B.C. team did not remain at Fairlawne much longer that morning. Cazalet was not amused. It was the third time that Fairlawne had come near to winning a National and fate had stepped in to stop it—Davy Jones through a broken buckle to a rein in 1936, Cromwell, owing to Lord Mildmay's damaged neck, and now Devon Loch.

Queen Elizabeth did her best to alleviate the pain and grief. She sent Cazalet a cigarette box 'as a memento of that terrible and yet glorious day last Saturday—glorious because of Devon Loch's magnificent performance and terrible because of that unprecented disaster when victory seemed so sure. We must now pray that such a gallant horse will go on to another great race, perhaps next year. . . . I am sure that you know,' added Queen Elizabeth, 'how deeply I feel for you. I am beginning to learn more of the immense amount of thought and work that goes into the preparation of a horse for racing and I can understand a little of the anguish you must have felt at such a cruel blow. I send my heartfelt sympathy to you and all in the Fairlawne stable. We will not be done in by this, and will just keep on trying.'

Four days after the National, Queen Elizabeth went down to Fairlawne to see Devon Loch. Francis was there to ride him in the park and to school Queen Elizabeth's other horses, and soon afterwards Francis was summoned to go to Windsor Castle where Queen Elizabeth gave Francis a cheque and a cigarette box as a memento of the race that was so nearly won. It was a lovely box and there was a charming inscription on its lid. Dick Francis, unspoilt by his great success as a writer, produced it out of its case when I went to see him recently. Twenty-four years later it is still, I feel, his most treasured possession.

5

The Late 1950s

THE FOLLOWING season of 1956–57 did not start as had been Peter Cazalet's wont with a lot of runners at the West Country meetings in August and September. In Lord Mildmay's day there were always Cazalet winners early on at Newton Abbot, at Devon and Exeter, and at Buckfastleigh—all within easy motoring distance of Lord Mildmay's Devon home at Mothecombe. Some of the horses would stay down in the West Country for two or three races and be stabled at Buckfastleigh racecourse, and after racing there would be cricket in the evening between Lord Mildmay's XI and an eleven composed of owners, trainers, and jockeys. In Dick Francis's first successful year for Fairlawne in 1953–54, Cazalet had a Newton Abbot treble on the first day of the new season and nearly a dozen West Country winners in the first month of the season. In the future, the pattern was to change; he did not have his horses ready quite so early, and he was to concentrate more on the meetings round London and in Kent and Sussex, to which Queen Elizabeth and his other owners could most conveniently come.

Queen Elizabeth's first runner in the new season was at Hurst Park in October, and the Queen and Queen Elizabeth both came to see the new horse Double Star make his début in England in the Mayflower Novices Hurdle. A dark brown, almost black gelding with a small star and three white socks, Double Star was an exceptionally good-looking horse, and he was to take the place of M'as-tu-vu. In Freeman's opinion, M'as-tu-vu had definitely lost his zest for racing and he was sold soon after the 1956 Grand National to Mr Hugh Craig-Harvey, a keen amateur rider who was later to form the Broomhill Manor Stud in Cornwall.

Double Star, bred in County Kildare, was originally trained by Charlie McCartan of Moynalty in County Meath. He won a two-mile bumper for four-year-olds only at Leopardstown in January 1956, having previously had two or three outings over hurdles. By Arctic Star out of the good brood-mare Bright Star, who was the dam of half a dozen winners, Double Star was brought for Queen Elizabeth by Judge W. E. Wylie, a leading figure in Irish racing and in the show ring for many years. Double Star on breeding was certainly entitled to gallop, for Arctic Star was a well-bred Nearco horse and Double Star's second dam (grand-dam), Sharp

The Lingfield Treble, 9 December 1961 : The Rip, Double Star and Laffy. Painting by Peter Biegel.

Peter Biegel's sketch of Laffy for the above painting.

The Rip, painting by Peter Biegel.

Makaldar, painting by Peter Biegel.

Kitty, was a half-sister (having the same dam) to the 1929 Lincolnshire Handicap winner Elton and the 1931 Irish Two Thousand Guineas winner Double Arch. Moreover, Double Star's full sister, Stella Coeli, had shown herself already a good staying handicapper in Ireland.

Double Star arrived at Fairlawne in the spring of 1956. When he was vetted on Queen Elizabeth's behalf, there was a scare that his sight was defective and an eye specialist came down to examine his eyes; he prescribed two kinds of drops to put in each day for a fortnight—one sort in the morning, the other at night. At the end of the period, Double Star's eyes passed the vet's examination and the purchase went ahead. The new arrival carried his head high. Fairgrieve drove him over hurdles in a long rein to get his head down and make him look at the obstacles, but he was a very hard puller to start with. Nevertheless he worked so well that Cazalet thought he would win first time out if he could be made to settle. It proved to be a big 'if'. Most horses settled well for Dick Francis. Double Star was an exception. Three horses with winning form opposed Double Star at Hurst Park, and on this occsion he would not settle and did not win what was the first of his fifty races for Queen Elizabeth.

A week later, Devon Loch went up to Nottingham to run in the Bulcote Hurdle, another novice hurdle, though the distance was two-and-a-half miles instead of the customary novice hurdle distance of two miles. Traffic Cop, who had finished in front of Double Star at Hurst Park, Northern King, who was to prove himself one of the best novice chasers of the season, and Twin Star, a half-brother to Killarney and Roddy Owen were thought likely to have too much speed for the ten-year-old Devon Loch. Half way through the race, Devon Loch was so far out of his ground that it did not look as if he could win. At the last flight of hurdles, he was still nearly ten lengths behind the leader, but in the end he won his one and only hurdle race by two lengths from Northern King. The victory showed that he was apparently none the worse for the Grand National incident seven months before.

None the worse for this unexpected victory, Devon Loch reverted to fences—his real game—in November. He was engaged in three-mile chases both at Sandown and at Kempton, and as he was better handicapped at Kempton, to Kempton he went to take on the 1954 Cheltenham Gold Cup winner Four Ten and the previous season's Cheltenham Gold Cup winner, Limber Hill, trained in Yorkshire by Bill Dutton of Tipperary Tim fame. Also in the field were Key Royal, recent winner of the Grand Sefton, and Sundew, due to win the following year's Grand National. The race proved to be a tremendous duel between Devon Loch and Key Royal. Devon Loch just led at the last but hit it. Francis, however, got his horse going again so quickly that he went a length up, but was then caught and beaten half a length in the last thirty yards. The ten pounds he was giving to Key Royal just turned the scales

29 Devon Loch (R. Francis), the winner, and the 1953 Grand National winner Early Mist (B. Marshall) in the Ewell Chase at Sandown in December 1956.

against him. The same afternoon, Lester Piggott, having just celebrated his twenty-first birthday, won over hurdles.

At Sandown a fortnight later, Devon Loch and the 1953 Grand National winner Early Mist fought out a match in the Ewell Chase at level weights. Early Mist, both ridden and trained by Bryan Marshall, forced the pace, but Devon Loch definitely jumped the better of the two and won on merit. On the final day of the week at Hurst Park, with ten Cazalet winners in the bag in ten days and the stable thus in great form, Dick Francis hoped to win on Double Star and on King's Point, another new purchase of Queen Elizabeth's. King's Point had also been bought in Ireland by Judge Wylie after the horse had finished second in a bumper at Leopardstown in November 1955 as a six-year-old. King's Point was by the Windsor Lad horse Queen's Eyot out of the Steel Point mare Steel Girl, dam of three other humble winners in Ireland, and he certainly looked a chaser in the making.

King's Point was one of a big field in the Henry VIII Chase, then one of the hottest races for novice chasers in the first half of the jumping season, but Queen Elizabeth's newcomer was probably out of his depth in such company so early in his career. At any rate he gave Francis a bad fall at the first fence, dislocating Francis's left shoulder, which had been out several times before. Francis had won the previous race on Crudwell, one of his favourite steeplechasing friends, and he hoped to win the last race of the afternoon on Double Star. A dislocated shoulder is one of the most painful of dislocations and with many people the shoulder does not go back easily without an anaesthetic. Francis knew that if he did not keep quiet about his dislocated shoulder he would lose the ride on Double Star to Cazalet's second jockey, Arthur Freeman, so his wife Mary was found and brought to the ambulance room. She had learnt how to put the dislocated shoulder back in spite of the pain her husband was in. This required courage from both, but it was done.

'I remember well going out for that last race,' said Dick Francis. 'I was heavily strapped up, but Double Star was still a terrific puller. I knew that I was going to be a complete passenger, that Double Star was an odds-on favourite, and that the betting public had not the slightest idea of my predicament. In the circumstances, I could not begin to hold Double Star. I was in front most of the way and I won all right, but it was just as well it was not a tight finish.'

There was snow over most of the country at Christmas 1956 and the only racing on Boxing Day was at Fontwell. The King George VI Chase at Kempton was postponed until the following day and Fairlawne was represented in the race by Devon Loch, ridden by Francis, Lochroe, ridden by Freeman, and by an unexpected third string in Rose Park, considered to be at his best over two miles. Owned in partnership by Guy Lawrence and Dick Wilkins, Lawrence was in favour of running Rose Park over the sharp Kempton three miles, Wilkins was not keen, and Cazalet was definitely against doing so. Lawrence's wishes prevailed, however, and Michael Scudamore, who was to win the 1959 Grand National on Oxo, was engaged. Scudamore was lucky to get to the course in time, for there were deep snowdrifts round his Herefordshire home, and he only got out with the use of a tractor. Queen Elizabeth, avoiding the snow-bound roads, came by train from Sandringham. Devon Loch

30 Galloway Braes (F. Winter) leads Devon Loch (R. Francis), Wise Child (G. Milburn) and Lochroe (A. Freeman) in the King George VI Chase at Sandown on 27 December 1956. Rose Park, also Fairlawne-trained, was the winner by two lengths from Devon Loch.

was favourite for the race and that brilliant chaser Galloway Braes, owned by Sir Percy and Lady Orde, was second favourite. He had already won the race in very fast time and had been second the two previous years but this front-runner was now approaching twelve and possibly past his best.

Rose Park appeared to have lost his form the previous season and Lawrence and Wilkins had decided to pension him off but, as no one was keen to have him, they had changed their minds. In the King George VI Chase he made the running as usual and was clear at half way passing the stands. Soon afterwards Galloway Braes made a bad mistake which put him out of court. With a mile to go, the three Fairlawne runners were clear of the others with the race between them. With two fences to go, Devon Loch lay second about four lengths behind Rose Park. Lochroe blundered at this fence and the race lay between Rose Park and Devon Loch. Rose Park still led by about three lengths at the last, and although he was weakening in the run-in he held the challenge of Devon Loch by two lengths, to the great disappointment not only of Queen Elizabeth but of the large holiday crowd.

Queen Elizabeth had not met the joint owners of Rose Park before. Having beaten Queen Elizabeth's favourite horse Devon Loch, seeking a consolation prize after his cruel luck in the Grand National, it cannot have been an easy occasion for Lawrence and Wilkins to receive Queen Elizabeth's congratulations.

Francis was of the opinion that Deven Loch had lost a bit of his dash and was not quite as good as in the previous season. Although Kempton was rather a sharp course for Devon Loch, Francis felt that he would have caught Rose Park if he had been as good as he was on Grand National day.

The race was marred by Galloway Braes falling, breaking a leg, and having to be put down. Queen Elizabeth, having suffered similarly with Monaveen, wrote quickly to Lady Orde on Kempton Park note paper to catch her before she left the course. 'I have just heard the terrible news,' wrote Queen Elizabeth, 'and I feel I must send you my deepest sympathy. I know how much you loved your wonderful horse, and my heart is full of sadness for you.'

Ten days later, Francis went up to Leicester to ride Crudwell to victory in a three-mile chase and soon afterwards at Hurst Park he was beaten on Double Star in a novices' hurdle—his last ride for Queen Elizabeth. At Newbury on January 11, he had a spare ride in the colours of Captain E. J. Edwards-Heathcote on the handicap hurdler, Prince Stephen, whom his owner was then training himself in Somerset. Prince Stephen fell at the second last flight when up with the leaders and Dick Francis had a very bad fall, breaking his right wrist and being badly kicked in the stomach and spleen, which meant a long spell of pain and discomfort to follow. To rub salt in the wound, King's Point, Freeman up, won his first race for Queen Elizabeth at Newbury the next day. The following week at

Sandown, Freeman again took the place of the injured Francis and brought off a Fairlawne double on Double Star and Lochroe.

31 Double Star (A. Freeman), the winner, leading Renaldo (W. Rees) in the Novices' Chase at Sandown on 22 November 1957.

The next day, Devon Loch made his second attempt to win the Mildmay Memorial Chase, now carrying top weight. Freeman was well back in the early part of the race but after jumping the water second time round Devon Loch began to improve his position. I can see him now moving up steadily through his field, jumping superbly. At the bottom end of the course, approaching the Pond fence, he looked to have a great chance but at the second last, which he jumped in front with Mr H. J. Joel's Glorious Twelfth he faltered, and Glorious Twelfth just led him going to the last. Arthur Freeman, now based on Newmarket, still remembers the race well. 'Devon Loch jumped perfectly throughout,' recalled Freeman. 'I felt I had hit the front too soon but going to the last he was still disputing the lead, and I remember saying to him, "Steady, boy, steady," and we really "pinged" it. Then half-way up the run-in he suddenly faltered and down he went almost on his knees, and if his head had not come up at the last moment, I would have gone. By the time we had recovered, three horses had passed us and we had lost and only finished fourth. Although he was lame after the race, I felt at the time that some spasm or something like it had attacked him in the run-in, rather like it had possibly done at Aintree.' It was an intensely exciting race with much cheering, and whether poor Devon Loch was again alarmed by the hub-bub, and this caused him to falter in the way described by Freeman, I do not know.

The following day, Peter Cazalet announced that Devon Loch had broken down during the Mildmay Memorial—in my view, probably at the seond last fence when he faltered. A tendon had gone again as it had four years before. He went from Fairlawne to Miss Norah Wilmot's stables at Binfield Grove in Berkshire to have electrical treatment from Sir Charles Strong, who was by now making a great name for himself dealing with horses as well as humans. Strong got Devon Loch sound again but it is doubtful if he would have stood up to a lot more racing and Queen Elizabeth wisely decided that his racing days were over. She gave him to Sir Noel Murless at Newmarket as a trainer's hack, but he was still a bit too lively to be ideal for the job. After a time, he went to Sandringham to end his days peacefully. In his last winter, it was clear that he was not able to hold his own and Queen Elizabeth gave permission for this top class but desperately unlucky horse to be put down at the age of sixteen. What is not often remembered is that if Devon Loch had galloped on to victory normally up that long Aintree straight in the 1956 Grand National, Queen Elizabeth's great chaser would easily have beaten Golden Miller's record time for the race, which was subsequently broken by Red Rum in 1973.

Queen Elizabeth would have liked to have had another of the progeny of Devon Loch's dam Coolaleen, but Coolaleen had died young after producing four foals by Devonian. The first, Donaleen, a bay colt, had been sold cheaply as a yearling and had gone to South Africa where he had proved himself a useful mile handicapper; the second was Devon Loch. The third foal, Devon Colleen, a bay filly, also went to South Africa, took time to develop like Devon Loch, and started winning races as a four-year-old.

Coolaleen's fourth and last foal, Queen of Devon, another bay filly, went to the yard of the Currah trainer Michael Dawson, who had bought her on behalf of his daughter and son-in-law Joe Canty, the former Irish jockey. Queen of Devon won as a three-year-old in Ireland in 1951, but it was decided to send her hurdling and, four years later as a seven-year-old, she won a novice hurdle at Naas. A week after the Devon Loch disaster at Aintree, Queen of Devon as an eight-year-old—two years Devon Loch's junior—ran unplaced in a hurdle race at Phoenix Park. As Devon Loch's full sister and a winner on the flat and over hurdles, she was then worth a lot of money as a potential brood-mare, but it was decided to go on running her, and a month later, again in a novice chase at Naas, she fell at the last fence when winning, broke a leg and had to be put down. Spring 1956 was a sad time for two of Coolaleen's progeny of four. Coolaleen herself had died in 1949 after slipping twins to Devonian. She had retained an afterbirth, and that had proved fatal.

Ten days after Devon Loch had broken down and run his last race, Dick Francis announced his retirement from race riding. He was badly injured internally by his fall at Newbury. He was thirty-six at the time, and if Devon Loch had not broken down, he would probably have tried to continue. He then decided to write and his first book, his autobiography *The Sport of Queens*, was to come out the following year. As a writer, he has never looked back. The retirement of Francis and Devon Loch was the end of a chapter for Fairlawne. Arthur Freeman was to be the stable jockey for the rest of the 1950s as Queen Elizabeth slowly increased her involvement in racing, and during this period Double Star was the only outstanding horse. The supporting cast, bought either in Ireland as stores or as made horses who had already shown promise on the Irish racecourses, were on the whole rather disappointing.

Queen Elizabeth had approved the scheme whereby Hill-Dillon bought yearlings in Ireland and then sent them over to Norfolk where they made their way to Major Eldred Wilson at Harpley Dams for making and breaking. The first two of the stores to appear were Gipsy Love and Flamingo Bay, both sons of the Lincolnshire Handicap winner Flamenco, who stood for a long time in County Kildare. Gipsy Love, who was rather small and rather scatty, went to Fairlawne and did not make the grade.

Flamingo Bay had more scope, plenty of good looks and seemed full of promise. After being hunted by Eldred Wilson as a four-year-old, he went down to Mr Roy Trigg, a member of a well-known Hampshire farming family. Roy Trigg, after migrating from Hampshire to Sussex, had ridden a lot of point-to-point winners and he looked on Flamingo Bay as a real chasing prospect, and so did Cazalet. As a six-year-old in 1956, he was placed in a couple of steeplechases but he lacked stamina, went point-to-pointing with Eldred Wilson without success and then went as a gift from Queen Elizabeth to Major Peter Borwick, Master of the Pytchley, where he really found his niche, just as the reluctant Billposter had done in the north several years before. During the summer, Flamingo Bay used to come down to Ascot to act as starter's hack to Mr Alec Marsh, the Jockey Club starter, who was always immaculately turned out for the Royal meeting. As Flamingo Bay waited patiently for the starter in the paddock, some time during most racing afternoons Queen Elizabeth would go to talk to him. After all, she had known him since yearling days in Norfolk.

Nine more stores were to follow, of which only one, Wild West, won under National Hunt rules when trained at Fairlawne. One of the last four, however, included a highly-strung gelding called Gay Record, who was a failure at Fairlawne. He had latent ability and he was to show it in the 1960s. The fact remained, however, that eleven yearlings had been carefully chosen, broken and made by experts and only one of the eleven was to make his name as a chaser. Queen Elizabeth loved having the stores close at hand at Sandringham, but the experiment had not really worked out well, so it was abandoned at the end of the 1950s.

With the stores unproductive, Cazalet had to find made horses to back up Double Star. In the 1956–57 season, Double Star only ran over hurdles, winning two novices ridden by Francis and one ridden by Freeman. The next season he was put to chasing, and Queen Elizabeth saw him win his first novice chase at Sandown in November. A week later at Newbury, he appeared in a new race—the Tote Investors Cup for novice chasers. The prize was large for the times and seven of the field of eight had won novice chases in the preceding few weeks. Norton, from Crump's Yorkshire stable, who had beaten Double Star over the Newbury course in October, Caesar's Helm from Renton's Yorkshire stable, Cheltenham winners in Le Siroco II and Wartown, the Champion hurdler Clair Soleil, and the Windsor winner Brunel II were thought to be the pick of the novice chasers of the new season. Double Star was becoming less headstrong, and Freeman got him to settle well in this Newbury race and come from behind to beat Brunel II and Clair Soleil. Afterwards Mr J. P. Phillips of the Dalham Hall Stud, Newmarket, well-known as an owner-breeder and the then chairman of Tote Investors, had the pleasure of presenting to Queen Elizabeth the first racing cup Her Majesty had won.

As the Old Year went out, Queen Elizabeth was preparing for her 1958 tour of New Zealand and Australia, in which she flew over 25,000 miles round the world—the first King or Queen to do so. In New Zealand, she

32   A week later, Queen Elizabeth receiving her first trophy after Double Star had won the Tote Investors Cup at Newbury on 30 November 1957. Mr J. P. Philipps makes the presentation.

went racing at Trentham, near Wellington, where the Queen and Prince Philip had been racing four years before. The principal race of the day was the St James's Cup which was won by Sir Ernest Davis, a former Mayor of Auckland, with his good stayer Bali Ha'i III. As Queen Elizabeth came down the steps to present the Cup to Sir Ernest, Colonel Sir Martin Gilliat, who had been appointed private secretary and equerry to Queen Elizabeth in 1956, was able to whisper to her at the last moment that he understood Sir Ernest was intending to present Bali Ha'i to her. Queen Elizabeth gave the cup to Sir Ernest, whereupon Sir Ernest went to the microphone and said that he had suddenly decided to present Bali Ha'i to Queen Elizabeth, adding that the horse was a present for 'the greatest lady in the world' and he would send Bali Ha'i to England for Her Majesty with his special delicacy peppermints to keep him happy! It was a charming gesture, made on the spur of the moment, and it brought the crowd to their feet. Throughout her time in New Zealand Queen Elizabeth had been given a tremendous reception, and it was equally overwhelming in Australia.

It had originally been planned that Queen Elizabeth would get back to England on March 10 on the eve of the National Hunt meeting at Cheltenham, but her aeroplane was held up by engine trouble and she arrived back three days later than planned, and missed seeing the victory of Edward Cazalet, Peter Cazalet's only son by his first marriage, in the Kim Muir Cup for amateur riders on the Fairlawne favourite, Lochroe.

Queen Elizabeth also just missed seeing the first victory of her new horse, King of the Isle, who had been bought by Cazalet the previous spring from his Irish breeder, Dr W. J. Purcell. Cazalet, at the same time as buying King of the Isle, had bought at Queen Elizabeth's suggestion his own sister, Queen of the Isle, who was one year his junior. Cazalet did not like training mares. He felt that they upset the opposite sex. It looked as if Queen of the Isle would win races but she was an excitable mare in training and she fell in each of her first three chases and never again ran with the promise she had originally shown. She was, however, to prove Queen Elizabeth's outstanding brood-mare. At the end of her racing days, she looked a bad buy. At the end of her breeding days, she had proved herself a good one.

Arthur Freeman won the 1958 Grand National on Mr What. The week before he did so, Mr What's full brother Inquisitive Pete, who was two years younger, won a two-mile bumper at Phoenix Park. He was owned and trained by Mr J. J. Prendergast. Inquisitive Pete was down the course in a similar race at Baldoyle a month later, but on paper, as a full brother to a Grand National winner, he looked an attractive proposition, and Cazalet bought him soon afterwards for Queen Elizabeth.

Double Star had been bought from Mr C. McCartan of Moynalty, and Cazalet went back to McCartan to buy from him a big tall bay gelding by

33 King of the Isle (A. Freeman) and Mr J. M. Whitney's Belgrano (D. Ancil), the winner, fighting out the finish of the Newtown Hurdle at Newbury on 10 January 1958.

Owenstown called Out of Town, who had run in the same bumper at Phoenix Park as Inquisite Pete. Out of Town, standing 17 hands, was Moynalty-bred, his dam Dismissal being a Flamenco mare who bred a couple of other winners. Cazalet also bought from McCartan in 1959, the four-year-old Battle Front who had shown promise in his only race in Ireland, a maiden hurdle at Leopardstown, and was a half-brother to French Brave, a useful two-mile chaser who had been winning races in England in the 1957–58 season. His other purchase of note for Queen Elizabeth in the late 1950s was Sparkling Knight. He was in training in Ireland with Charlie Rogers, a great name for many years in Irish racing, and was already the winner of two bumpers in 1957 and a three-mile novices' chase at Baldoyle early in 1958.

With these Irish purchases back in England, Queen Elizabeth had eight horses in training at the start of the 1958–59 season. Double Star, with six victories already to his credit, was again the star performer. He started the new season by winning a two-mile chase at Newbury from the great Mandarin, from whom he was receiving a lot of weight. In December, he returned to his favourite course Lingfield to make light of soft going and of top weight in the Ashdown Handicap Chase. This was the meeting for which, from 1956 onwards, Queen Elizabeth usually came to stay at Fairlawne for the weekend and at which Cazalet naturally hoped to saddle a number of winners.

Double Star had won on the first day of Queen Elizabeth's first Fairlawne weekend in 1956, and it was hoped that Sparkling Knight would do likewise in 1958, but he was a most uncertain jumper, and he fell near the finish of his race when no longer a fighting factor, giving the wretched Freeman the second of five crushing falls he endured from Sparkling Knight during the season. How different was Double Star who, to the best of my knowledge, never fell in his fifty races for Queen Elizabeth, over forty of which were over fences!

In the first week in 1959 at Hurst Park, Queen Elizabeth had her first racing double. Double Star, in spite of having to hump round over twelve stone in soft going, managed to give a stone and a beating to Delmacare from the neighbouring Kent stable of Chris Nesfield at Charing in the Star and Garter Chase. An hour later, Sparkling Knight, carrying top weight in the Tolworth Handicap Chase, just got the better of a desperate finish with Beau Chevalet. In between giving Freeman five falls during the season, he did win three steeplechases, so perhaps one should not be too hard on him. The sad thing was that he had the scope to be a good chaser if only he could have learnt to jump.

The following day at Newbury, Queen Elizabeth nearly had another double. The newcomer Out of Town, running for the first time under National Hunt rules, was an unexpected winner of the Newtown Hurdle,

34 Double Star (A. Freeman), the winner, leading Delmacare (F. Winter) in the Star and Garter Chase at Hurst Park on 8 January 1959—the first leg of Queen Elizabeth's first racing double. Sparkling Knight won the second leg.

owing much to Freeman's strong driving. Half an hour later the grey Classiebaun, bought in Ireland on the recommendation of Judge Wylie, was second in the Elcot Park Chase for novices, which was as close as this disappointing horse ever got to winning a steeplechase. At the end of the day, there was frost in the air and practically no more racing took place in England during the month of January. Then, just before Queen Elizabeth left for Kenya, Double Star and Out of Town both won again—her last victories under National Hunt rules for nearly a year.

The New Zealander Bali Ha'i was, however, to do well during the 1959 flat racing season. Bali Ha'i had won seven races in New Zealand, including the Great Northern St Leger and the St James's Cup, when Sir Ernest Davis suddenly decided on his gift. The horse was shipped from Trentham in March 1958 and arrived in England towards the end of April, going into training with Sir Cecil Boyd-Rochfort at Freemason Lodge. Unfortunately, he cracked a sesamoid bone in his near fore soon after he arrived, so he could not race in England during 1958. Queen Elizabeth came down to Freemason Lodge early in 1959 with Sir Martin Gilliat. Bali Ha'i was completely sound again and fairly forward in condition. Early in May, his Royal owner flew up to Chester to see him run in the Ormonde Stakes against strong opposition and finish fourth, and then she saw Sir Humphrey de Trafford's subsequent Derby winner Parthia win the Dee Stakes for Freemason Lodge. At the same meeting, Agreement won the Chester Cup for the Queen.

The following week, Bali Ha'i appeared in the Coombe Stakes over thirteen furlongs at Sandown. The high-class French horse Vacarme, who had just beaten Sir Humphrey de Trafford's St Leger winner Alcide in the Jockey Club Cup at Newmarket, was meeting Bali Ha'i at level weights and started an 8-1 on favourite. Dick Wilkins's hurdler Le Petit Roi from Fairlawne, who had won on the flat at Aintree in March, was the only other with winning form on the flat in the field, the two other runners being basically hurdlers. Harry Carr, then stable jockey to Boyd-Rochfort, was in the north at Haydock Park riding two fancied runners for the Queen, so Willie Snaith, a good lightweight, rode Bali Ha'i. Bill Rickaby on Le Petit Roi helped the cause of Bali Ha'i by setting a strong gallop and, on rounding the bend into the Sandown straight, Snaith pushed Bali Ha'i into the lead, made for home, and to the amazement of the crowd held the challenge of Vacarme by three-quarters of a length. Queen Elizabeth immediately sent a telegram to Sir Ernest Davis in New Zealand: 'Delighted to inform you Bali Ha'i has won his first race here . . . Everyone enchanted, including his owner.'

Bali Ha'i next ran at Royal Ascot, seeking to win the Queen Alexandra Stakes of two-and-three-quarter miles—the longest race of the meeting, which Sir Harold Wernher's Brown Jack, Steve Donoghue up, made a

habit of winning in the 1930s. Above Suspicion and Pindari had both won for the Queen earlier in the meeting and everyone hoped that Bali Ha'i would be the third Royal winner. Harry Carr on Queen Elizabeth's horse rode a waiting race and came from behind to challenge the Irish-trained Smiley. Bali Ha'i looked at one moment like winning comfortably but in the end was all out to beat Smiley by half a length. He was probably feeling his legs on the hard going, but he did win amidst much rejoicing.

At the beginning of October, Bali Ha'i was much fancied again in the Newbury Autumn Cup and may well have been unlucky not to win, the top weight Red Dragon, owned and bred by the Princess Royal, defeating Bali Ha'i by half a length. Some onlookers thought that Breasley on Red Dragon could not prevent his horse interfering with Bali Ha'i in the final furlong and that Bali Ha'i should have got the race, but the stewards did not object and the result was allowed to stand. In view of the hard going, there was then considerable doubt about risking Bali Ha'i in the Cesarewitch ten days later. Unfortunately it was decided to run him and Bali Ha'i finished a creditable third, changing his legs several times and obviously hating the going. Sadly, he broke down as a result and was on the side lines throughout 1960. He appeared to be sound again in 1961 but, after a promising first race, he broke down again. In accordance with the wishes of Sir Ernest Davis, Queen Elizabeth then had him sent back to New Zealand so that he could end his days in Sir Ernest's own paddocks.

In October 1959, in the week following Bali Ha'i's brave showing in the Cesarewitch, Sparkling Knight was in action again at Hurst Park. After

35   The New Zealander Bali Ha'i III in the unsaddling enclosure at Ascot after winning the Queen Alexandra Stakes for Queen Elizabeth in June 1959. In the foreground are Queen Elizabeth, Princess Margaret and the Duke of Norfolk. Behind, left to right: Mr D. Parker-Bowles, the Princess Royal, Sir Eric Miéville and Sir Martin Gilliat.

36 Sparkling Knight (A. Freeman) and Spring Moss (F. Winter) rise at the last hurdle together in the Mayflower Hurdle at Hurst Park on 19 October 1959. Sparkling Knight finished first but hung badly and lost the race after an enquiry.

the falls he had given Freeman in the previous season, it was decided to revert to hurdling and Sparkling Knight ran in Division II of the Mayflower Novices Hurdle. After a long duel with the favourite Spring Moss, ridden by Winter, Sparkling Knight and Freeman finished first by one length, but Sparkling Knight had hung left in the run-in, going across Spring Moss. The stewards promptly lodged an objection, relegating poor Sparkling Knight to second place. It is the only time in over thirty years that Queen Elizabeth has lost a race on an objection.

Freeman was plagued by injury in December and could not ride at the Lingfield December meeting nor at Hurst Park just before Christmas. Mr Edward Cazalet took Freeman's place on his favourite Double Star in the Westminster Handicap Chase, came the shortest way home but just failed to give over two stone to Certain Justice, owned and trained by Mr A. S. Neaves at Faversham in Kent. At the end of the day, Mr Neaves completed a long-priced double with Certain Danger, Sparkling Knight again just failing.

Queen Elizabeth's run of thirty consecutive losers over fences was ended in January, appropriately by Double Star, Freeman up, when winning Sandown's Londesborough Chase under top weight. At Sandown again a month later he won the Gainsborough Chase equally easily, and hopes were high that he would complete a hat-trick in the two-mile Champion Chase at the National Hunt meeting at Cheltenham.

Fortria from Tom Dreaper's Irish stable was favourite, and Double Star was most fancied of the English. Double Star was moving up to challenge, full of running, when he hit the fifth fence from home so hard that it looked a miracle that the horse stayed on his feet and that Freeman was able to stay aboard. That sadly put paid to his chances, and Fortria won from the Fairlawne second string Blue Dolphin.

In the middle of April, Freeman announced that on medical advice he was giving up race riding at the end of the season, at the age of thirty-four. His last winner for Queen Elizabeth was Mr What's full-brother, Inquisitive Pete, in a novice chase at Fontwell at the end of March. Mr What had given Freeman perhaps his greatest thrill when he had won the Grand National on him, but his successes for Queen Elizabeth had given him similar pleasure. Statistics are sometimes revealing. Over six seasons riding for Fairlawne, he had had 140 rides for Queen Elizabeth and had won twenty-two races for Her Majesty, including ten on his favourite Double Star out of the twenty-two times he had ridden him. He and Double Star had never parted company in their twenty-two races but on other Royal horses he had no less then twenty-two falls—Sparkling Knight, King of the Isle, Queen of the Isle and Inquisitive Pete being the worst offenders. Arthur Freeman was tough and very courageous, but the human body can only stand so much. His retirement was the end of another chapter for Fairlawne.

37 Double Star (Mr E. Cazalet) going out to run in the Westminster Chase at Hurst Park on 18 December 1959, in which he was second.

6

The Rip and Company

PETER CAZALET had been leading trainer for the second time at the end of the 1959–60 season with fifty-eight races won with twenty-five different horses. No other trainer reached the half-century of winners that season. Neville Crump, who saddled the Grand National winner Merryman II, was runner-up in the trainer's table, and Verly Bewicke, then training near Alnwick in Northumberland, was third. Cazalet was a long way ahead of any of his contemporaries in the south. His leading owner was Mrs A. T. Hodgson, who lived at Cowfold in Sussex and was an ardent supporter of Fairlawne for many years. Another woman owner, Mrs Mildmay-White, was still winning races with Lochroe, who was only just beaten in the 1960 Cheltenham Gold Cup at the age of twelve.

Not only did Freeman retire at the end of the season, but Edward Cazalet, godson of Lord Mildmay, did likewise after ending up fourth in the amateur riders' list. Cazalet had won twice on Lochroe in the first part of the season and Mrs Mildmay-White had agreed that he should ride her horse in the Cheltenham Gold Cup. A bad fall with serious concussion on the eve of Cheltenham put an end to the plan and an end also to Edward Cazalet's race-riding career. It also gave Peter Cazalet's second jockey, David Mould, the chance to show his ability for, taking Edward Cazalet's place at short notice on Lochroe, he rode a first-class race in the Cheltenham Gold Cup and was only just beaten by Bill Rees on Pas Seul. Mould was improving fast but at the time he had not enough experience to be first jockey to a big stable and Cazalet needed a replacement for Freeman.

The new stable jockey was Bill Rees, a member of a famous racing family, and son of L. Bilby Rees, who had won the 1922 Grand National on Music Hall and the second running of the Champion Hurdle in 1928 on Brown Jack. Bill Rees's uncle was Dick Rees, five times champion jump jockey in the 1920s and the star performer of his time. His grandfather, Brycham Rees, was a veterinary surgeon at Tenby in Pembrokeshire and rode with success in point-to-points. Bill Rees was certainly bred to be a good jockey in the same way as was Lester Piggot and, in the view of all, Cazalet had made a first-class choice.

Inch Arran (R. Dennard) going out on to the course at Newbury on 25 March 1972.

Inch Arran (A. Branford) taking the water ahead of Land Lark (R. Smith) at Newbury on 23 March 1974.

Queen Elizabeth with Mrs Fulke Walwyn, Terry Biddlecombe and Fulke Walwyn in Cheltenham's
unsaddling enclosure after Game Spirit had come third in the 1974 Gold Cup.

Game Spirit (W. Smith) leading, on the right, Bula (J. Francome), Lean Forward
and Soothsayer in the Hermitage Chase at Newbury, 23 October 1976.

With the exception of Manicou and M'as-tu-vu, nearly all Queen Elizabeth's winners in the 1950s had been Irish-bred. Horse-breeding in Britain had been drastically curtailed during the Second World War, as it had been in France, but henceforward Queen Elizabeth was to have a mixture of English-, French- and Irish-bred winners.

Appropriately, perhaps, Bill Rees's first winner for Queen Elizabeth was The Rip, who was to become a great favourite in the stable and was found by his Royal owner only a few miles from Sandringham. The Rip's story starts with a hunting hotelier Mr Jack Irwin, whose family have been at The Red Cat Hotel at North Wootton near Sandringham for fifty years. A member of an old King's Lynn family, many of whom were seamen, Jack Irwin's grandfather was a horse carrier in King's Lynn. His father was London-orientated for a time and when Jack Irwin was at King Edward VII School at King's Lynn, he used to go whenever possible to ride the ponies of his cousin Leslie Howard, a great sulkyman and a dairyman just outside the town. At the beginning of the 1930s, his father, Horace Irwin, came back to Norfolk, and bought The Red Cat Hotel, which lies beside the old railway line from King's Lynn to Hunstanton by way of North Wootton and Wolferton.

Jack Irwin, being keen on horses, then went as a lad in his teens to help a friend start a riding school at Pound Farm, Esher, near Sandown racecourse, and the two moved later to a covered school at Thames Ditton. When the war came, Jack Irwin grew a moustache to make himself look older and joined the East Surrey regiment at the age of seventeen. After the war he was soon back at The Red Cat, helping his father run the hotel, but also starting his own riding school, aided by a gift of £150 from the War Office to start a business. The pupils at the riding school paid five shillings an hour and he took them out hunting with the West Norfolk hounds of which Major Bob Hoare was then a highly friendly master.

Jack Irwin was friendly with Leonard Bradley, stud groom at the Royal Stud at nearby Wolferton where Aureole went when he finished his racing days in 1954. 'I was on the look out at this time for a couple of point-to-point horses,' recalled Irwin, 'and went to the 1952 Newmarket December sales where I took a liking to a good-looking filly called Joyful, who was out of the Tetratema mare Tamasha, one of the fastest two-year-old fillies of 1937. She had been knocked down for 35 guineas to a cat's meat man. Bradley remembered Tamasha and advised me to get hold of her, so I gave the cat's meat man a £10-profit and £6 for delivery to The Red Cat and Joyful was mine. She came to me as thin as a rake but after worming she eventually came up like a little apple, very quick, very sharp, and she became a beautiful hunter, but then she got tetanus and died. I have never been so upset in my life.

'Luckily at the sales, I also bought a ten-year-old mare called Easy

38 Mr Jack Irwin, breeder of The Rip, on his hunter Decoy, arriving home after a 29-mile hack across country in March 1977. The parish church of All Saints, North Wootton, is in the background.

Virtue for 45 guineas, hoping to make a hunter out of her, but she was impossible. As soon as you put a saddle on her, she was up in the air. I asked Bradley for advice, and he said that as she was unridable, the only thing to do was to breed from her, and he would arrange for her to be covered in the spring of 1954 by Queen Elizabeth's steeplechaser Manicou, who was at Sandringham after breaking down. Easy Virtue held to her second or third service to Manicou, she was stitched after the service as advised by the vet and a colt foal was born the following year after an easy delivery.

'I started showing Easy Virtue and her foal in the breeding classes at various Norfolk shows. I got several firsts, and at one of the shows Queen Elizabeth noticed my Manicou colt who was, I think, the first Manicou colt to be foaled. When Queen Elizabeth was next looking round the Wolferton Stud, Bradley happened to say that my colt was doing well, so the agent Captain Fellowes telephoned me and said that Her Majesty would like to come over to see Easy Virtue and her foal. When he was weaned, I bought another colt foal to run with him. Queen Elizabeth came over several times and I eventually understood from Captain Charles Moore, the Manager of the Royal Studs, that Her Majesty would like to buy him. I said I thought there should be one condition: he must pass the vet first, which he did. Captain Moore asked what I wanted for him. I said I thought £500 would be a fair price. He said he thought £400 would be correct and I understand that Her Majesty said that 400 guineas seemed to be a reasonable compromise. I felt very honoured that she should want him.'

Jack Irwin had named the Manicou colt, Spoilt Union. Queen Elizabeth renamed him The Rip, and The Rip, rising two after he had changed hands, went from the paddocks by The Red Cat to Major Eldred Wilson's farm at Harpley Dams, as had done the stores from Ireland before him. Wilson's farm is mostly arable but there is chalk round the house; there is a big paddock above the house and there is the Long Meadow below the house, through which or under which the Harpley Dams river flows. For three years out of five, the Harpley Dams river is well below the surface of the Long Meadow, but whether on or below it, it finds its way to the sea via Castle Rising and through part of the Sandringham estate to Wolferton Marshes. Wilson liked to have his young horses out in all weathers, keeping them hardy and fit. He held that there was less risk in frosty weather if there was no question of them belting off first thing in the morning after being in stables all night.

Wilson reported to Queen Elizabeth soon after he got The Rip: 'I am afraid that he is rather a plain, clumsy, ponderous two-year-old and I think he may be a bit bone-headed. We are taking him very steadily and I am intending to give him a lot of long-rein work.' Wilson also reported that his right-hand man, Ben Lloyd, a good horseman, stableman and feeder, was spending a lot of time with The Rip. Later Wilson was able to report that he was taking him hunting as a four-year-old, and that he was definitely beginning to improve. He was, in fact, a late developer.

The Rip went to Fairlawne in the late spring of 1959, and Cazalet's first report was that he was rather slow. Six months later, ridden by Freeman, The Rip made his racecourse début at Sandown. It could hardly have been less auspicious, for he was badly crossed at the third flight of hurdles, was unsighted and came down. He reappeared at Fontwell the next week and showed he was none the worse for his fall at Sandown for he was only just beaten in a four-year-old hurdle by a more experienced opponent. He ran seven times in his first season over hurdles, showing that he still needed more time but that he might do well in his second season.

Ridden by Rees, The Rip made his first appearance in his second season in the Mayflower Novices Hurdle at Hurst Park—the event in which Queen Elizabeth's Sparkling Knight had been disqualified in favour of Mr J. U. Baillie's Spring Moss a year before. This year, Mr Baillie's Devon Squire looked likely to beat The Rip at the final flight of hurdles, but The Rip ran on very stoutly for Rees to win in the end from Mr Edward Courage's Border Flight, Devon Squire being third. It was the first of over fifty winners Rees was to ride for Queen Elizabeth, and it was the first and only race The Rip was to win over hurdles. His attention was now to be turned to steeplechasing. The Rip was improving in looks and ability, and John Lawrence who had come rapidly to the fore as a leading amateur rider, reported in *The Daily Telegraph*, prophetically: 'The Rip has grown into a fine big five-year-old with the substance to make a chaser.'

Later in the week Rees was to ride Freeman's favourite Double Star in public for the first time in Newbury's Evenlode Chase. With top weight to shoulder in very heavy going Double Star struggled valiantly but was beaten a head by Stan Mellor on Quick Approach in a desperate finish. Rees and Double Star were to have some noteworthy Lingfield days together, Lingfield above all other courses being Double Star's happy hunting ground.

Cazalet took The Rip up to Nottingham for his first race over fences, which he won well, and took him to Birmingham for the second. With odds of 4 to 1 laid on him, the opposition on paper looked weak. The Rip led at the second fence, but almost stopped and then bucked violently at an angle over the jump, leaving Rees with no chance of staying aboard. He clearly needed another race quickly to restore his morale, and this he got a week later at Kempton. On this occasion, in the Middlesex Novices Chase, the gods were on the side of The Rip, for the favourite Silver Dome, a hard puller and ridden by Alan Oughton, brother-in-law of Bill Rees, refused to settle and fell early on which made The Rip's task the easier. Nevertheless, Rees had to ride The Rip very hard indeed before he got the better of Gallant Barney in the colours of Mr Gay Kindersley, at the time the leading amateur rider. 'The Rip jumped well,' reported Rees after the race, 'but he really needs blinkers to liven him up.'

The Rip ran in a novices' chase for the last time at Lingfield at the beginning of December. This was the meeting for which Queen Elizabeth usually stayed at Fairlawne and at which naturally Cazalet liked to have a fleet of runners. Queen Elizabeth would drive straight down from London to Lingfield in time for lunch with the Beckwith-Smith family, who then owned the course. After racing, there would be tea at Fairlawne by a fire in the hall. Queen Elizabeth always got up early before breakfast on the Saturday morning to see her other horses at work on the gallops.

The whole party would go racing again on the Saturday, and on Sunday after morning service at Shipbourne, when Peter Cazalet read the lessons, Queen Elizabeth would make a tour of the yard, see each horse stripped off, talk to the lad responsible, have a word with 'Bunny' Dunn, the blacksmith, Maurice Butchers, Cazalet's old batman, Joe Hills, the gallops' man, Alan Whiffen, a sterling secretary, and other members of the racing team. Queen Elizabeth would then walk back to the house, and friends would probably come in for a chat before lunch. During the weekend, there was plenty of racing chat, much of it very light-hearted. All the strange incidents and characters, which make racing such a fascinating sport, were noted and enjoyed, and even the setbacks were found to have a funny side. This atmosphere of friendly relaxed enjoyment Queen Elizabeth thoroughly appreciated. Cazalet always did his best to make racing fun for his owners, although he was an efficient man below the surface.

On Sunday afternoon, weather permitting, there was a highly competitive game of croquet, at which Queen Elizabeth would partner her trainer—who would have been in the top class of croquet players had he given the time to it. After dinner on Sunday evening there would be entertainment of some sort, one of the guests normally rising to the occasion. The house party usually had diverse interests, some with a bent towards sport, some interested in politics, some in the theatre. Noel Coward was often an asset to the party. He definitely preferred singing songs after dinner to watching horses at early morning work!

At the December meeting at Lingfield in 1960, Fairlawne had not much luck on the first day, but a treble on the second. The only Cazalet winner on the Friday was Queen Elizabeth's new French-bred hurdler, Jaipur, who had been owned in France by Prince Aly Khan and trained at Longchamp by Alec Head. After winning two three-year-old handicaps on the flat in France in the autumn of 1959, he had been confidently recommended both by his owner and his trainer as a suitable horse for Queen Elizabeth. His success at Lingfield was his second over hurdles for Queen Elizabeth, but when it came to steeplechasing he did not have the courage to shine.

It had been a disappointing day for Fairlawne on the Friday but three out of the four Cazalet runners won on the Saturday. Double Star, in spite of top weight and heavy going, gave over a stone to Mr G. Strakosch's good horse Rosenkavalier in the Ashdown Handicap Chase. Mrs Hodgson's Scottish Flight II won the three-mile handicap chase, and the French-bred Corredjidor II the Juvenile Hurdle for Dick Wilkins. The one failure was The Rip, who disgraced himself by jumping indifferently and falling in the Oxted Novices Chase—a rare occurrence for The Rip.

At Kempton on Boxing Day, bearing in mind the surprise victory of the two-miler Rose Park over Devon Loch, Cazalet started Double Star, ridden by Rees, in the King George VI Chase as well as Lochroe, ridden by Mr R. McCreery in place of the injured Mould, and the six-year-old King, ridden by Dave Dick. In very soft ground, Double Star clearly failed to stay, Lochroe ran moderately but King was second on merit to Saffron Tartan, subsequent winner of the Cheltenham Gold Cup.

In the New Year, Queen Elizabeth bought from the Lingfield vet, Mr Gerry Langford, his good novice chaser Silver Dome, a liver chestnut and a full brother to Dargent, who was also to carry Queen Elizabeth's colours in the future. Both Silver Dome and Dargent were by the versatile horse Domaha, who stood at Langford's Ardenrun Stud at Lingfield. Silver

Dome's dam, Silverina, was a half-sister by the 1943 Irish St Leger winner Solferino to a fast mare in Radiopye, trained by Sam Hall at Middleham to win several sprints of note in the north. Silver Dome's second dam, Silversol, was closely related to the Maharaja of Rajpipla's 1926 Irish Derby winner Embargo. Silver Dome, thus, on breeding was certainly entitled to have speed which, in fact, he did.

The first time Silver Dome carried Queen Elizabeth's colours was in the Londesborough Chase at Sandown where he beat Flame Gun, a brilliant performer at Sandown, and Sir William Piggott-Brown's Newby. Although Queen Elizabeth's new horse was getting weight from both, it was a highly creditable performance on the part of Silver Dome, who was only a novice. 'I was third going to the Pond fence, and he went by them as if they were standing still,' reported his rider, Rees.

Meanwhile, The Rip, when his novice chases were over, was given a rest until the spring, but in his next two races his jumping was moderate and he was under a cloud, as indeed was his breeder, Jack Irwin of The Red Cat. This strong supporter of the West Norfolk had a young horse out and the horse, short of experience, put his foot in a rabbit hole. The horse turned turtle and rolled on Irwin, who looked in very poor shape. No one liked to move him and an ambulance was sent for. Just then, up came the Master, Mr T. H. Barclay, son of a famous hunting parson, the Reverend Humphrey Barclay who often visited many of his parishioners on horse back. His father had taught the Master of the West Norfolk a thing or two and in particular, if a man can twiddle his toes, he is probably not too bad. Tim Barclay noticed there was movement in Irwin's feet, and said in a voice loud and clear: 'It is not worth sending for an ambulance. Let's dig a hole straightaway and bury him.' Whereupon Jack Irwin, who was only badly winded, got up in double quick time before being buried!

The Rip, like his first master, also suddenly improved when spring came. His last race of the season was in the newly sponsored Fremlin's Elephant Handicap Chase at the Folkestone April meeting which Cazalet always supported. The new race was the brain-child of Lord Cornwallis, president of Fremlins Brewery, a friend of Queen Elizabeth, and a regular visitor to Fairlawne. Cazalet also saddled in the race Mr R. E. Goodfellow's Blue Dolphin, already the winner of fifteen races and a son of Domaha, like Silver Dome. Blue Dolphin, ridden by Rees, was favourite. The Rip was being ridden for the first time in public by David Mould. With no success yet to his name in handicap company, The Rip was one of the outsiders in a big field. Eldred Wilson was on hand to watch his protégé, for he had saddled his good hunter chaser Essandem in the United Hunts' Cup earlier in the afternoon. On fast going and suited by the right-handed course, The Rip jumped much better than he had done in recent races. Mould took up the running soon after half way and as they went to the last fence, the race lay between The Rip and Regal Arch,

39 The winner Silver Dome (W. Rees) left and Sir Michael Sobell's Flame Gun (F. Winter) at the last fence in the Londesborough Chase at Sandown on 14 January 1961. Newby (Sir William Pigott-Brown) is lying third, half-hidden by Flame Gun.

40 Tim Brookshaw on Lady Sherborne's Bengal Scroll leading the field at the water in the Fremlin's Elephant Chase at Folkestone on 20 April 1961. D. Mould on The Rip is just behind him.

trained by Bryan Marshall at Lambourn. Regal Arch hit it, and The Rip went away to win decisively. Wilson was able to report to Cazalet that he had seen The Rip cocking an ear as he passed the racecourse stables as if he were thinking: 'It would be nice to run out here and finish now.'

Queen Elizabeth was far away in the White Highlands of Kenya in the middle of an official tour when The Rip won the Elephant Chase, so Lord Cornwallis and Peter Cazalet arranged that news of The Rip's victory would go to Buckingham Palace and thence to Government House in Kenya. Her Majesty was on the governor's train at the time near Equator Station and the staff of the governor, Sir Evelyn Baring—later Lord Howick—were able to send a message, which came in during dinner, to say that The Rip had won the Elephant Chase. Appropriately enough, his owner was not far off elephant country at the time. Mould's victory on The Rip was his first success in a steeplechase for Queen Elizabeth. His only previous victory in the Royal colours was on King of the Isle in a long-distance handicap hurdle at Kempton a year before. Mould for the first time was amongst the dozen leading National Hunt jockeys of the season. Bill Rees was in fifth place with fifty-two winners to his name.

41   Minutes later, D. Mould and Cazalet stand beside The Rip, the winner, in Folkestone's unsaddling enclosure.

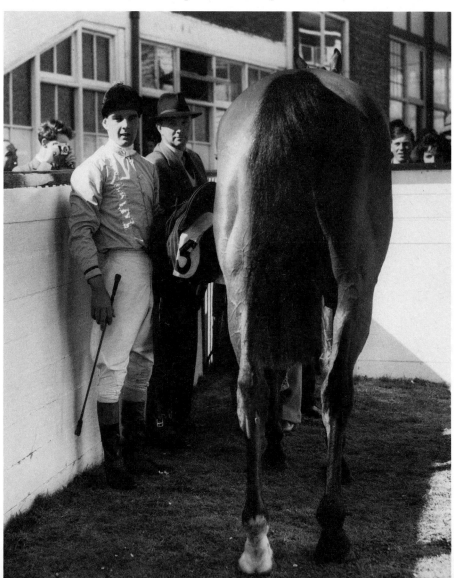

The next season of 1961–62 was to be an outstanding one for Queen Elizabeth. Double Star was still going strong; Out of Town, now a seven-year-old, was about to strike form; Silver Dome and The Rip were improving chasers from the previous season; Young Rajah was an ex point-to-pointer Cazalet had brought on behalf of Queen Elizabeth from Tom Yates, then training at Letcombe Bassett on the Berkshire Downs. Last but not least, Cazalet, accompanied by Sir Martin Gilliat, had been to France to seek the advice of Colonel Wladyslaw Bobinski, the gallant Polish cavalry soldier who was responsible for most of Cazalet's French purchases. Bobinski, his home burnt by the Russians, had settled in England after the war. His link with the Cazalet family came through his brother's friendship with General Sikorski killed in the same aircrash as Victor Cazalet. Bobinski had a great eye for a horse. He had discovered the brilliant two-miler Rhetorius in France, brought him to England, schooled him and eventually sold him to Fairlawne. M'as-tu-vu was another Bobinski horse.

When Sir Martin Gilliat and Cazalet met Bobinski on a winter day at the end of 1960, it was explained that Queen Elizabeth wanted a horse with the scope to make a chaser. His recommendation was the French-bred Laffy, who had won a flat race and three hurdle races as a four-year old when trained at Maisons Laffitte by Noel Pélat, a member of a well-known French racing family. Laffy was bought and made his first appearance in Queen Elizabeth's colours in the autumn of 1961. Before the end of the season his name was to be well-known on both sides of the Irish Sea.

The Rip, who had ended his 1960–61 season with a victory as a long-priced outsider at Folkestone, started the 1961–62 season with a victory as a long-priced outsider at Hurst Park in the Grand Sefton Trial Chase, a race in which Cazalet saddled the winner five times in its short life—thrice with the gallant Lochroe, once with Mariner's Dance and now in its final year, before the course disappeared, with The Rip. At the beginning of the 1960s when the valuable sponsored steeplechase was still a rarity, Cazalet was inclined to start more than one chaser in the few valuable chases and on this occasion saddled a hot favourite in the French-bred King, who had run well in the Cheltenham Gold Cup the previous spring. Nicolaus Silver, the 1961 Grand National winner, was also in the field and in such company The Rip was still near the foot of the handicap. Ridden by Rees, King looked to be going well for most of the race but made a bad mistake, broke down and had to be pulled up, and The Rip, well ridden by Mould, led throughout the last circuit of the course and won from Double Star's old rival, Certain Justice.

The sharp right-handed courses of Folkestone and Hurst Park suited The Rip. When he went to left-handed Newbury for his next race, three weeks later, he jumped badly to the right most of the way, made mistakes, but still had enough in hand to win. Carrying a penalty at right-handed

42 The Rip (W. Rees) hits the last fence hard before going on to win the Cottage Rake Chase at Kempton on 23 November 1961. Rees does well to stay aboard.

Kempton a fortnight later in the Cottage Rake Chase, The Rip jumped much better till he blundered badly at the last but Rees sat very tight and all was well. 'The Rip could butcher a fence and get away with it, he was so strong,' was Rees's comment.

The Rip won this Kempton race from Malacca, trained at Findon by Ryan Price, at the time a worried man since his hurdler, Scarron, who had started favourite in the Rank Challenge Cup at Fontwell, had just been found to have been doped with a stopping drug. Detectives were seeking, so it was reported, a dark-haired young woman with a foreign accent who had visited several stables where horses were thought to have been doped. Cazalet had reacted by locking his intended runners in special boxes on the night before they were due to run.

The Cazalet horses and the stable jockey Bill Rees were at the top of their form as December dawned. At Windsor on 1st December, Rees won four races off the reel for Fairlawne. The fifth Cazalet runner was Dick Wilkins's Orbiquet in a division of the three-year-old hurdle. In a desperate finish, Orbiquet was beaten by inches by Vitamin who, in Rees's view, had definitely interfered with him. 'Only object if you feel certain you will get the race,' said Cazalet to his jockey. Bill Rees objected for bumping and boring and did *not* get the race. It was before the days of the camera patrol, which has made the duties of stewards much less difficult.

For Queen Elizabeth's annual weekend visit to Fairlawne for the Lingfield December meeting, there were three Fairlawne runners on the first day and five on the second. On the first day, Queen Elizabeth's Out of Town in his fourth season at Fairlawne suddenly came good as a chaser after many disappointments. He was winning his third chase of the season when making light of a penalty in the Blindley Heath Handicap Chase. The other Fairlawne runners, Gort and Fier Chimiste, owned by Dick Wilkins, both failed. Wilkins, a stock jobber in the city of London, large, jovial, friendly and generous, was a popular member of the Fairlawne December weekend. He enjoyed life and wanted others to enjoy it, too.

On the Saturday, Queen Elizabeth had four fancied runners—the French-bred pair Jaipur and Laffy in the two divisions of the Oxted Novices Chase, Double Star in the Ashdown Handicap Chase and The Rip carrying a penalty for his Kempton victory in the Eridge Handicap Chase. The day began badly, for Jaipur, carrying a penalty for a highly promising victory at Sandown, fell on the far side of the Lingfield course. As Jaipur was attempting to give weight to Mr Gay Kindersley's future Grand National runner-up Carrickbeg, it is doubtful if he would have won at any rate. Half an hour later, Laffy jumped well to win Division II of the same event. It was his third race in England. He had shown promise in the other two, so he was expected to win.

Double Star, appearing in the Ashdown Handicap Chase for the third time in four years, was not so well backed as Mr J. E. Bigg's Barberyn, who had won the Grand Annual Challenge Cup at the National Hunt meeting at Cheltenham in the spring. Unlike his early days when he pulled

43   Out of Town (W. Rees) winning the Blindley Heath Chase at Lingfield unchallenged on 8 December 1961, on the eve of Queen Elizabeth's famous Lingfield hat-trick.

like a train, Double Star was now much more amenable, and Rees was able to settle him, to ride a waiting race and to come from behind to beat Barberyn and company. 'At this stage of his career, Double Star did not like one being tough with him.' recalled Bill Rees. 'He was much better if you let him do it on his own. He had become very experienced. He liked to see plenty of daylight, and then he would get to the other side of a fence in the most economical fashion and, after the last fence with nothing more to jump, he would find a real turn of foot even in heavy going.'

The Rip was Queen Elizabeth's last runner of the afternoon. Laffy and Double Star had won the two previous races. Would The Rip, carrying an eight pounds' penalty in heavy going, be up to defeating his four experienced opponents and completing a hat-trick for Queen Elizabeth in the Eridge Handicap Chase? To all four opponents, The Rip was having to give nearly two stone in weight, including Wily Oriental, who had been second in the Mildmay Memorial Chase at the beginning of the year, Domstar from Frank Pullen's stable at Fleet in Hampshire, and Trinidad, a well-known performer at local meetings in Sussex and Kent. But The Rip was on the crest of a wave, improving all the time, and he was fully equal to giving away the weight after both Domstar and Wily Oriental had made a good deal of the running, hoping to make their light weights tell.

It was a great day for Queen Elizabeth and to commemorate the treble, Honor Beckwith-Smith, widow of General M. Beckwith-Smith, and only child of Mr J. Blundell Leigh who created the Lingfield course, presented to Queen Elizabeth a picture by Peter Biegel of Double Star, The Rip and Laffy at Lingfield on that great day, as a souvenir of the occasion. The picture now hangs in Clarence House as a permanent reminder to their Royal owner of three of her favourite horses, the lads who did them and others in the Cazalet team. Lingfield was still a family course in beautiful surroundings and Queen Elizabeth enjoyed its friendly atmosphere, mingling with young and old, all intent on enjoying their day's racing.

Queen Elizabeth had a very promising young horse this winter in Young Rajah who, as a six-year-old in 1961, had won two point-to-points in the Duke of Beaufort's country where competition was hot. Young Rajah, a grey, by the grey Blandford horse Rajah II who stood at Sir William Cooke's Wyld Court Stud near Newbury, was out of a mare who had already bred a good handicapper in Operatic Society. At the time, the biggest prize of the jumping season for novices was the National Hunt Chase for amateur riders at Cheltenham in March—a race for novice chasers who had not won a steeplechase at the time of the race closing about two months beforehand. Owners with a likely horse for this four-mile chase could not win a novice chase before the race closed in January. Cazalet thought that Young Rajah might well be a potential winner of the National Hunt Chase. He wanted to give the horse racing experience over regulation fences in the autumn and provisionally engaged Mr R. McCreery, then one of the leading amateur riders as his jockey, for a race which was then sometimes known as the amateur riders' Grand National.

Bob McCreery, son of General Sir Richard McCreery, who had won two Grand Military Gold Cups in the 1920s, had already twice been the leading amateur rider of the National Hunt season, and to get to know Young Rajah, McCreery was asked to ride the horse in the Ewell Chase at Sandown in December. He had to tackle experienced handicap chasers in King's Nephew and Hedgelands and a stable companion in Cupid's Charge, who had just won the Molyneux Chase at Liverpool for Mrs Hodgson. Queen Elizabeth came to see the race. 'The plan is to run Young Rajah in the National Hunt Chase at Cheltenham,' said Cazalet to McCreery, 'and we are very hopeful that he will run well.' Queen Elizabeth's new horse was leading at the water second time round, going well and looking a possible winner but he made a terrible mistake soon afterwards and McCreery did extremely well to stay aboard. McCreery reported to Queen Elizabeth after the race that, in his opinion, Young Rajah was a good horse in the making and but for his bad mistake on the far side of the course he might well have beaten the winner King's Nephew and plans for the National Hunt Chase would have had to have been revised!

The following month, Young Rajah was asked to take on the Cheltenham Gold Cup winner Pas Seul at Sandown, but it was asking a lot of a young horse and, Rees up, he did not jump well. Entries for the National Hunt Chase had closed when Young Rajah ran in his first novices' chase at Newbury, ridden by McCreery. Opposition was strong

44   The grey Young Rajah (Mr R. McCreery) gets the best of a photo-finish with Lord Ashcombe's Aberdonian (A. Dennis) and Mr Herbert Blagrave's Milo (W. Rees) in the Wantage Chase at Newbury on 20 January 1962.

and included Milo who, on autumn form, was superior to Queen Elizabeth's Lingfield winner Laffy, but in a tight finish Young Rajah just won from Aberdonian and Milo. A month later in another novices' chase at Newbury, Young Rajah was going well when he suddenly broke a blood vessel very badly. McCreery came back covered with blood. Young Rajah's heart was also affected. His racing career was at an end after one more race in which he was pulled up.

Cazalet had entered both The Rip and Out of Town in the 1962 Grand National. Out of Town, in the middle of January, ran well for a long way in the Mildmay Memorial Chase at Sandown but he had gone in the wind, had to be hobdayed and showed no form again till two seasons later. At the end of January, it was decided that The Rip, with four consecutive victories to his credit, would take on the famous Mandarin at a difference of only eight pounds in the Walter Hyde Handicap Chase at Kempton Park. As Mandarin had won the Hennessy Gold Cup with a big weight in his previous race and had two King George VI Chases already to his credit, it meant that The Rip was going to be very near the top of any handicap if he acquitted himself well against Mandarin. In fact, The Rip, jumping better than he had ever done before, gave Mandarin a terrific race at Kempton. The two were never far apart and rose at the last fence together, Mandarin eventually getting home all out by a bare half length. 'Mandarin just found that little bit extra in the run in,' reported Rees, 'but it was a tremendous performance on the part of The Rip, who was only a seven-year-old.'

45   The Rip (W. Rees) and Mandarin (F. Winter), the winner, at the last fence in their thrilling duel in the Walter Hyde Chase at Kempton on 25 January 1962.

The racing days of Hurst Park were numbered. Cazalet had saddled a lot of winners there and he sent both The Rip and Laffy to run at Hurst Park's last February meeting. With no Mandarin in opposition, The Rip gave away over a stone to all his opponents in the Morden Chase and won comfortably in spite of a bad blunder early on. It was decided that he needed more experience before running in the Grand National but that he would take his chance in the Cheltenham Gold Cup. Laffy took on some of the best novices of the season in the New Century Chase. Mill House, making his début over fences, was expected to win but fell at half way. Completing a double for Queen Elizabeth, Laffy took the lead two fences from the finish and won from School for Gamble from Jack Fawcus's Middleham stables. It was then provisionally decided that Laffy's next race would be the Monaveen Chase at Hurst Park's final jumping meeting in mid-March. It would be highly appropriate for Queen Elizabeth to win the race named in honour of her first chaser. Unfortunately it was not to be.

During Newbury races, one winter day, the Fairlawne stable had had unexpected visitors. 'One late afternoon at stable time,' recalled Jim Fairgrieve, 'a chaffeur-driven car came to the yard and out stepped a very expensively dressed, attractive lady. She spoke with an accent and seemed surprised that I did not know she was coming. She told me that she was sending two horses to be trained at Fairlawne and they were on their way from France. She also said she had spoken to the guv'nor the previous evening and made arrangements with him to look round the stables. Mr Cazalet had said that he would be at Newbury, but he would let me know to expect her. "I expect he forgot to tell you," she said. This did not sound like the guv'nor to me, as he never forgot things like that. At the same time it was possible, and I did not want to offend a prospective patron. With some misgiving I showed her round and I must say I found her very charming and, what is more, she was charming to all the lads. Going round the yard, she was accompanied by her chauffeur wherever she went, and he took notes, and eventually they said they must leave, and she would look forward to seeing me again. I know the whole staff felt that they would look forward to seeing her again, too.

'The guv'nor rang on his return from Newbury and I told him of our attractive visitor. He exploded at the end of the telephone, and made it clear that he should have warned me of the attractive woman who was reported to be going round doping horses. The sequel came on the morning of March 17 when the Monaveen Chase was to be run at Hurst Park. As a result of the doping scare, Fairlawne had five security boxes with alarms on the door and the windows and, as a fancied runner, I had locked Laffy in "security" the night before the Monaveen Chase. All was well when I looked round the last thing before going to bed. I always believed, like the guv'nor, in feeding horses early in the morning to enable them to feed in peace and quiet before the lads started work, and I unlocked the security and switched the alarms off at 5.15 a.m., fed the horses in there, including Laffy and, when I had completed the feeding round the yard, came back to lock up the security boxes again. The lights went on in the lads' quarters and I heard one or two of them come down into the yard and go into the tack room to look at the board to see what horses they were riding. As they were about, I saw no reason to lock up and so I went back to my house for a cup of tea.

'All was well when the first lot went out. The guv'nor and I were both riding out. Bill Braddon was left in to lead out that day's runners and prepare them for travelling. When we came back with the first lot, Bill was standing with a look of concern on his face."I was glad to get Laffy back in his box," he said, "I thought he would fall down." The guv'nor and I looked at the horse and jumped to the same conclusion. Laffy was doped. We got the vet, and he thought the same as we did. He took a saliva and blood sample, signed a certificate to say the horse was unfit to run and told me just to let the horse rest. The analysis of the blood sample proved that Laffy was full of dope. This was a case of mistiming by the dopers. Obviously they would want to dope a horse in the middle of the night, so that to all appearances he would seem all right in the morning. As the stable was locked up, they—or he, or she—had to wait until I opened up in the morning. Laffy must have been done between 5.15 a.m. and 5.30 a.m. How and by whom will always remain a mystery. Every lad was thoroughly interrogated by the investigating detectives, including me, but we never found out who did it.'

Fortunately, as Laffy did not run and was rested, he recovered very quickly and, in fact, ran five days later at Lingfield, where he won a three-mile handicap chase under top weight. The racing public, unaware of the drama at Fairlawne, made Laffy favourite and he showed he had thrown off the effects of the dope very quickly by winning well.

It was decided that Laffy would have one more race during the season. Queen Elizabeth was to go to Ulster in the first week of April to visit, amongst other engagements, the 9th/12th Lancers at Omagh and to Enniskillen for the 350th anniversary celebrations for the granting of a Royal Charter. It had also been suggested by Lord Glentoran that she might have a runner in the Ulster Harp National at Downpatrick, which is associated with one of the oldest hunt clubs in the British Isles, with records going back over 200 years. The most senior inhabitants recalled that there had not been a Royal runner at Downpatrick since Edward VII's Grand National horse Flaxman in 1906. Lord Glentoran's father and uncle Sir Thomas Dixon had been among the leading owners in Ulster in the 1930s.

Laffy, none the worse for his fluent victory at Lingfield, left Fairlawne for Ulster a week before the Downpatrick race, being flown from

Cambridge to Ulster in the charge of Bill Braddon, the travelling head lad, with nearly twenty years' service at Fairlawne already behind him. Laffy was based on the home of Captain John Corbett, a well-known horsebreeder and a past master of the East Down hounds with an attractive home at Tyrella a few miles from the course. 'Laffy needed a good deal of knowing,' recalled Bill Braddon. 'He periodically suffered from kidney trouble and on occasion used to walk out, crippled right up. He also had an unpleasant habit of dropping a shoulder on the gallops without any warning, and getting rid of most of the lads who rode him. When we got to Tyrella, I used to work Laffy on the sands within sight of the Mountains of Mourne.

'One day in particular I shall never forget, for I took Laffy down towards the shore, intending to work him on the sands. I was just going through an open gate leading to the sands when he suddenly dropped me and went scampering off up the sands. Luckily for me, the guv'nor was miles away at Fairlawne and there were three chaps in a rowing boat, laying lobster pots. When they saw the riderless Laffy coming towards them, they dropped their lobster pots for the moment and managed to catch Laffy. They were obviously used to handling horses and was I grateful to them! On the day of the race, I took Laffy in the captain's trailer to the course. At the time, the Downpatrick course stables were a bit primitive, and his box on the course was so small that I had to get Laffy almost on his knees to get him into it. The Rip would certainly never have made it!'

Downpatrick has mixed racing. The stands, the finishing post, and the parade ring are all on top of a hill and it is a sharp right-handed course up hill and down dale with the runners disappearing behind the hill on one part of the circuit. Knowledge of the course is important and Cazalet thought it politic that an Irish jockey should ride Queen Elizabeth's horse, so engaged for Laffy one of the top Irish jockeys in Willie Robinson instead of the disappointed stable jockey Bill Rees. Queen Elizabeth was staying with the governor Lord Wakehurst, Sir Martin Gilliat and the Cazalets with Lord Glentoran near Doagh in County Antrim. The Downpatrick programme consisted of three hurdle races at the start of the afternoon, two steeplechases in the middle and two flat races at the end. Before a big race, Robinson always liked to have a previous ride in a minor race and had been engaged to ride a novice hurdler Tyrone Star for Paddy Sleator in the second race. The mare had won a bumper on the course in the autumn and was a hot favourite, but unfortunately gave Robinson a bad fall at the final flight of hurdles. Robinson was kicked by another horse and it looked as if he would not be fit to ride Laffy an hour later.

Apart from the flat race for amateurs, the field for the Ulster Harp National was the biggest of the day with Laffy, who was still a novice, being required to give weight to all his fourteen opponents. The Ulster

National had been in abeyance for several years and had been revived this
year as a sponsored race and it had brought out a number of chasers well
known in Ireland at the time—Roman Folly, trained by Jimmy Brogan,
who had run well at the National Hunt meeting at Cheltenham, his stable
companion Gold Legend, ridden by Pat Taaffe and winner of the 1958
Irish Grand National, Moyrath from Paddy Sleator's yard and a recent
winner at Mullingar, The Proud Servant, one of the old men of the party
but still fast enough to win a handicap hurdle at the age of thirteen and the
second favourite Court Taster, trained by R. A. Hoey.

'Robinson's bad fall in the second race was very worrying for Cazalet,'
recalled Sir Martin Gilliat. 'He knew of no other jockey on the spot to take
the ride on Laffy at the last moment, and his misgivings were redoubled when
he gave Robinson the leg up on Laffy in the parade ring before the race,
for he was like a deadweight, and we feared the worst. In fact we need not
have worried, as he proceeded to ride a super race.'   The race itself was
full of incident. The thirteen-year-old Connkeheley, who had been a
useful chaser, had a bitless bridle, and his jockey could not help steering
an apparently highly erratic course, appearing to run out at one fence but
still continuing in the race to the bewilderment of the spectators. When
the Irish race-reader announced during the race that 'the first horse is the

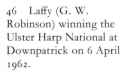

46   Laffy (G. W.
Robinson) winning the
Ulster Harp National at
Downpatrick on 6 April
1962.

second, if you see what I mean', the position to many did not become any clearer! He meant apparently that the leading horse—the bitless one—was to be disregarded, and the horse lying second was the leader. 'The Irish-trained horse which finished first past the post, had missed out a fence on the far side of the course, unnoticed by most of the racegoers,' confirmed Lord Glentoran. 'He had terrified me by crossing Laffy twice, running out and then charging back into the race. When the crowd realised that Laffy had definitely won, Queen Elizabeth received a wonderful reception and was completely mobbed at the unsaddling—Peter Cazalet at the front of the horse and Queen Elizabeth at the back, unable to move.'

'I have never forgotten the occasion,' recalled Bill Braddon. 'The Queen Mother had lost her bodyguard and there were a seething mass of people round her. I remember vividly one woman rushing up with her twin daughters and asking the Queen Mother to bless them. The crowd was completely out of control, and I remember, too, saying to the Queen Mother: "Hang on to my arm, Your Majesty, we will stay with the horse," and stay with the horse we did, till the seething crowd began to disperse. By this time, poor Laffy had lost a lot of hairs out of his mane and tail. The Laffy expedition was one of the greatest experiences of my life, although I must admit that I had to report to the guv'nor at Downpatrick that I had been keeping up his good name and was stony broke. "I hear you have been a marvellous ambassador," the guv'nor replied, and gave me some more money without a murmur.'

The one person who has no clear recollection of Laffy's great victory at Downpatrick is his jockey Willie Robinson, grandson of the breeder of The Tetrarch, with a host of victories on Mill House, Team Spirit, Anzio and other Fulke Walwyn stars still ahead of him. Whether Robinson was slightly concussed when he won on Laffy nobody will ever know. He knew the course and no doubt he instinctively rode a first class race. Cazalet was very apprehensive before the race but all was forgotten after the race. Laffy won officially by five lengths from Roman Folly with The Proud Servant third and Gold Legend fourth. The following day, Queen Elizabeth returned by air to England. It had been a very happy expedition.

Laffy had certainly earned a rest and so had The Rip after finishing unplaced behind Mandarin in the Cheltenham Gold Cup. Queen Elizabeth went racing for the last time that season on the last day of April at Folkestone to see Silver Dome finish second in the Fremlins Elephant Chase, which The Rip had won so unexpectedly a year before. Lord Cornwallis and Colonel Arthur ffrench Blake, the senior steward, were on hand to welcome her, and she enjoyed her day. At the end of the season Queen Elizabeth, for the first time, was high up in the list of winning owners in fourth place with more races won than anyone else. Ten of her horses had won twenty-four races between them, The Rip and Laffy being her big winners of the season.

To The Rip's breeder, Jack Irwin of The Red Cat, Queen Elizabeth sent a silver salver and engraved on it were the details of the five steeplechases The Rip won during 1961. In a charming letter to Jack Irwin, Queen Elizabeth said: 'I am so proud of The Rip and I am so grateful to you for breeding such a fine courageous horse. . . . I do hope that someday we shall see another foal at The Red Cat.' The Rip's story was far from finished but there were vicissitudes ahead. Every steeplechaser with a long racing life has his ups and downs and The Rip was no exception. To Willie Robinson, Queen Elizabeth gave a pair of gold links to commemorate his victory on Laffy in the Ulster Harp National. That eventful day at Downpatrick Queen Elizabeth was not going to forget, and nor, for the matter of that, was Cazalet's resourceful head lad, Bill Braddon.

There is one postscript to the Laffy story of 1962. Six months after Laffy's triumph at Downpatrick, Mademoiselle Micheline Emilenne Lugeon, aged twenty-six, daughter of a Swiss cemetery superintendant, together with several men, stood trial at Lewes Assizes in Sussex, accused of 'conspiring together and with others to dope racehorses'. Mr Owen Stable, QC, prosecuting, said: 'These conspirators had at their disposal enough dope to dope effectively 600 to 900 racehorses . . . I shall endeavour to establish the doping by this gang of over forty horses, some of them more than once. A young and attractive Swiss beautician, working in league with this horse-doping gang, exploited her good looks and got into twenty-three stables in different parts of the country in forty-seven astonishing days. She visited stables as far apart as Charing in Kent and Roxburghshire in Scotland, playing a difficult role with incredible intelligence. She was a close friend of one of the accused men, William John Roper, and originally came to this country as an *au pair* girl.'

The judge, in passing sentence, referred to the case as 'a wicked conspiracy—one of the biggest horse-doping conspiracies ever known in British racing. . . . Roper was the brains of the conspiracy. Mademoiselle Lugeon merely a tool of someone else.'

Jim Fairgrieve, who gave evidence at the trial, saying that Mademoiselle Lugeon had visited Major Cazalet's Fairlawne stables and 'made notes as she went round', wrote a poem in memory of a remarkable visitation.

THE LADY DOPER

Well groomed, trim figure, fair of face,
Demure, sweet and serene,
The lady swept into our place
In chauffeured limousine.

I touched my cap, 'Good afternoon,
Can I of service be?'
'I'm looking for the man in charge.'
'Your servant, Ma'am, that's me.'

'I have two horses coming here
To train for steeplechasing.'
'The Guv'nor is away, I fear,
He's gone to Newbury, racing.'

'I know he has, he said last night,
Upon the telephone,
If I looked round t'would be all right
Although he would have gone.'

I showed her round, a pleasant task,
She praised the horses' coats,
And many questions she did ask
Whilst making copious notes.

She paused at every stable lad,
Spoke to them and smiled.
When she moved on, they worked like mad
And whistled as they toiled.

The trainer rang on his return,
I told him of our guest,
His language made my eardrums burn—
Draw curtains o'er the rest.

'That charming lady took you in
She goes round doping horses,
She should be punished for her sin
And warned off all racecourses.

'Alarm bells fix, locks—change the lot,
Take up action stations,
For all intruders make it hot
With guards and fierce Alsatians.'

When we'd recovered from our fright
And were secure again
Or so we thought, until one night
She struck, but God knows when.

I've learnt my lesson. Now I know
Why great men sometimes fail.
The female species, to my woe,
Is deadlier than the male.

7

Gay Record and Jack O'Donoghue

THE RIP, Laffy, Double Star and Out of Town all won three or more races for Queen Elizabeth during that successful season of 1961–62—Her Majesty's thirteenth as an owner of steeplechasers. There was a fifth horse who also did well for Queen Elizabeth that season—the former failure Gay Record, who as a young horse was too neurotic and difficult to make the grade in a big stable like Fairlawne, and had been sent back in disgrace to spend the summer of 1959 at Sandringham. From Norfolk, he was then sent to be trained at Reigate in Surrey just south of Epsom Downs by an Irishman Jack O'Donoghue, who had a way with difficult horses and had made his mark in no uncertain terms by saddling the mare Nickel Coin to win the 1951 Grand National.

Gay Record, a dark bay with no white about him, was by Arkle's sire Archive, and had been bought by Colonel Hill-Dillon for 410 guineas as a yearling at Goff's and sent as a store to Norfolk to be broken and made by Major Eldred Wilson. He was one of the second lot of stores bought by Hill-Dillon for Queen Elizabeth and the one who was—after an unpropitious start—a great success. The other two who came from Ireland to Norfolk with Gay Record were Kingsville Star, who was also a failure at Fairlawne but did well as a point-to-pointer when hunted and trained by Jack Irwin of The Red Cat, and Brig O'Dee, who was no good for racing, but had a long, useful life as a police horse.

Eldred Wilson, after an interval of a quarter of a century, still remembers very vividly the difficulties which beset him with Gay Record. 'He arrived from Ireland,' he recalls, 'having been badly kicked on the way, with the equivalent of a splint, and as a result he had long spells of lameness. However, he looked the part of a potential chaser, was tough and wiry and I thought it was well worth persevering with him, but it was three years before he really became sound. He was not difficult to break but when I eventually took him out hunting he was very excitable indeed in the company of others.

'Gay Record eventually went to Fairlawne as a six-year-old in 1958, and Peter Cazalet reported back that he intensely disliked going out in a string and was almost unmanageable. He also apparently took a poor view of going by horse box to the races and worked himself up into a nervous lather when boxed. Cazalet told me that a motorist had once stopped his box driver and told him his box was on fire, but it was only Gay Record getting steamed up!'

In spite of all this, Gay Record definitely showed sufficient latent ability at Fairlawne to be worth persevering with, if only his temperament could be improved. As a half-brother to the 1957 Champion hurdler Merry Deal, it was to be expected that he would have some speed, and in his third and final race when trained at Fairlawne he was second in a big field of novice hurdlers at the April meeting at Wye. Queen Elizabeth and Eldred Wilson, who had had Gay Record for five years, were keen to persevere, and Eldred Wilson suggested to Her Majesty that Jack O'Donoghue might be the man for Gay Record. He had recently had great success with a chaser called Trapeze II, who had an even more fervent dislike of horse boxes then Gay Record, and Trapeze II, under O'Donoghue's care, had become a reformed character. 'Gay Record has settled down at Sandringham,' wrote Queen Elizabeth to Cazalet in the summer of 1959, 'and when he has got a bit of meat on him, to quote Scallan, our Irish stud groom, I thought it would be worth sending him to O'Donoghue, who . . . specialises in "difficult" horses. If he does not respond to that treatment, he will have to go hunting, which he loves.'

So, thanks to Queen Elizabeth's perseverance, to O'Donoghue's Priory Stables, at Reigate, went Gay Record in the autumn of 1959. It would be difficult to think of two more dissimilar yards than Fairlawne and Priory Stables. Reigate lies on the old Pilgrim's Way by which the Canterbury Pilgrims went from Southampton via Winchester, Alton, Guildford, Dorking and Reigate to Wrotham and Canterbury. To the south of the town originally lay a thirteenth-century priory, and on its site had been built, two hundred years ago, a mansion known as The Priory, the home before the Second World War of Admiral of the Fleet Lord Beatty, Commander-in-Chief of the Grand Fleet in the second half of the First World War. Lord Beatty, besides being an outstanding sailor, was keen on racing and farming and had two yards near The Priory—one for horses and one for cows—and it was these two yards Jack O'Donoghue had taken over after the Second World War.

O'Donoghue's home as a child was near Mallow in the south-west of Ireland, where his father farmed. He had started riding in donkey races, had won his first point-to-point at the age of fourteen and in the 1920s joined Jack Lombard, who then had the reputation of being the best point-to-point rider in Ireland. One of his contemporaries and friendly point-to-point rivals was Collis Montgomery, a cousin of the Field-Marshal, a long-distance runner of note, and himself winner of over a hundred point-to-points in Ireland. O'Donoghue crossed the Irish Sea in 1929, feeling there were more opportunities for a man keen on horses and racing than in Ireland, and came to work near Reigate for Mr A. G.

Cowley, who had point-to-pointers, and later to work for Mr A. E. Berry who, in the late 1930s, had Kingsland and other chasers in training with 'Towzer' Gosden near Lewes. Kingsland was a contemporary of Anthony Mildmay's Davy Jones.

It was in 1948 that O'Donoghue took on Lord Beatty's two yards and made his home in an Elizabethan cottage, which had been the old gate house for The Priory, and which overlooked the top yard where Lord Beatty had had his cows. His bottom yard was on the other side of a small road leading to The Priory, and this Lord Beatty had built for his brood-mares. By the time Gay Record joined Priory Stables, O'Donoghue had built on another row of boxes in the bottom yard, had made a covered school adjoining it, and had between twenty-five and thirty horses in training. A couple of hundred yards from the stables, he had made a schooling ground with every sort of obstacle in a disused chalk-pit; he used to exercise his horses either on Walton Heath between Reigate and Epsom on Walter Nightingall's old family gallops or in Heathfield Park near the golf course on ground which had belonged to Mr Arthur Rank.

'I remember very well going to collect Gay Record at Sandringham in the autumn of 1959,' recalled O'Donoghue, in his quiet voice with an Irish twang. 'Scallan, the Sandringham stud groom, told me to expect an uncomfortable journey back, with Gay Record working himself up into a nervous wreck. Later I had very good advice from Queen Elizabeth. Her Majesty felt that Gay Record wanted an open box looking on to a yard so that he could see all that was going on and could be kept interested, the boxes at Fairlawne being nearly all enclosed. She also felt that as Gay Record was such a bad traveller, it might be as well to take him to two or three courses without running him, to get him more used to the sights and sounds of the racecourse, and therefore less apprehensive. They were good pieces of advice and I followed them. She also told me that I was to take my time trying to get Gay Record right.

'Luckily, I had had recent experience of another horse who hated a horse box—Trapeze II—who was so bad in a box that he could originally only run at racecourses within walking distance of his Epsom stables. George Duller, the famous hurdle race jockey, was training him at the time and got fed up with him, and I told his owner we would take him on, so I went to Epsom to collect him and hacked him back across the Downs. I used to put Trapeze out in a paddock with one of my home-bred spotted donkeys and hack him around quietly. I then put the horse box out, leaving the sides open, and I always fed him in the horse box. After a few months, we had the horse box in the paddock and from then on travelling to race meetings was no worry to him. Trapeze was transformed, winning four races in five weeks in one season.

'When we got Gay Record back to Reigate, I put him in a box in the top yard facing the back door of our house, so that he could see the canaries

47 Jack O'Donoghue, trainer of Gay Record, feeding his home-bred spotted donkeys Molly and Neddy at his Priory Stables at Reigate.

and golden pheasants in my aviary and could see everyone who came in and out of our house and all that was happening. I also hung a brick in the centre of the door of his box to stop him weaving. We treated him rather as we had treated Trapeze and he soon got as fond of one of my donkeys as Trapeze had done. I also asked my old friend Collis Montgomery if he would come over from Ireland to take charge of Gay Record, and try to settle him down. At the time, he was managing a farm for his sister in County Cork, but he sportingly agreed to come and he did Gay Record almost all the time he was in training with us. He was undoubtedly a great man with horses.

'To start with, Collis used to take Gay Record out each day, jogging him along country lanes. Then after he had settled down a bit, he started hacking him to meets of the Surrey Union, perhaps up to ten miles away. He would have him out two or three hours with hounds and then hack him another ten miles or so home. He would take perhaps two and a half hours getting to the meet, and a similar time getting home. To start with Gay Record got very excited in company out hunting but after six weeks of long hacks to the meet and back we really got to the bottom of him and he gradually got less excited and started to settle down.

'Once he was used to the horse box, we began to take him to nearby racecourses. We didn't run him, but just let him walk round the paddock.

48 Collis Montgomery out hunting with the Surrey Union on Gay Record.

We also took him to Fontwell and Kempton to school. I remember on one occasion at Kempton, the jockey who was to have ridden Gay Record failed to turn up at the last moment, so Collis Montgomery took his place, though he was on the wrong side of sixty, and rode him very well indeed in a couple of schools.'

Four months after his arrival at Priory Stables, in mid-February, 1960, O'Donoghue and Montgomery took Gay Record to Fontwell for his first race over fences. The Irishman, Johnny Lehane—'Tumper' to his friends, because his frequent expression was 'Bejabbers, I'll tump ye'—had been engaged to ride. The chief race, the Robert Gore Memorial Challenge Cup, had ended in a desperate duel between Freeman on the Fairlawne chaser Scottish Flight II and Lehane on Miss Popsi-Wopsi, which Freeman had won. As O'Donoghue often fed Gay Record in his horse box, Gay Record was always in a hurry to get in and had travelled like a lamb going to Fontwell. The favourite in Gay Record's novices' chase was the Fairlawne-trained Cupid's Charge, who had already run in half a dozen chases that season. Ayala, a future winner of the Grand National, was among the outsiders. Gay Record, looking all the better for his spell of hunting, a change of scene, and ten months' absence from the racecourse, was thought to be in need of a race. Lehane let him settle down and have a good look at his fences but, finding that he was jumping well, he took him to the front soon after half way. As in the previous race, the finish again only concerned Freeman and Lehane, with Freeman on Cupid's Charge winning all out by a length from Gay Record.

Less than a fortnight later at Kempton, with a novices' chase at his mercy, Gay Record fell three fences from home when in the lead, and it was decided to wait until the autumn before he appeared again. It was at the 1960 October meeting at Fontwell that Gay Record made his third appearance over fences, again ridden by Lehane. This time Gay Record made no fatal mistake, led throughout and won his first race from Pure Whisky, ridden by Ian Balding, who a few years later was to take over the Kingsclere stable of Captain Peter Hasting-Bass and train for the Queen. It had been seven years from the time when Gay Record had arrived in Norfolk from Ireland until he gained his first victory on the racecourse—a very long haul in which Eldred Wilson and his henchman Ben Lloyd, Peter Cazalet and his staff at Fairlawne, Scallan at Sandringham, O'Donoghue and Montgomery at Priory Stables and 'Tumper' Lehane had all played their parts with much patience and much expertise, which at last had begun to bear fruit.

Gay Record did not win again that season. Lehane was injured and the horse seemed to miss him on at least two of the three occasions on which he finished second, and it was annoying also to finish second twice to runners from Fairlawne. He was having his twelfth race of the season when he finished fourth in the Abergavenny Challenge Cup at Plumpton on Easter Monday. He was in need of a rest and he was to get it.

'Tumper' Lehane was attached to the North Country stable of Verly Bewicke in the new season of 1961–62. O'Donoghue was in need of a new jockey for Gay Record and his choice fell on E. F. 'Gene' Kelly, a Warwickshire man who had been apprenticed to Joe Lawson at Manton

49 Gay Record (J. Lehane) taking part in the Weald Chase at Lingfield on 17 February 1961. Gay Record finished fourth to the Cheltenham Gold Cup winner, Linwell.

and had done Lord Astor's Archive, sire of Gay Record, and also Lord Astor's remarkable old warrior High Stakes. Kelly had joined Hector Smith's Snowshill stable near Broadway in Worcestershire one Friday in the autumn of 1955, had ridden a couple of winners for Hector Smith in the next two racing days, had met the girl he was destined to marry, and from that weekend he had not looked back.

Gay Record's first race of the new season was at the mixed meeting at Hurst Park in mid-October. O'Donoghue, seeking permission from Sir Martin Gilliat to engage Kelly for the Molesey Handicap Chase, was able to inform him that Kelly had been down once a week riding work for him and that he seemed to get on well with Gay Record. Starting an outsider in a field of ten, Gay Record ran well for a long way, finishing in the middle of his field. At Fontwell at the beginning of November, Gay Record ran considerably better to finish second in a two-mile handicap chase. When Sir Martin rang up Kelly to find out on Queen Elizabeth's behalf the next morning how he had gone, he was first of all told by Mrs Kelly that her husband was too busy cleaning the windows of their Worcestershire home to come to the telephone, but on hearing the enquiry came from Clarence House, Kelly dropped his window-cleaning materials, hurried at the double to the telephone, and was able to report to Sir Martin that he thought Gay Record would go very close to winning his next race, which was at the Sandown November meeting. He also reported that, except for a mistake at the first fence, Gay Record had never put a foot wrong at Fontwell, was running on well at the end of the race and, he thought, would stay the extra distance of the Withington Stayers Handicap Chase at Sandown in ten days' time.

Queen Elizabeth came to Sandown to see Silver Dome and Jaipur from Fairlawne and Gay Record from Priory Stables carry her colours on the first day of the Sandown November meeting. Silver Dome, who showed some of his best form at Sandown, failed to give the weight to Mr Basil Samuel's Some Alibi in the Littleworth Chase, but Rees on Jaipur just got the better of a desperate duel, with Stan Mellor on Sir George Bailey's Firecracker in the Novices Chase. Cazalet also had expectations of winning the Withington Stayers Chase with Hal's Hope, but luckily for Queen Elizabeth, Jack O'Donoghue and Gene Kelly, Hal's Hope was shouldering a seven pounds' penalty for winning a minor chase at Worcester.

Some jockeys are superstitious, some are not. Kelly, when race-riding, always used to wear his wife's silver horseshoe and the badge of St Christopher, the patron saint of travellers. On that morning, he had set out for Sandown from home without them but had time to return to get them, and perhaps inwardly that made all the difference. Jack O'Donoghue was also ready for the occasion. He for once had dug out his hunting bowler in honour of Queen Elizabeth, and many thought it a

50   Gay Record (Gene Kelly) and Burton
Tan (F. Winter) disputing the lead in the
Withington Stayers' Chase at Sandown on
17 November 1961.

51   Minutes later, Gene Kelly on Gay
Record, the winner, returning to the
unsaddling enclosure—Kelly's first victory in
the Royal colours.

52 Queen Elizabeth and Jack O'Donoghue at Sandown after the race.

good omen for Gay Record when they saw him sporting it on Sandown racecourse. In the race itself, Gay Record was in the lead and jumping boldly for Kelly almost throughout. For a moment, Fred Winter on Commander H. S. Egerton's Burton Tan headed Gay Record on the far side of the course and in the run-in from the last fence Hal's Hope and Bill Rees for a moment looked like catching Gay Record but O'Donoghue's ewe lamb struggled on gallantly for Gene Kelly and the penalty Hal's Hope was carrying just anchored the Fairlawne horse to the delight of the crowd. It was Gay Record's race by a bare one length, and it was much his best performance to date. O'Donoghue received much praise for the transformation he had wrought in the former 'bundle of nerves'.

Early in February 1962, O'Donoghue took Gay Record to Windsor for the Herne The Hunter Handicap Chase. The figure-of-eight Fontwell course seemed to suit Gay Record, and O'Donoghue thought the somewhat similar Windsor figure-of-eight course would also be to the horse's liking. He was correct, for Gay Record jumped quickly and confidently and in the end won unchallenged. It was clearly worth bringing him to Windsor again, and so back he came at the beginning of March to run in the Runnymede Handicap Chase over the same distance. Some Alibi, Silver Dome's conqueror at Sandown, was a hot favourite, but was no match over three miles for Gay Record, who was always in front and, except for one mistake in the final mile, jumped superbly. He won in the then record time for this distance at Windsor of 6 minutes 5 seconds.

After the race, it was found that Gay Record had twisted a plate badly during the race. O'Donoghue removed it and put it in his coat pocket, and shortly afterwards O'Donoghue and Kelly were asked to go and wait by the entrance to the members' enclosure as Queen Elizabeth wanted to have more words with them before leaving the course. Her Majesty appeared suddenly, catching O'Donoghue off-guard with his hands in the pockets of his overcoat. Queen Elizabeth put out her hand to say goodbye and congratulate O'Donoghue again on Gay Record's fluent victory, and out came O'Donoghue's right hand still clutching the twisted plate, which he proceeded to 'plonk' in Her Majestry's hand to the surprise and great amusement of all concerned!

The course record broken by Gay Record that day had stood for fourteen years since the 1949 Grand National third Royal Mount had lowered it in the same race in 1948. 'If Gay Record had not twisted a plate and I had given him a kick in the ribs, the time record he established that day would have lasted a lifetime,' was Gene Kelly's comment afterwards. It was perhaps the best performance of Gay Record's career. He was not destined to win three handicaps in a season again.

The 1961–62 season had been a marvellous one for Queen Elizabeth. She had had more victories to her name than that of any other owner and her growing support of National Hunt racing was undoubtedly adding greatly to its popularity. It looked on paper as if the prospects for 1962–63 were equally good. Double Star, Laffy, Out of Town, Silver Dome and The Rip, Queen Elizabeth's principal winners at Fairlawne, remained in training. Much was thought of Silver Dome's full brother Dargent, who had won a handicap hurdle for Queen Elizabeth early in 1962 and was expected to make a novice chaser of great ability, and Her Majesty had a new horse from Ireland in Super Fox, a half-brother by the Ascot Gold Cup winner Supertello to the versatile Farrney Fox, winner of the Irish Lincolnshire, and just beaten in the Irish Cesarewitch and the Champion Hurdle in successive years.

Jack O'Donoghue had also found a new horse in Ireland for Queen Elizabeth in Sunbridge, a gelding by the staying Solario horse Foroughi out of the Archive mare Archstar. She had won a maiden plate in Ireland as a three-year-old in 1953 for her owner, breeder and trainer Mr O. T. V. Slocock of Castletown, Ballylinan, County Kildare. Archstar was herself a half-sister to three other small winners in Ireland, whilst Foroughi, who had won at Royal Ascot for the Aga Khan in the late 1930s, stood at Mr Slocock's stud.

Queen Elizabeth, thoroughly enthused by her successes of the past season, gave her approval for Cazalet to buy another young horse for her during the summer. This was bought from Mr Jack White of Clonsilla, County Dublin, a veterinary surgeon, well-known and respected on both sides of the Irish Sea. The newcomer was Arch Point, an Archive gelding out of the Solferino mare Sol Point, who had been spotted by Judge Wylie, now an octogenarian, looking out for a likely young horse for Queen Elizabeth. Although Judge Whylie did not know it at the time, Sol Point was out of Point to Point, a mare bred by King George VI during the Second World War and later discarded by the Royal Stud. She was a half-sister by Foxhunter to the King's good stayer Rising Light, winner of the Newmarket St Leger and second to Chamossaire in the 1945 St Leger. Arch Point traced back both on his sire's side and on his dam's side to one of Lord Astor's foundation mares the illustrious Popingaol, dam of the full sisters Book Law, from whom Archive descended, and Book Debt, from whom Point to Point descended. Arch Point was, therefore, an appropriate horse to join Queen Elizabeth's team. He was so good looking as a two-year-old that Judge Wylie suggested that he should remain with Jack White during the summer of 1962 and should be shown at the Dublin Horse Show. Not only did he win his two-year-old hunter class but he also won the Laidlaw Challenge Cup for the best young horse in the show.

During the summer, Queen Elizabeth visited Canada for the third time when she flew to Montreal to present new colours to the three battalions of The Black Watch (Royal Highland Regiment) of Canada on the occasion of their centenary celebrations. During this trip to Canada, she was the guest of the Ontario Jockey Club for the 103rd running of Canada's most famous race—the Queen's Plate—run at Woodbine on the outskirts of Toronto. King George VI accompanied by Queen Elizabeth had been the first reigning monarch to see the Queen's Plate when they visited Woodbine in 1939, and Queen Elizabeth II and Prince Philip had watched the 100th running in 1959. Now, in 1962, Queen Elizabeth was making her second visit to watch the race for Canada's classic three-year-olds, staying as a guest of Mr E. P. Taylor, the leading Canadian owner-breeder.

Soon after her return from Canada, Queen Elizabeth went up to Newcastle to watch the Northumberland Plate, the big race of the Gosforth Park summer meeting and the Durham Plate which her own three-year-old Harvest Gold was expected to win. The Queen had a fancied runner in Optimistic in the Northumberland Plate, but she was unluckily beaten by a short head, her rider mistiming his challenge. Harvest Gold, who had shown ability at home, was a failure in the Durham Plate. He seemed to swallow his tongue when under pressure, and after he had won a minor race at Brighton in September, it was unfortunately decided to sell him instead of giving him the chance to see if he would take kindly to hurdling. With hindsight, it was the wrong decision, but everyone makes the wrong decision sometimes in racing and it usually pays to get out of horses who frequently disappoint.

A month after Harvest Gold had won his one and only race for Queen Elizabeth, The Rip made his first appearance of the new 1962–63 season in Manchester's valuable Emblem Chase over three miles. After his forward showing at Kempton against the Cheltenham Gold Cup winner Mandarin, he was bound to be near the top of the handicap. He ran well, was in the lead three fences from home, but finished third, very leg weary. He had broken down, had to be fired, and was out for the season. It was a very sad blow. The same day, however, Super Fox appeared for the first time in the Royal colours and shaped with much promise.

Queen Elizabeth came racing for the first time in the new season for the November meeting at Sandown where Super Fox, Silver Dome, Double Star and Dargent were all to carry her colours on the opening day. Super Fox had won a bumper at Naas as a four-year-old in the spring of 1961 when trained by C. Weld, so had come to Fairlawne fully accustomed to the life of a racing stable. Now over eighteen months later, ridden by Mould, he was one of a field over twenty strong in Division I of the Waterloo Novices' Hurdle. The more experienced Grey Gauntlet, whose owner Major D. Vaughan had just failed to win the 1948 Grand National with First of the Dandies, was thought to be the probable winner. In fact, there was a desperate finish between Super Fox, Grey Gauntlet and Skate In. Super Fox, jumping cautiously, had been left with a lot of ground to make up but was gaining fast when he propped, swerved, and landed asprawl after jumping the last flight of hurdles. It looked as if he had lost his chance, but somehow Mould got him going again in time, and he just caught Grey Gauntlet near the line. To win under such circumstances showed that Super Fox was a horse of great potential.

Half an hour later Silver Dome and Double Star both appeared in the two-mile Littleworth Handicap Chase against other old two-miler rivals in Flame Gun, King's Nephew, Some Alibi, and Barberyn—Rees was on Silver Dome, who was the better suited by the distance, and Double Star was partnered by Mould. Double Star was never in the hunt, Silver Dome always was, and in fact held on all out to defeat King's Nephew and Some Alibi. Two-mile steeplechases at Sandown with proven chasers in competition are nearly always thrilling to watch. This race was no exception.

Cazalet was hopeful that he would saddle Silver Dome's full brother Dargent to complete a hat trick and treble for Queen Elizabeth in the novices' chase which followed. Dargent had been schooling well at home and was much fancied but at the first fence, and for no apparent reason, he came to grief. He was to be very disappointing throughout the season. The following week, Laffy appeared at Cheltenham and, like Dargent, fell at the first. The December meeting at Lingfield was abandoned owing to frost, so neither Double Star nor Laffy could go to their happy hunting ground. The Old Year went out with Super Fox and Silver Dome Queen Elizabeth's only winners in mid-season. With no racing in England between Boxing Day and the second week in March owing to snow and frost, National Hunt owners were faced with a disastrous season.

Queen Elizabeth, however, had good news early in the New Year when the New Zealander Mr James Wattie announced that he wished to lend Her Majesty his outstanding stayer Even Stevens to run in England. Even Stevens, the winner of both the Melbourne and the Caulfield Cups of 1962, was to come over to England for two years to be trained by Boyd-Rochfort at Newmarket and was to attempt to win for Queen Elizabeth the Ascot Gold Cup and other races. At the end of two years, he was to return to Mr Wattie's stud in New Zealand. Even Stevens had been only the fifth horse to complete the Caulfield Cup-Melbourne Cup double, and Queen Elizabeth was very appreciative of Mr Wattie's magnanimous plan. He was due to leave New Zealand at the end of January, but a few days beforehand he broke a sesamoid bone in a foreleg whilst exercising at his New Zealand stable and the whole plan had to be quashed.

After a hold-up of seventy-five days, racing resumed in England at Newbury on March 8. The Fairlawne horses usually did well after a break in the weather. Cazalet was adept at keeping them fit and raring to go. The tipster Prince Monolulu, part and parcel of the English racing scene for nearly half a century but now in his eighty-fourth year, appeared at Newbury, announcing as usual that he had a HORSE and, seeing Queen Elizabeth, proceeded to advise all and sundry to support the unpredictable Dargent in Division I of the Burford Novices' Chase and Her Majesty's Gay Record in the Snelsmore Handicap Chase for amateur riders. As John Lawrence, then high up in the amateur riders' table, was riding Gay Record, the latter part of his advice seemed to be reasonable.

For a long way it looked as if Prince Monolulu's suggestion to support Dargent was going to prove inspired. With the leaders throughout, Dargent came to the last fence disputing the lead with Rise and Shine, and going the better, but he got too close to the fence, hit it hard and collapsed on landing. It was the third time he had fallen with Rees in a novice chase. A couple of hours later Gay Record, giving weight to all but one of his opponents, proceeded to go well for John Lawrence in the Snelsmore Chase. He appeared the likely winner two fences from the finish, but then two rivals near the foot of the handicap proved too much for him.

Fortunately Queen Eliabeth did not have to wait long for a winner, for on the following day Double Star, ridden with determination by Rees, just got the best of his old rivals King's Nephew and Barberyn in the Paddington Handicap Chase which was run over Double Star's best distance of two-and-a-half miles. Double Star was but one of six Cazalet winners at the meeting—Prince Rajsinh of Rajpipla's Sinin and Mrs

Robert Evans's Dali on the first day, Sir Winston Churchill's Kemal, Mr F. C. Penney's Thornfield, Queen Elizabeth's Double Star, and Mrs A. Hodgson's Nymphellor on the second—a notable piece of training.

Queen Elizabeth had no runner at the National Hunt meeting at Cheltenham when Mill House won the Cheltenham Gold Cap. As Mill House in his previous race had only defeated Laffy by three lengths, giving him a mere two pounds, Laffy looked a handicap certainty when he appeared two days later in the Coventry Handicap Chase at Kempton. Rees and Mould both being on the the injured list, Cazalet called on Willie Robinson, who had not ridden Laffy since his triumph in the Ulster Harp National. In the Kempton race, Laffy hit the first fence hard, hit the second fence harder still, twisting in the air, and unseating Robinson. Laffy, ridden by Mould, fell again early on in his next race but, ridden by Robinson again, he finished fourth in his final race of the season at Cheltenham. It was the only season in five in which he failed to win a race for Queen Elizabeth, but then there was no steeplechasing at Lingfield throughout the season owing to the foul weather.

Double Star also missed Lingfield that spring. He was asked to hump 12 stone 8 lbs in the Richard Marler Handicap Chase for amateur riders at Newbury at the end of March. Cazalet expected that Nicholas Gaselee, at the start of a successful career as an amateur rider, would be able to claim seven pounds in the race, but the conditions were obscure and, at the last moment, it was ordained that Gaselee was not allowed to claim. In spite of the weight, Double Star was still in the hunt three fences from home and finished a creditable fourth. A month later towards the end of April, Double Star was asked to take on Mill House in the Mandarin Chase at Newbury over three-and-a-quarter miles—a distance which had always proved too far for him. Rees kindly pulled him up well before the finish when his chance had gone. He was not enjoying himself, and if horses could talk I think he would have told his trainer, as he had implied to Rees, that he was beginning at the age of eleven to get a bit long in the tooth. It was the forty-sixth time he had carried Queen Elizabeth's colours.

Gay Record at the same age was definitely not feeling his years to the same extent. After several near misses he appeared at Sandown towards the end of March at the Grand Military meeting, which Queen Elizabeth always supported. In the long-distance Sandown Handicap Chase he came to the last fence disputing the lead and looking the winner. 'I gave him a slap and he took off a stride too soon and came down', reported Gene Kelly dejectedly to Queen Elizabeth after the race. 'It was my fault, ma'am, I should have won. I feel heartbroken. I am extremely sorry.' 'Bad luck, Kelly, that's racing,' replied Queen Elizabeth, sympathetically. Six weeks later at Fontwell at the beginning of May, Gay Record won for the first time that season after being narrowly beaten on three occasions. It was some compensation for his consistency.

53   Gay Record and a small friend at Priory Stables.

Bill Rees unfortunately had no reward for his fortitude in riding the unpredictable Dargent. At Newbury at the end of March he came to the last fence but one, full of running and looking all over the winner, but fell yet again. At Cheltenham in April, with Rees on the sidelines, Dargent fell for the fifth time in a novice chase and fractured a pedal bone. His racing was at an end. Queen Elixabeth only won five races in the season so grievously interrupted by the weather. There were much better days ahead.

8

Makaldar

QUEEN ELIZABETH had had twenty different horses who had won races for her under National Hunt rules in her first fourteen years as an owner. They had all basically been steeplechasers as opposed to hurdlers. She had yet to have a top class hurdler to carry her colours, but it was the French-bred hurdler Makaldar who was to be her star performer in the 1963–64 season.

Makaldar was discovered in France by Colonel Bobinski, now in his early sixties and a most loyal friend to Peter Cazalet. Makaldar was bred in the south of France near Lyons. His sire Makalu was a jumping stallion. Makaldar was out of the Marsyas mare La Madouna of M. Marcel Boussac's breeding. La Madouna had been barren for four years when she was sent to Makalu as a last hope. The resulting foal, Makaldar, who was, in fact, La Madouna's last foal, went into training at Maisons-Laffitte and was bought by Cazalet from M. P. Mercier after he had run well in a hurdle race at Auteuil, carefully noted by the observant Bobinski.

A chestnut with big lop ears, standing 17 hands, he was to prove himself a horse of great stamina, which no doubt he inherited in large part from his dam's sire Marsyas, the winner on no less than four occasions of the Prix du Cadran—the French equivalent of the Ascot Gold Cup—as well as several long-distance races of note in England.

Makaldar joined Fairlawne in the spring of 1963. He was a colt when he arrived and Cazalet had him gelded. He first ran in Cazalet's name in the Hedge Hoppers' Hurdle at Newbury at the end of October when there were four penalised hurdle race winners in the field. The favourite Kirriemuir, in the colours of Mrs T. Beddington, jumped well and made all the running. Queen Elizabeth, watching the race on television, noted that Makaldar came from behind to take second place, was duly impressed, rang up her principal trainer and bought Makaldar. One is apt to associate a particular jockey with each of Queen Elizabeth's star performers in her first fifteen years as an owner—Tony Grantham with Monaveen, Bryan Marshall with Manicou, Dick Francis with Devon Loch, Arthur Freeman with Double Star, Bill Rees with The Rip, and now, I feel, David Mould with Makaldar.

54 David Mould going
to post on his favourite,
Makaldar.

Mould had had his first ride for Queen Elizabeth on that erratic jumper King of the Isle in the Henry VIII Chase at Hurst Park on a December day in 1958. Arthur Freeman was then stable jockey and rode Moretons, the more fancied Fairlawne runner, in the same race. King of the Isle had fallen in his previous race over hurdles, so Cazalet was asking a lot of King of the Isle in sending him out to race against some of the best novices in the country. Sadly he was brought down when going well, Mould breaking his collar bone.

Mad keen on ponies from an early age, Mould was apprenticed for three years to Staff Ingham at Epsom. Ingham, a product of the Wootton school of jockeys, had in his day been a brilliant hurdle race rider and he evidently considered Mould showed plenty of promise for, when he grew too heavy for the flat, he arranged for Mould to move to Fairlawne as a lad, hoping that Cazalet would give him the chance to become a jump jockey. A few months later Cazalet gave Mould his first ride in public on Mr F. C. Penney's mare Straight Hill in a handicap hurdle at the November meeting at Plumpton. He had obeyed orders and come from behind to win his first race narrowly. Cazalet was evidently so impressed that he was content for Mould to wear the Royal colours for the first time only a month later on King of the Isle. It was to prove good judgement for in the end Mould was to win more races for Queen Elizabeth than anyone else.

It was just over a year later when Mould rode for Queen Elizabeth again. He now had eight victories to his credit on Straight Hill and had won on nothing else, and Cazalet put him up on King of the Isle in a long-distance handicap hurdle at Kempton in January 1960. With the help of the seven pounds' allowance, King of the Isle and Mould just got the better of a desperate finish with Belgrano in the colours of the American Mr J. H. Whitney, who had been supporting steeplechasing in this country from the days of the great Easter Hero at the end of the 1920s. Three months later, when still in his teens, Mould was just beaten on Lochroe in the Cheltenham Gold Cup, and had definitely arrived in the steeplechasing world.

When Makaldar appeared on the scene, Mould had five victories to his credit for Queen Elizabeth—three on The Rip, one on King of the Isle, and one on her promising young horse Super Fox in a novice hurdle at Sandown in November 1962. At Folkestone towards the end of September 1963, nearly a year later, Mould brought off his first double for Queen Elizabeth on Super Fox in a long-distance handicap hurdle and Out of Town in the Whitelaw Gold Cup. Super Fox gave away weight to all his opponents. Out of Town, having been hobdayed, found his form again after a blank season in 1962–63.

At Wye a week later, Silver Dome, preparing to go up to Liverpool to run in the Grand Sefton in October, won a two-mile handicap chase under top weight, starting at odds on and looking in a different class to his opponents. In the Grand Sefton on soft going, Superfine, ridden by Sir William Pigott-Brown, then the leading amateur rider, and Peacetown, owned by Mrs F. Williams, daughter of Sir John Jarvis, were the joint favourites whilst Mr Edward Courage was hopeful of winning with Border Flight. Two fences from home, Border Flight was out clear but fell as he began to tire, leaving Silver Dome in front. At the final fence Silver Dome was six lengths in front of the second horse, April Rose, and looked sure to win, but he tired in the long run-in as many had done before him, and was passed in the last fifty yards by Team Spirit, finishing strongly. Silver Dome's rider, Bill Rees, was very disappointed. He reported that he hit the first fence hard and several others but got away with it. But for that he felt he must have won. The fact remained that Silver Dome had had heart trouble at the end of the previous season, and probably, as a result of that, was apt to weaken suddenly at the end of a race. With hindsight, it was no disgrace to be beaten by Team Spirit, who was destined to win the 1964 Grand National.

Makaldar carried the Royal colours for the first time in the 1963 Toll House Hurdle at Sandown. Before the race, Mould reported to Queen

Elizabeth that Makaldar had given him a tremendous feel in his race at Newbury and he thought it would take a very good novice hurdler to beat him that season. He won the Toll House Hurdle comfortably and half an hour later Gay Record, ably ridden by Kelly, made every yard of the running to win the Walton Green Handicap Chase—his only success of the season. A fortnight later, Makaldar won another three-year-old hurdle at Kempton and was then aimed at the December meeting at Lingfield to which Queen Elizabeth was to come as usual.

On the first day of Lingfield, the only Cazalet winner was the Contessa di Sant' Elia's French-bred Orinoco II. After racing, Rees went north to Newcastle to ride the Contessa's Antiar in the valuable Gillette Handicap Hurdle, which he won in an exciting finish between four horses. In Rees's absence, Mould had five fancied rides for Cazalet at Lingfield on the Saturday and just failed to bring off another Lingfield treble for Queen Elizabeth. He was beaten on Dick Wilkins's Cosmoudan in Division I of the Oxted Novices' Chase, but won Division II on the same owner's Gort. Then came the big disappointment of the day when Queen Elizabeth's favourite Double Star, seeking his eighteenth victory and his seventh at Lingfield, was just beaten by the six-year-old Double March in the Ashdown Handicap Chase. Double Star had won this particular race in 1958, ridden by Freeman, and in 1960 and in 1961, ridden by Rees. In his

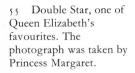

55   Double Star, one of Queen Elizabeth's favourites. The photograph was taken by Princess Margaret.

old age, Double Star needed humouring and Rees was adept at getting the best out of him. Cazalet felt he undoubtedly missed him on that December day. Nevertheless, Double Star, rising twelve, was getting arthritic and had had trouble with his feet. He had his fiftieth and last race for Queen Elizabeth at Lingfield in the New Year when, lumping twelve stone in holding going, ridden by Rees, he could only finish fifth. He was then retired—with seventeen victories to his name. A year later he was becoming infirm and miserable, and it was decided that the kind thing to do was to put him down.

Queen Elizabeth's other two runners from Fairlawne at that Lingfield December meeting both won. Laffy, plagued by back trouble, had lost his confidence in the previous season and had failed to win a race, but Mould gave him a very good ride in the Eridge Handicap Chase and in the end he outjumped his opponents. Mould ended the day by landing the odds-on Makaldar in the Juvenile Hurdle. Two Epsom-trained winners—Baliol from Ron Smyth's stable and Cupboard Love of Ingham's—were both fancied to beat Makaldar, but Makaldar was too good for them and for more than a dozen other novice hurdlers in the same race.

Makaldar was not to be allowed to while away his time in contemplation. He went to Fontwell at the end of the year to win his fourth three-year-old hurdle in the space of seven weeks and to Sandown less than a fortnight later for the Village Hurdle for four-year-olds, which brought out a field of twenty-five. It was in this race that Makaldar really showed his mettle, as John Lawrence clearly put it, reporting the race in *The Daily Telegraph*: 'Makaldar put up an extraordinary performance to win the Village Hurdle. Looking beforehand as if he could do with a rest, he was off the bit soon after halfway and then, having made up a mass of ground, blundered horribly at the second last. For any normal horse it would certainly have been the end, but, says Mould emphatically, "This is the best horse I have ever ridden." He could well be right, for picking himself up as if nothing much had happened, Makaldar scooted home to win by an almost unbelievable four lengths from Cocky Boy . . .' 'He has never made a mistake before,' observed Queen Elizabeth, as she greeted Makaldar and Mould on their return to the winner's enclosure. It had been a very exciting race to watch.

Queen Elizabeth was due to leave England early in February for a seven weeks' tour of Canada, New Zealand and Australia. On the eve of her departure by air for Canada, she had to have an emergency operation for appendicitis and there was no alternative but to cancel her tour. 'All along the route from Vancouver to Adelaide and from Auckland to Fiji, which Queen Elizabeth was gaily preparing to traverse, there has been keen disappointment that her visit must be postponed,' wrote a leader writer at the time. 'Hers is an unsurpassed popularity throughout the Commonwealth; she won it in the first days of her emergence as a public figure and has worn it with easy grace for more than forty years . . . In the years of her widowhood she has travelled untiringly . . . She plays her ceremonial part with natural majesty, but she speaks to all sorts and conditions of men and women from the warm simplicity of the heart. At most times her endearing ways are taken for granted without comment, but there are occasions like the present when the millions of her daughter's subjects have an excuse to send her their love and good wishes.'

At Sister Agnes's in London, where the operation took place, Fairlawne did not forget their principal owner. Lilac, daffodils and tulips arrived in profusion from Double Star and The Rip and there was a lovely bouquet of baby roses from Makaldar and her new horse, Rochfort. A few days after the operation, Queen Elizabeth wrote a light-hearted letter to thank Peter and Zara Cazalet, saying: 'I cannot tell you what a sensation these glorious flowers have caused, and I think Double Star and The Rip showed enormous taste in their choice. Great boughs of lilac and daffodils and tulips were exactly right for two such esteemed characters to order, and I am sure that, if there was one, they would be members of the equine Turf Club. . . . Makaldar's and Rochfort's lovely bouquet was also absolutely right. Please thank them from their loving and grateful owner, and tell them what very real pleasure she derived from this imaginative, amusing and beautiful present. . . .'

Meanwhile, whilst Double Star and The Rip, Makaldar and Rochfort, were basking in reflected glory from their owner's appreciative letter of thanks, things were not going well for the Countessa di Sant' Elia's Antiar, who was due to carry Queen Elizabeth's colours in the future. The day following the news that the operation on Queen Elizabeth had been carried out successfully, Antiar went down to Wincanton to take on moderate opposition in the Kingwell Hurdle. He was one of the favourites for the Champion Hurdle at the time, following his success in the Gillette Hurdle, and on form he looked a racing certainty for the Wincanton race, starting an odds-on favourite.

Bill Braddon had taken Antiar down to Wincanton the day before. 'I did the horse at evening stables on the course,' he reported later. 'I looked in to see if all was well at 10 p.m. He was all right and had eaten up, and I then left the course to go into the town of Wincanton, where I was staying. I went up at 6.30 a.m. the next morning. There had been a hard frost. In fact, it was so hard that I could not exercise Antiar normally. I eventually cantered up a field with long grass. Before racing started, Bill Rees and I walked the course and we both felt the horse should not run. It was obviously touch and go whether it was fit to race, as racing was put back half an hour. Antiar on his form in the Gillette Hurdle should have trotted up but I felt he was the sort of horse who would be scared if the conditions were not right. When the guv'nor arrived, I reported that I thought the horse should be withdrawn, and David Mould, who won the first race on a novice chaser, was of the same opinion. The guv'nor, however, decided to let Antiar take his chance; he completely failed to show his form and he fell at the last hurdle when beaten, Bill Rees fortunately escaping with a shaking. The Wincanton stewards failed to order a dope test, but the guv'nor felt Antiar must have been doped and arranged a private test, the samples being sent to the Royal Veterinary College.'

Cazalet's suspicions were correct. Poor Antiar was not fit to run again until April—a month after he should have competed in the Champion Hurdle. When he did run, he failed to show his true form. The dope tests showed that 'he was suffering from a considerable dose of some drug of a depressant nature'. No doubt the dopers and those associated with them gloried in their ill-gotten gains, and no doubt it did not worry them that they had put at risk the lives of Antiar and his rider Bill Rees. 'I was cross-examined for a long time by detectives afterwards,' added Bill Braddon. 'They were naturally suspicious until I told them I had tried to persuade the guv'nor not to run Antiar.' Racecourse security at the time was primitive. It was to be tightened up in the future.

In the middle of February, Queen Elizabeth left hospital after her successful operation, her doctors insisting that she should take on no public engagements for two months. She was cheered up a week later by the victory of Laffy in the Manifesto Chase at Lingfield. Rees had had a bad fall on a Cazalet novice chaser the previous afternoon, so Mould rode Laffy, who won impressively. It was decided to let Laffy take his chance in the Grand National.

Towards the end of the month, the Queen, shortly expecting her fourth child—Prince Edward who was to be born on March 10—went down quietly to Priory Stables at Reigate to see Gay Record and also Her Majesty's own National Emblem, a five-year-old by the Ascot Gold Cup winner Zarathustra out of the Big Game mare Maple Leaf, who had won for the Queen and was a half-sister to the Queen's Doncaster Cup winner Agreement. National Emblem had proved a complete failure in training with Boyd-Rochfort and on his only appearance on the flat as a big and backward three-year-old in a maiden race at Newmarket, running in a hood, had finished tailed off last in a big field, refusing to co-operate. The Queen, however, had rightly thought that he might be worth persevering with and had sent him to O'Donoghue to join Gay Record to see if a spell of hunting might cause him to change his outlook, as it had done that of Gay Record. 'I remember the occasion vividly,' said O'Donoghue. 'The Queen sat in Park Road, resting on a tree stump just by the entrance to my top yard. We discussed National Emblem by the roadside, and people passed by without beginning to realise to whom I was talking.'

Meanwhile, Queen Elizabeth the Queen Mother was about to set out to convalesce in the Royal yacht in the Caribbean, and the Queen, after her visit to O'Donoghue, was able to report on the well-being of Gay Record, now a twelve-year-old, and on the novice Sunbridge, whom O'Donoghue had bought on Queen Elizabeth's behalf after seeing him win in the show ring in Ireland. He had engaged John Lawrence to ride Sunbridge in the National Hunt Chase at Cheltenham in the first week in March. Lawrence already had the 1959 National Hunt Chase to his credit on Sabaria. Queen Elizabeth's long-distance hurdler Super Fox, already the winner of four long-distance handicap hurdles that season, and Sunbridge, were Queen Elizabeth's only runners at the National Hunt meeting of 1964. Makaldar was in reserve for Haydock Park's valuable Victor Ludorum Hurdle at the end of the week.

O'Donoghue had first noticed John Lawrence's skill as a rider at the November meeting at Plumpton in 1957 when he had won a novice chase for his future father-in-law Major 'Ginger' Dennistoun on Foolish Man. As a result, O'Donoghue had put him up on the one-eyed Trapeze later in the season, and Lawrence had delighted O'Donoghue by winning. Three years later, he nearly won the 1961 National Hunt Chase for O'Donoghue on Nickel Coin's son King's Nickel, so that it was not surprising that he had successfully sought to engage him for Sunbridge in the 1964 National Hunt Chase. On one occasion, Sunbridge had run really well in a novice chase at Sandown but the rest of his form on paper that season had looked very moderate and he was a 33-1 outsider for the race in a field of thirty. Nevertheless, John Lawrence felt that Sunbridge probably stayed well and on a good day was capable of jumping well.

'I determined to ride a waiting race on Sunbridge,' Lawrence recalled recently. 'In this particular race, there are usually some of the field going too fast out in front early in the race and I felt I wanted to go to sleep on Sunbridge at the back of the field for the first circuit. At the end of the circuit I was, in fact, lying about tenth, ten lengths or so off the leaders, and at the first fence down the hill, going away from the stands, Sunbridge suddenly saw daylight, "pinged" it, and gained lengths. He did the same thing at the very next fence, and there was I in front much too soon. I realised that I had made a nonsense. Sunbridge was a very good jumper when he was going well, but I could not expect him to be in front for so long, and two fences out Dorimont and Pontoeuvre came from behind to run me out of it. If I had been able to cover Sunbridge up till well in line for home, I should nearly have won.'

Unfortunately, during the summer Sunbridge injured himself when out at grass, was fired on both forelegs, and was never the same again.

A couple of days after Sunbridge's narrow defeat in the National Hunt Chase, Sir Martin Gilliat and Peter Cazalet went up to Haydock Park by train to see Makaldar run in the Victor Ludorum Hurdle for four-year-olds. Cazalet had not been to Haydock Park since he had had a very bad

56   A superb picture of
Makaldar (D. Mould)
in action at
Cheltenham with
Cleeve Hill in
the background.

fall on his father's home-bred hurdler Shipbourne in the middle 1930s.
Makaldar and Mould had won five hurdle races off the reel and Queen
Elizabeth's horse was an odds-on favourite in a field of eleven. Gilliat and
Cazalet parted when they got to the course. Sir Edward Hanmer was the
guiding light at Haydock in those days. One of his assistants took Sir
Martin Gilliat off to have lunch in the owners' dining room and Cazalet
went to the trainers' dining room. They met later and compared notes on
their respective lunches! Mould had had a fall on a spare ride in the selling
chase an hour before the big race but was fortunately unhurt.

Makaldar had competitors from all over the country. From Newmarket
came Mr Stanhope Joel's Stem Turn and the Royal Ascot winner Master
Cappelle, a son of Red Rum's sire Quorum, and carrying the colours of Mr
R. Midwood, whose family had won the 1930 Grand National with Shaun
Goilin. From Yorkshire came Vintage and Mr Clifford Nicholson's Corn
Cockle, from Cheshire Lord Leverhulme's Number Please, trained by
George Owen, from Epsom C. J. Benstead's Vicky Joe, Rimell's Ballet

Painting from Worcestershire, and Fortune Hunter from Denys Smith's successful stable in County Durham. 'I needed a very strong gallop for Makaldar,' recalled David Mould, 'and Brian Taylor on Master Cappelle won it for me without him knowing it, for he went like a bat out of hell from the start. If you were on the bridle with Makaldar in the first mile, you then knew you would probably *not* win. In this Haydock Park race, I was twenty lengths off the leaders at half way, but the pace was so strong that I felt confident already that I would come through and win, as indeed I did from Master Cappelle and Ballet Painting.' It was Makaldar's last race of the season, and Queen Elizabeth's ninety-ninth success under National Hunt rules.

Queen Elizabeth was recuperating in the Royal yacht in the Caribbean when Silver Dome and Laffy went up to Aintree for the Grand National meeting—Silver Dome, ridden by Rees, to attempt to win the Topham Trophy and Laffy to run in the Grand National itself.

In the Topham Trophy, Silver Dome looked the winner two fences from home. 'I was galloping over them, going to the second last,' reported Rees to Cazalet after the race, 'and then he weakened suddenly as if it was heart. He jumped much better than he did when beaten by Team Spirit in the autumn.' Sadly, Mr Paul Mellon's Red Tide, the winner, and Renton's Siracusa had both taken Silver Dome's measure before the last fence.

Rees fancied Laffy considerably in the Grand National two days later. The going was soft which did not usually worry him. 'Laffy could be a brilliant jumper,' said Bill Rees, 'but if the ground was the slightest bit slippery, he just did nothing at all and was capable of barely taking off at a fence. Therefore, although I felt Laffy was capable of going really well in the National, one had to realise that he might lose heart and barely rise at a fence. In fact, I knew my fate very soon, for he barely rose at the second fence, I could not stay on, and he fell riderless at the fourth.'

Queen Elizabeth heard the Grand National broadcast on board the Royal yacht *Britannia* anchored off Plymouth, the capital of Montserrat in the West Indies. Cazalet rang up by radio to report to Queen Elizabeth what had happened to Laffy and to say that Silver Dome's old rival Team Spirit was the winner. Queen Elizabeth, thanking her principal trainer by letter, said: 'It was very disappointing that the radio was so bad on Saturday night. I really could not hear you. I was so anxious to know whether Rees and Laffy were all right, and when I asked you the answer came back in a short squeak like "*eeeek*", which I took to be "Yes", so I was satisfied. I heard the race quite well on the radio. The only comforting thing was that, if Laffy had to fall, it was better to get it over early. . . . I have had wonderful weather and have been to a lot of islands and seen some very beautiful ones. I rather fell for the Virgin Islands. They are marvellous, rather remote, divine white beaches and perfect sun and cool

57 Laffy (W. Rees) leaving the paddock at Aintree to run in the 1964 Grand National.

58 Laffy clearing the first fence with Rees silhouetted by the chimney. Laffy came to grief soon afterwards.

evenings. . . . I do hope the horses are well? What about Silver Dome having a summer out in a field, to see if a change and a rest would bring back that little bit of staying on? He usually jumps so beautifully. . . .'

Queen Elizabeth was back from her convalescence in the Caribbean in time to come to Sandown to see Laffy perform with credit in the Whitbread Gold Cup at the end of April. In a big field, three horses singled themselves out from the remainder approaching the Pond fence at the bottom end of the course—Laffy, the top weight and favourite, Mill House, who had been beaten by Arkle in the Cheltenham Gold Cup, and Mrs D. Wells-Kendrew's Dormant, trained by Crump at Middleham. 'Laffy ran a really good race,' reported Rees to Queen Elizabeth. 'He hated the water, as he always does—I think it hurts his back—but I got him over it and was moving up well at the bottom end of the course, when Mill House, looking like an elephant, came passing by.' Later still, Dormant, in receipt of three stone from Mill House, also came by and caught and beat Mill House.

Queen Elizabeth's total of ninety-nine winners under National Hunt rules was to remain static till the following season. Her Majesty was seventh in the winning owners' list, seven horses contributing to her eighteen races won—with Makaldar and Super Fox contributing ten between them, Laffy, Out of Town and Silver Dome two each, and Gay Record and The Rip one each. The Rip was under a cloud again in the second half of the season. He went in the wind and was hobdayed. Cazalet was third in the trainers' table behind Fulke Walwyn and Bob Turnell. Mould had rocketed up to second place in the jockeys' table behind the champion jockey Josh Gifford, and ahead of Terry Biddlecombe.

9

A Great Season

THE 1964–65 season—Queen Elizabeth's sixteenth as an owner of steeplechasers—was to be her most successful at Fairlawne. She ended it third in the winning owners' list with more races won than any other owner. In fact, five women were the five leading owners' of the National Hunt season—the American Mrs M. Stephenson, owner of the Grand National winner Jay Trump, Anne Duchess of Westminster, owner of the Cheltenham Gold Cup winner Arkle, Queen Elizabeth with Makaldar one of several to shine, Mrs T. Beddington, owner of the Champion Hurdle winner Kirriemuir, and Mrs J. Rogerson, owner of the top class hurdler Salmon Spray, who fell unexpectedly in the Champion Hurdle. Peter Cazalet was leading trainer for the third time. The only disappointing fact was that Fairlawne's jockeys, Rees and Mould, were both seriously injured during the season.

It was a very dry autumn in the south in 1964 and Cazalet had comparatively few runners in September and early October, but three times during that period he hoped to saddle Queen Elizabeth's 100th winner, first when the four-year-old Arch Point was a moderate third in a novices' hurdle at Fontwell in mid-September and again when Arch Point was a moderate second of four at Fontwell a fortnight later. At Worcester in mid-October, Cazalet again hoped the 100th winner would come when Super Fox, winner of six hurdle races and with the scope to make a top-class chaser, was risked on hard ground in a hurdle race but could only finish third of four.

The following week, old Gay Record was in a handicap chase at Folkestone with the probability of a very small field. He had been coughing and therefore unable to run, but he had nearly recovered and was an acceptor for the Sevenoaks Handicap Chase at Folkestone on October 20. Queen Elizabeth was still in Scotland, so O'Donoghue rang up Sir Martin Gilliat for advice. 'I reported to Sir Martin that Gay Record, now rising thirteen, had no temperature but he still had a slight cough—like an old man's cough—which I did not think signified much. I asked for advice and Sir Martin said, after consultation, "Let's take a chance and run," so we did. The one sad point was that Gene Kelly, who had ridden Gay Record in practically all his races during the previous three seasons,

59 Gay Record (H. Beasley) leading Irish Deal (R. Williams) at the last fence in the Sevenoaks Chase at Folkestone on 20 October 1964 before going on to gain Queen Elizabeth's 100th victory under N.H. rules.

had fractured a vertebra in his back and had a broken collar-bone after a fall on the hard ground at Worcester, and was not able to ride. In his place I booked Bobby Beasley. He had ridden Gay Record at Sandown in the spring when unplaced, but with a Grand National, a Cheltenham Gold Cup and a Champion Hurdle already to his credit, he was clearly a man for a special occasion.'

Gay Record's two opponents that October day at Folkestone were Irish Deal, trained by Bill Rees's brother-in-law Alan Oughton at Ditchling in Sussex, and Woodlands II, whose form was very moderate. 'I said to Beasley,' continued O'Donoghue, "We are trying to get Queen Elizabeth's 100th winner. Do your best. Let him stride along in front." During the race I was so nervous that I stood at the back of the stand all by myself, and I could hardly bear to watch the race. I felt Gay Record was sure to do something wrong. Woodlands was leading at the fourth when he fell, and I think that Gay Record made the rest of the running and I don't think that he made a mistake.' Gay Record won eventually by three lengths from Irish Deal, and that evening O'Donoghue had a telegram from Queen Elizabeth in Scotland: 'So delighted that it was Gay Record who gave me my century of winners, and many congratulations to the trainer.'

The going had much improved by the third week in October and the Queen and Queen Elizabeth both came to Newbury to see Laffy run in the

Capital and Counties Handicap Chase, in which Laffy outjumped his much fancied rival Beau Normand, owned by Mr H. J. Joel. Queen Elizabeth did not go up north the following week to see Silver Dome tackle the Aintree fences for the third time in the Becher Chase, which was run over a slightly shorter distance than the Grand Sefton. Cazalet had followed Queen Elizabeth's suggestion and had sent Silver Dome away from Fairlawne up to Sandringham for a change of scene at the beginning of May, and he had stayed at Sandringham for three months.

60 The winner Laffy (W. Rees) leading Beau Normand (J. King) in the Capital and Counties Chase at Newbury on 24 October 1964.

In the Becher Chase field, there were a couple of fancied Irish runners— the grey Loving Record, owned by Mr J. McDowell whose family had won the 1947 Grand National with Caughoo, and King Pin, trained by J. McClintock and ridden by Pat Taaffe. Loving Record, another Archive gelding, and a very experienced chaser, was favourite. Threepwood and Barleycroft, a half-brother to Prince Barle and Iron Blue, were also in the field. Formerly owned by Colonel B. Hornung and a winner at Ascot as a two-year-old, Barleycroft had later won over hurdles and fences for Mr Guy Lawrence of Rose Park fame and after a lean spell had struck winning form again, whilst Captain N. Ansell was riding his own horse Threepwood on which he had won the Grand Military Gold Cup six months before.

In the race, Threepwood was disputing the lead till he fell at a fence going away from the stands, leaving Silver Dome and Bill Rees in front with Barleycroft now second and Loving Record improving. As they came to the last fence, the race lay between Silver Dome on the rails and Barleycroft, who just led as they jumped the last. Bearing in mind that Aintree's long run-in had twice been Silver Dome's undoing in the past, it looked long odds on Barleycroft, ridden by Phil Harvey. As the two came to the elbow in the long run-in, Barleycroft began to hang to his left, cutting off Rees and Silver Dome. In a trice, Rees switched Silver Dome to the outside and in a finish of tingling excitement, Silver Dome caught and beat Barleycroft in the last two strides. There is little doubt that Rees would have got the race on an objection if he had not caught Barleycroft, but I still remember vividly Rees's trigger-quick reaction in a nasty predicament. It was to me a brilliant piece of race-riding. The sea breezes at Sandringham certainly seemed to have revived Silver Dome. Queen Elizabeth's suggestion had borne fruit.

A week after Queen Elizabeth's first victory at Aintree, Her Majesty went to Folkestone to see Gay Record in action again and to watch fancied Cazalet runners in five of the other six races. Gay Record now had much stiffer opposition in the Canterbury Chase than when recording his owner's 100th success, and most people thought that Trinidad, who was equally experienced and of the same age, would beat him. With Kelly still *hors de combat*, Beasley again rode Gay Record and again he won decisively. Queen Elizabeth had two other runners during the day—Arch Point in the Marden Novices' Hurdle and her long-distance hurdler Super Fox appearing over fences for the first time in the Chilham Novices' Chase. Arch Point, hard ridden by Rees, won his race all out by a length. Super Fox's race came towards the end of the afternoon. Ridden as usual by Mould, Super Fox won to complete a treble for Queen Elizabeth—her second treble coming nearly three years after that Lingfield treble when Double Star, Laffy and The Rip had all won in the Lingfield mud.

'With the first real chill of winter in the air,' reported John Lawrence 'the presence and evident delight of their Royal owner in the victories of Arch Point, Gay Record and Super Fox made Folkestone seem a warm and cheerful place. Super Fox was her seventh winner of the season—a better start that she has ever made before. For a moment after Super Fox pulled up, it seemed that this highly successful first effort over fences was going to end in sadness, for Mould dismounted quickly and the seven-year-old walked back definitely lame. By the time the saddle and bandages were off, things looked a good deal brighter. Afterwards Super Fox trotted away apparently sound and was perhaps only slightly jarred. I certainly hope that this is the case for this stout-hearted bay stays really well and today jumped clean and fast. . . . He has about him the stamp of a future Grand National horse . . .' Queen Elizabeth's grandchildren were thrilled at the news of the treble a fortnight after her 100th winner. 'Will Granny get a gold medal?' asked the four-year-old Prince Andrew.

I have told how the distinguished physiotherapist Sir Charles Strong, on Queen Elizabeth's suggestion, had used his electrical treatment on Devon Loch, Laffy and company through a technique known as R.M.C.—Rhythmic Muscular Contractions—by which an unsound horse is provided with a form of exercise which speeds the injury's healing. The theory behind R.M.C. is that the repair of damaged tissue depends on a good circulation of the blood. At the end of the 1963–64 season, Cazalet had suggested to Sir Charles Strong that he bought the special equipment for Jim Fairgrieve to use on Fairlawne horses with strains and sprains, experience having shown that it is all-important for a horse to be treated within twenty-four hours of having heat in a leg or showing other signs of unsoundness. It so happened that Super Fox was one of the first horses Fairgrieve treated, and during the 1964–65 season, he treated sixteen horses—exactly a third of the horses in training at Fairlawne at the time.

Super Fox had ended the 1963–64 season sound but had injured a tendon in his off-fore when turned out. After three week's electrical treatment from Fairgrieve, he was again sound, and four months later Cazalet had risked him on the hard going at Worcester, when he had weakened rather ominously in the run-in. John Lawrence had feared for his future when he had come in lame after winning on firm going at Folkestone three weeks later on Queen Elizabeth's treble day and unfortunately his fears were well-grounded, for this time he had a badly sprained tendon in his near-fore. The next day, Fairgrieve started daily

61 Arch Point, the first of Queen Elizabeth's three winners at Folkestone on 4 November 1964, the others being Gay Record and Super Fox.

electrical treatment, followed by twenty minutes standing in a running stream below the stables at Fairlawne, followed by exercise, and Super Fox seemed sound again a fortnight or so later.

Having won his first novice chase, Super Fox had other novice chase engagements of which Cazalet wanted him to take advantage. How soon to risk a horse who might well make a top-class chaser, and who was only a seven-year-old? It was the sort of difficult decision trainers have to take, owners normally following the professional advice of their trainers on such matters.

Meanwhile, with Super Fox temporarily out of action, Queen Elizabeth went to the Sandown November meeting with the going still firm and fields much smaller than usual. Both Laffy, Rees up, and The Rip, Mould up, were running for Queen Elizabeth in a new sponsored steeplechase, the Senior Service Trophy, on the second day of the meeting, Laffy carrying a five pounds' penalty for his victory over Beau Normand at Newbury. Fort Leney, owned and bred by Colonel Sir John Thomson and the first foal of his illustrious mare Leney Princess, had crossed from Ireland for the race and, like Laffy, was carrying a penalty, having recently won a race at Punchestown. The third penalised runner was Mrs L. Brotherton's Prudent Barney. The Rip had not run since being hobdayed in the spring and was among the forlorn outsiders in the race, whilst Laffy was third favourite.

Like many steeplechases at Sandown, this was a tremendous race to watch with Fort Leney, Prudent Barney, Laffy, The Rip, the Grand National third Peacetown, and John O'Groats all still in the race as the six came to the Pond fence at the bottom end of the course. At this fence, Fort Leney and Prudent Barney were in trouble and Peacetown led, but he then weakened and John O'Groats, a remote outsider from L. S. Dale's Epsom stable, took the lead, hotly pursued by Laffy and The Rip. In the run-in, The Rip seemed to me to finish the fastest of the three, but the winning post came just too soon. He failed by a neck to catch John O' Groats. A few minutes later, Queen Elizabeth presented the trophy to Dale. She did so with her usual charm and grace, but she must have wished dearly that the race could have been a few yards longer and The Rip had got up. It certainly seemed the wish of the majority of the onlookers.

A fortnight later, Cazalet took half a dozen runners down to Folkestone again for the November meeting, including Queen Elizabeth's five-year-old Mel, bred, like The Rip, by Jack Irwin of The Red Cat and, like The Rip, a son of Manicou and therefore of particular interest to Queen Elizabeth. Mel had been foaled four years after The Rip. Irwin had had The Rip's dam Easy Virtue put down after the vet had pronounced that she was barren again. When she was opened up it was found that the vet had erred and she was, in fact, carrying a colt foal by Manicou, who would thus have been a full-brother to The Rip.

Shortly after this piece of bad luck, Mr W. Sutton, a farmer friend of Upwell near Wisbech, offered Jack Irwin a four-year-old Honeyway mare, Sweeter and Sweeter, in foal to Manicou. Bred at Newmarket by Mr J. P. Phillips of the Dalham Hall Stud, Sweeter and Sweeter was a bit of a cripple and Jack Irwin bought her at the asking price of £30, but the resulting Manicou colt foal got very badly kicked by his mother and had to be put down. Irwin, however, sent Sweeter and Sweeter to Manicou again and the resulting colt foal was called Mel. Queen Elizabeth went to see Irwin's new Manicou colt and bought him as a foal for 350 guineas, and sent him, like The Rip, to Eldred Wilson to make and break.

Irwin asked Bradley, the Wolferton stud groom, if he thought Queen Elizabeth would like to have Sweeter and Sweeter as a brood-mare as he was over-horsed. The reply was in the negative and he sold her to a friend, Mr S. W. Bridge, after Mel had been weaned. The following year, Sweeter and Sweeter's half-brother, Ayala, by the stayer Supertello, trained by Keith Piggott, father of Lester, showed himself a useful chaser and then won the 1963 Grand National. It was bad luck on Queen Elizabeth that she did not buy Ayala's half-sister for a song and also on Jack Irwin that he did not keep the mare longer.

Meanwhile, Mel, a bright chestnut of substance, had taken time to mature, like The Rip. Queen Elizabeth was to report to Cazalet after seeing him at Harpley Dams in the summer of 1963 that Eldred Wilson was hoping there would be room for him at Fairlawne. 'He will need to be taken slowly, I suppose,' wrote Queen Elizabeth, 'for he is a big fellow. He is quiet and has been ridden about but has done nothing. He has one peculiarity which I must warn you about! He is a great roller, and the moment he comes in or goes out in a field, he rolls and rolls! Have you got a nice big box where he can roll without destroying himself? Or a sand pit—they adore sand pits.' Cazalet had room for Mel and he went to Fairlawne in August 1963. He made his first appearance in a novice hurdle in the December of his four-year-old days, four months later, but he was too backward to shine in his first season.

On firm going in November 1964, Mel ran for the first time in a novice chase. Bill Powell, Cazalet's claiming jockey, rode him in a three-horse race at Birmingham and won. Powell rode him again in a similar race at Plumpton a fortnight later and fell at the first fence. Bill Rees rode him for the first time over fences a week later in the Channel Tunnel Novices Chase at the Folkestone November meeting when he was one of half a dozen Cazalet runners. It was a race of decidedly mixed blessings for Fairlawne for, although Mel won again, David Mould had a bad fall on Gay Kindersley's Mythical Prince in the same race, broke his right leg in two places and was out for a season in which his services were much needed. Mel was useful but definitely not of the calibre of The Rip, reported Rees to Cazalet.

Queen Elizabeth came to Lingfield as usual for the two-day meeting held at the end of November this year although normally in the first week of December. With Mould in hospital, Rees had five fancied rides for Cazalet on each of the two days and had mixed luck, riding two winners on each day. On the Friday, he won on Queen Elizabeth's Arch Point—Cazalet's 100th winner for his favourite owner—and also on the Contessa di Sant' Elia's Antiar, who was winning his first race since being nobbled at Wincanton ten months before. On the Saturday, Queen Elizabeth had four fancied runners—Mel and Super Fox in the two divisions of the novices' chase, Laffy in the Eridge Chase, and the newcomer Lochmore, closely related to Lochroe, in the three-year-old hurdle. Mel gave Rees an unpleasant ride in the first division of the novices' chase, pecking badly twice, and was beaten by Mythical Prince. 'Mel hung on my hands,' reported Rees, 'and I would prefer not to ride him again.' Nor he did.

Super Fox was started in the second division of the novices' chase only three weeks after breaking down at Folkestone. In spite of Fairgrieve's hard work in getting Super Fox sound, Cazalet seemed to be taking a grave risk in running him again so soon. Super Fox won his race at Lingfield but the horse was lame again on his near-fore afterwards. Electrical treatment was resumed but each time after work he now went lame. Two months later, Cazalet decided to fire Super Fox, but sadly he did not stand training and never won under rules again.

Queen Elizabeth's Lingfield Saturday banker was Laffy in the Eridge Handicap Chase. He had won the race the year before and, like Double Star, he had shown a definite liking for Lingfield but, as Rees had already reported to Queen Elizabeth, if any course was slippery, Laffy was apt to lose his nerve and barely rise at a fence at all. It happened at Lingfield that day, Laffy slipping and falling at the first open ditch. Lochmore, the fourth string to Queen Elizabeth's bow, was second to Sir Freddy Laker's Blarney Beacon in the Juvenile Hurdle, after being unlucky in running. Lochmore was by the good middle-distance horse Mustang out of Loch May, a half-sister by the Ascot winner Ramtapa, to the Fairlawne favourite Lochroe. He was to strike winning form over hurdles a year later, but then broke down badly.

Mould and Makaldar had established a highly successful partnership during the previous season. With Mould in hospital, Rees rode Makaldar in the Morningside Hurdle for four-year-olds at Windsor a fortnight after Lingfield. On form he looked a racing certainty but he did not win like one. He flattened the second hurdle, hit the last one hard, and took a long time to get the best of the novices Palycidon and Season. 'The big Royal chestnut could hardly have been less impressive . . .' reported John Lawrence. 'He is the sort of horse who would make a race of it with a donkey, but who keeps pulling out a bit more. This is the sort that lasts. I hardly think, however, that he is going to be a champion hurdler either this or any season. Three miles over fences seems to be more his ticket.' Makaldar took a lot of knowing. Mould knew and loved Makaldar, and there seems little doubt that Makaldar missed Mould at Windsor that day.

Laffy had been a grievous disappointment at Lingfield in Queen Elizabeth's Fairlawne weekend but he made amends at Lingfield a week before Christmas. Not only did he give nearly a stone and a beating to Dorimont, who had beaten Sunbridge in the National Hunt Chase at Cheltenham in the previous March, but he came near to beating the then three miles' time record, set up by the great Golden Miller over thirty years before. Boxing Day racing was hit hard by frost and snow, and Laffy was Queen Elizabeth's last winner of 1964.

Cazalet lost three owners of note in the New Year. That great Englishman Sir Winston Churchill died in January. Queen Elizabeth and Sir Winston had had the two best novice hurdlers at Fairlawne in the previous season—Makaldar and Sir Winston's home-bred Sun Hat, a half-brother to Sir Winston's top class horse High Hat, an appropriate winner of the 1961 Winston Churchill Stakes. The grey Colonist II had been a previous winner of the Winston Churchill Stakes for Sir Winston, and it was on the initiative of Queen Elizabeth that the Queen arranged to buy Colonist II to stand as a stallion at Sandringham after Queen Elizabeth had heard that he was proving difficult to manage at Sir Winston's stud near Lingfield. King George VI and Queen Elizabeth had drawn very close to Winston Churchill in the Second World War. Sir Winston made his final journey from the lying-in-state at Westminster Hall on the last Saturday in January. There were Windsor races that day. Cazalet had various runners, but the Royal runners were withdrawn.

Cazalet also lost in January two of his women owners—Mrs A. T. Hodgson with her gruff voice and deep laugh, and the frail Lancastrian, the Contessa di Sant' Elia, owner of Antiar, whom the Contessa said in her will she hoped Queen Elizabeth would race. At the time of her death, Mrs Hodgson had a very promising French-bred horse in Worcran, who had good form on the flat in France but had yet to win a novice hurdle. In the first week in February at Kempton Park, Worcran, running in the name of the late Mrs Hodgson's half-brother, Mr R. Harvey, won a novice hurdle in good style, and later in the day The Rip, now a ten-year-old, fired and hobdayed, showed some of his old ability in winning the Walter Hyde Chase—the race in which he and Mandarin had had such a tremendous duel three years before. 'The Rip has always looked an Aintree horse,' reported John Lawrence, 'and never more than at Kempton today. . . . Though not nowadays a spectacular jumper, The Rip has acquired more cleverness with age and I do not think the Grand National fences will worry him. His fired forelegs have passed several searching tests and after one more warm-up race he should go to Aintree a thoroughly worthy bearer of the nation's hopes.'

A fortnight later at the Newbury February meeting, fate struck Fairlawne a cruel blow. Bill Rees, who had been riding in great form, was leading two fences from home on Queen Elizabeth's Arch Point in Division II of the Aldermaston Novices' Chase, when he had a bad fall, fracturing his skull. Cazalet's choice as a temporary replacement for Rees was Dave Dick, who had first come into prominence when winning the 1941 Lincolnshire Handicap as a lightweight at the age of seventeen, on Gloaming. He had, however, soon grown much too tall and heavy for the flat, and had been one of the leading National Hunt jockeys for nearly twenty years when Cazalet asked him to take the place of Rees on Colonel W. H. Whitbread's Dunkirk at Newbury on the day after Rees's fall on Arch Point. 'I remember well when Cazalet asked me out of the blue if I would ride Dunkirk,' recalled Dick. 'At the time, Dunkirk had the reputation of being a tearaway and a chancy ride. I said I would have a go, whereupon several people kindly told me that I would be "buried alive" by him. The next day Dunkirk took the first fence much too fast but from then on he measured his fences perfectly. I won in a trot, and I reported to Cazalet that in my view he had jumped brilliantly and I thought he would be hard to beat in the National Hunt Two-Mile Champion Chase at Cheltenham. Cazalet was apparently so pleased that he booked me to ride all his horses, when weight allowed, till Rees was fit again.'

Dave Dick went up to Birmingham two days later to ride Queen Elizabeth's hurdlers Rochfort and Ballykine in novice hurdles. Rochfort, bred by Major-General David Dawnay, Sir John Crocker Bulteel's successor as clerk of the course at Ascot, was by the Cheltenham Gold Cup winner Fortina, a very good sire of jumpers, and had good looks to recommend him but he failed on the racecourse and eventually went to Bob McCreery for point-to-pointing. Ballykine, by the French-bred Roi de Navarre II out of a staying mare Flowery Path, who had won on the flat and over hurdles in Ireland, was of Lady Barbara Smith's famous Verdict family from which came the Ascot Gold Cup winner Quashed. On Ballykine at Birmingham, Dave Dick won his first race for Queen Elizabeth, defeating a large field of fellow novices. Ballykine had been on the easy list with a sprained suspensory only three months before and Jim Fairgrieve had got him sound again after four weeks' electrical treatment, so his success at Birmingham was a particular feather in Fairgrieve's cap and an example of his great dedication to the cause of Fairlawne.

Queen Elizabeth had bought Worcran from Mrs Hodgson's executors, and Cazalet hoped that Dick would be free to ride the new purchase on the second day of the Birmingham meeting. Worcran was due to run in Division II of the Elmdon Hurdle, a condition race in which experienced and novice hurdlers could both compete. Dick, however, had been previously engaged in this race by Fulke Walwyn to ride the American-bred Exhibit A, who had been sent over from the United States to race in

England. Exhibit A had made a very promising début at Sandown in mid-February when fourth to the 1964 Champion hurdler Magic Court and ahead of Sun Hat, now running in the name of Sir Winston Churchill's son-in-law, the present Lord Soames. With Dick not available, Cazalet engaged Bobby Beasley to ride Worcran. Exhibit A was a front runner, capable of setting a very strong gallop throughout, and this is what Dick proceeded to do. Worcran, as the winner of only one novice hurdle, was being asked a big question in meeting Exhibit A at level weights. But, though Dick was setting a spanking gallop, Beasley on Worcran was still able to sit on his tail and shadow him with the rest of the field soon more or less out of contention. Two flights from home, Dick was already going as fast as he could on Exhibit A but he could not shake off Worcran. Beasley sent Worcran up to Exhibit A between the last two flights of hurdles and they jumped the last superbly side by side. Worcran was still full of running, and he drew away in the run-in to win by two lengths. It was apparent to all who watched the race that Queen Elizabeth had acquired a game and high-class horse who, on Birmingham running, was certainly entitled to take his place in the Champion Hurdle field.

Two former Champion hurdlers had, in fact, won that day at Birmingham—Sir Thomas Ainsworth's 1962 winner Anzio and the 1964 winner Magic Court. Anzio from the same stable as Exhibit A had won the other division of the Elmdon Hurdle, but had previously been on the shelf for over a year and was thought to be on the downgrade. His time for

62   Arch Point (D. Nicholson) No. 19, the winner, at the first fence in Lingfield's Sevenoaks Chase on 26 February 1965.

the course was very slow compared with that of Worcran. What was much more significant was that Magic Court, in winning the Champion Hurdle Trial as the then reigning Champion hurdler and the winner of four competitive hurdles already that season, returned a time four seconds slower than that of Worcran. Cazalet did not see Worcran win as he was attending a memorial service to Mrs Hodgson, but Beasley, thoroughly impressed, spoke of Worcran's high potential.

At Windsor the following day, Dick rode two more winners for Cazalet and at Lingfield a couple of days later won on another of Cazalet's novice chasers, but he could not do the weight on Queen Elizabeth's two runners on the first day of the February Lingfield meeting, so David Nicholson, son of 'Frenchie' Nicholson, took his place. Nicholson then proceeded to bring off a steeplechasing double for Queen Elizabeth with two of her novice chasers, Arch Point and Mel, on his first two rides over fences in the Royal colours. Nicholson had been just behind when Rees had had his ghastly fall on Arch Point at Newbury, so he knew the form when he got up on Arch Point. He was able to report to Cazalet after the race that Arch Point had never put a foot wrong.

Mel had jumped badly in his two previous races, and Nicholson knew he was not an easy ride. Now in the Old Mill Handicap Chase, he had to take on more experienced chasers including Babel in the colours of Mr J. C. Clay, for long a supporter of Chepstow, and Mrs L. Carver's Voleur, a recent winner in the Midlands. Babel had already won a dozen races and yet was being asked to give only seven pounds to Queen Elizabeth's novice. 'Mel pulled hard and galloped with his head on the floor, and was a bit hairy,' reported Nicholson. 'He took it up at the water and just lasted long enough to hold Babel.' It was a good performance on the part of Nicholson and Mel, and augured well for Mel's future, but unfortunately he broke down the following season and went back to Norfolk for hunting and point-to-pointing.

Having flown back from Jamaica overnight, Queen Elizabeth went down to her much favoured Lingfield on the Saturday to see Laffy perform in the Manifesto Handicap Chase, in which he was meeting Double Star's old adversary Double March and the Grand National horse L'Empereur, trained by O'Donoghue and ridden by his Polish owner, Mr John Ciechanowski who was based in France but was a frequent visitor at the time to England. Ridden by Dick, Laffy was again in jumping mood, and though he jumped to the right at the last three fences, he had enough in hand to win comfortably. His victory put Queen Elizabeth temporarily at the head of the winning owners' list with twenty races already won during the season.

During the afternoon, Dick also rode two young horses for Queen Elizabeth—Irish Rover and Finnea in the two divisions of the novices' hurdle. Finnea was to prove a failure as a racehorse. Irish Rover had racing ability. That same weekend, Gene Kelly had a very bad fall on a spare ride in a novice chase at Chepstow, breaking a bone in his back. His riding days were over. He had missed riding Gay Record in his two races in the autumn and his long and successful racing partnership with Gay Record was at an end. Shortly afterwards Kelly received a small parcel from Clarence House. In it was a pair of gold cuff links from Queen Elizabeth—'A memento to mark Her Majesty's appreciation of your successful association with Gay Record on so many occasions, with Queen Elizabeth's very sincere good wishes for your retirement.'

Queen Elizabeth had four runners at the National Hunt meeting at Cheltenham in the second week in March—Worcran in the Champion Hurdle, Antiar, carrying her colours for the first time, in the Spa Hurdle, Makaldar in the County Handicap Hurdle, and Ballykine in Division I of the Gloucestershire Hurdle. Dick was to ride all except Worcran. Neither Beasley nor Dick were available for Worcran, so Cazalet engaged David Nicholson, who had just landed his noteworthy double for Queen Elizabeth at Lingfield. Nicholson had never sat on Worcran before the day of the race.

The Champion Hurdle, as is often the case, looked open with the 1964 winner Magic Court favourite, Salmon Spray, who had a series of

63   Exhibit A (D. Dick) No. 12, leading Kirriemuir (G. W. Robinson) No. 21, Spartan General (T. Biddlecombe) and Worcran (D. Nicholson) at the final hurdle in the 1965 Champion Hurdle, in which the third, Worcran, was unlucky in running.

victories to his name, second favourite, and Spartan General, who was to become a good National Hunt sire, joint third favourite with Worcran. Nosey, trained by George Todd at Manton, the mare Wilhelmina Henrietta and Exhibit A were all considered likely outsiders. Kirriemuir, who had been close up third in the race a year before, was a 50-1 outsider. There were early casualties when Salmon Spray fell at the second flight, bringing down Nosey. Dave Dick on Exhibit A, as at Birmingham, set a spanking pace, with Nicholson on Worcran tracking them and lying about sixth. 'Basically Worcran was only a novice,' recalled Nicholson, 'but he was jumping super, and I had moved up third on the inside approaching the third last when I got squeezed for light by Exhibit A and as a result got too close and hit it hard, making a bad mistake at the wrong time in the race. If I had jumped it all right, I would have landed second and I think I would have won. I had no intention of trying to go up on the inside, as I would have been put through the wing.

'The mistake cost Worcran his momentum and several lengths and the only thing to do was to make my run on the outside. From the second last, I made up ground steadily, but I was still only fourth at the last where Exhibit A blundered and Willie Robinson on Exhibit A's stable companion, Kirriemuir, got through on the inside. Worcran ran on like Old Harry up the hill and I was gaining steadily on Kirriemuir, Spartan General and Exhibit A, but I could not catch the first two and could only finish third. I have always felt that with luck in running, Worcran would have won. He was a very good horse that day. The only thing was that he was lacking in hurdling experience.'

On the last day of the National Hunt meeting, Dick rode Makaldar and Antiar for Queen Elizabeth. The ground had become firm and it was all against Makaldar in the County Handicap Hurdle and he ran moderately. The firm going did not worry Antiar in the Spa Hurdle, and he came to the last flight with the race apparently won and Nicholson on Lord Sefton's Tobago the only danger. Antiar hit it hard, pecked on landing and Tobago passed him, but Dick rallied Antiar to some tune. Queen Elizabeth's new horse fought back gallantly up the hill and caught Tobago again in the last thirty yeards after all had seemed to be lost. Cheltenham was proverbially Cazalet's unlucky course. He won comparatively few races at the National Hunt meeting. After the narrow defeat of Worcran, it was poetic justice that the luck should be on the side of Antiar in the Spa Hurdle. It was Queen Elizabeth's first success at the National Hunt meeting.

Poor Bill Rees must have watched Antiar's success with mixed feelings, but he was recovering, and on the following day he had his first ride in public since his accident on Queen Elizabeth's novice hurdler Rochfort at Kempton. The following day he had a single ride on the front runner Silver Dome in a two-mile handicap chase, leaving Dave Dick to ride his

64   Antiar (D. Dick) leading Lord Sefton's Tobago (D. Nicholson) at the last hurdle before winning the 1965 Spa Hurdle at Cheltenham.

65   A few minutes later, Sam Manktelow leads Antiar into Cheltenham's unsaddling enclosure.

66 Frenchman's Cove (S. Mellor) leading the winner The Rip (D. Dick) No. 2, Sign Post No. 16, and Scottish Final in the Coventry Chase at Kempton on 13 March 1965.

favourite The Rip in the Coventry Handicap Chase—The Rip's preliminary race before the Grand National. Kempton suited The Rip, but it also suited Mr Stanhope Joel's Frenchman's Cove, a spectacular jumper who already had three victories to his credit that season over Kempton's three miles. In the dual between Mandarin and The Rip in the Walter Hyde Chase of 1962, Mandarin had just managed to give The Rip eight pounds and to beat him by half a length. Now Frenchman's Cove, ridden by Stan Mellor, was required to give seven pounds to The Rip. Like Galloway Braes, Frenchman's Cove was a thrilling horse to watch. Both were great crowd pullers, and I well remember Frenchman's Cove winning the 1962 Whitbread Gold Cup from John Lawrence's Grand National runner-up, Carrickbeg.

In this Coventry Chase field, the only other horse much fancied was Sign Post who had won the Lord Stalbridge Memorial Gold Cup at Wincanton in his previous race. In fact, the race soon become a duel between Frenchman's Cove and Queen Elizabeth's horse. 'The Rip was a lovely horse to ride. My favourite of the horses I rode for the Queen Mother,' recalled Dave Dick. 'Frenchman's Cove was a great jumper, very spectacular, and potentially a better horse than The Rip, but The Rip was the nicer horse, more of a man, and definitely the braver. The Rip gave me one helluva ride in this race. Frenchman's Cove made much of the running, but when I passed him with two fences to go, he had no answer.'

Most people considered The Rip had run a satisfactory Grand National trial.

Rees was feeling fit again. He went to Lingfield the following week and won on Laffy on the first day of the meeting and brought off a Fairlawne hat-trick on the second day. Later in the week, at the Grand Military meeting at Sandown, he brought off a chasing double on the Friday, winning on Queen Elizabeth's Antiar and Dick Wilkins's Wilminton II, and he had four rides at Sandown on the Saturday. The only big disappointment was that Worcran, pulled out again after his fine race in the Champion Hurdle ten days before, failed to reproduce Cheltenham form on very soft ground in the Imperial Cup.

Fairlawne had two runners for the 1965 Grand National—The Rip ridden by Bill Rees and Kapeno by Dave Dick. John Lawrence was to have ridden Kapeno but was in hospital after an operation and Dick, in spite of wasting hard, had to put up seven pounds overweight to ride Kapeno at 11 st 6 lbs. Freddie, owned and trained by Mr R. R. Tweedie on the Scottish borders, was favourite. He had won the Mildmay Memorial Chase at Sandown in January with The Rip and Kapeno close behind him. Although he was high up in the handicap, he had earned his place.

Queen Elizabeth made the long journey north to Aintree for the first time since Devon Loch's National nine years before. Cazalet and Rees were both hopeful. Jack Irwin of The Red Cat had come north, too, to see

67   The Rip about to go into the parade ring at Aintree before the 1965 Grand National in which he finished seventh to Jay Trump. Queen Elizabeth is with Lord Derby and Mrs Cazalet.

68 The entrance to the main yard at Fairlawne. David Mould is on the left with Retz.

The Rip run. The going was good and Rees's tactics were to go down the middle of the course rather towards the outside, so as to have plenty of horses racing on his left to attract him and to prevent his proneness to hang to the right. Unfortunately, The Rip hit the third fence—the first open ditch—very hard, and in Rees's view he did well to stand up. At the water at half way Rondetto, winner of the National Hunt Handicap Chase at Cheltenham, was the leader with Peacetown, the O'Donoghue-trained L'Empereur, Freddie, and the Fairlawne pair Kapeno and The Rip just behind. At Becher's second time round, Kapeno was crossed and brought down when going well and The Rip by now was beginning to weaken and Rees knew that his chance had gone. With three to go, the race lay between Peacetown, who was beginning to weaken, the American-owned Jay Trump and Freddie. Jay Trump led at the last from Freddie, who came again most gallantly, but Jay Trump held on to win by three quarters of a length. There was then a long gap to the third horse Mr Jones, and The Rip finished a weary seventh. Rees was in no doubt that the bad mistake The Rip made at the first open ditch had taken a lot out of him and was the reason he weakened with over a mile to go. It was, in fact, the only bad mistake The Rip made.

When April came, Cazalet's stable was hit by coughing. By the middle of April, he had saddled seventy-seven winners—only two behind the then record total of seventy-nine winners in a National Hunt season, saddled by Ryan Price in 1956–57. Early in May, at a mixed meeting at Newbury, Makaldar came back to form in a handicap hurdle to give Queen Elizabeth her twenty-sixth winner of the season. Cazalet was anxious to beat Price's record, and Queen Elizabeth was persuaded to keep Worcran in training and run him in the £212 Melody Man Hurdle at Taunton in the first week of May, one of the late Mrs Hodgson's horses, Moretons, being also engaged.

It was an evening meeting at Taunton but Braddon took Worcran and Moretons down the previous day. Their instructions on the morning of the meeting were to work in the middle of the course, which they proceeded to do. Luckily they were wide awake for they suddenly came across a rope stretched across the cantering ground. They proceeded to jump it in their stride like a hurdle and all was well. Sir Martin Gilliat and Cazalet came down to see Worcran and Moretons run in the evening and both horses won easily. Cazalet had beaten Price's total of seventy-nine. Someone suggested that it was the occasion for a drink. Cazalet related his father's story about the Royal jockey Joe Childs, who, when asked what he would like to drink on a racecourse, always said champagne. 'Why do you always say champagne?' asked William Cazalet. 'More likely to get a clean glass,' replied Joe Childs. So the drink at Taunton that evening was inevitably champagne.

Cazalet's final winner of the season was Moretons at Fontwell on Whit Monday. His total of winners was eighty-two, of which twenty-seven were in the colours of his principal owner Queen Elizabeth. Her old favourites The Rip, Gay Record, Silver Dome and Laffy had all won for her again. Makaldar, the star of the previous season, had won three races; Antiar and Worcran, her new horses, had both proved their worth; Arch Point, Mel and Ballykine were winning novices. It had certainly been a marvellous season for Queen Elizabeth and the whole racing world rejoiced.

A postscript. Dick Wilkins did not let Queen Elizabeth's 100th winner go by without giving a party of celebration in London. It took the form of a dinner-dance to which were invited the people involved in Queen Elizabeth's racing activities and other personal friends. The star performer was David Mould, who somehow wangled his way out of hospital, where he was nursing his broken leg, was dressed up for the occasion by the nurses and turned up on crutches.

During the evening, Sir Martin Gilliat arranged for all the jockeys who had ridden for Queen Elizabeth to go in turn to talk to Her Majesty. Mould, thoroughly enjoying his temporary release from hospital, requested Queen Elizabeth for a dance as the evening wore on. The crutches were put on one side and David Mould on the dance floor was given a very wide berth indeed! His leg somehow survived and he went back to hospital with morale greatly raised. Someone suggested at the time that the noise of the party would have drowned the roar of the successful Wilkins power boat *Tramontana*. That was an exaggeration, but it was certainly a very happy occasion.

10

The Late 1960s

AFTER a highly successful season, races are always harder to win in the season which follows. The good horses are higher in the handicap. The handicapper probably has their measure, and this happened to Queen Elizabeth in the 1965–66 season when, for the first time, she had twenty horses in training. At the end of the season, she had won a dozen races and only Makaldar had shone—and he only in the first part of the season. The Rip and Gay Record were feeling their years in the autumn of 1965 and both for a change had a blank season. Poor Silver Dome, whose heart had been suspect for a long time, died racing. Mel broke down. Queen Elizabeth offered him to Jack Irwin of The Red Cat, but he was over-horsed, so he went to another sporting Norfolk family. Ballykine started breaking blood vessels and had a blank season; Arch Point took a dislike to jumping and went back to hurdling, without success; Antiar had serious leg trouble and only ran once and worst of all, Worcran, a lovely horse, who looked a Champion hurdler of the future, also had leg trouble after running on the firm ground at Taunton in May, had to be fired and never regained his old form. Queen Elizabeth had to pay a heavy price for winning that Melody Man hurdle.

Queen Elizabeth had two new horses of French breeding to carry her colours—the grey Bel Ambre, another Bobinski find, and Oedipe, whom Her Majesty bought from Prince Rajsinh of Rajpipla, son of the Maharaja of Rajpipla, who had won the 1934 Derby with Windsor Lad. The Maharaja, familiarly known as Mr Pip, was a popular figure on the English Turf in the late 1920s and throughout the 1930s. Oedipe, trained by Cazalet for the Prince, had won half a dozen races for him before Queen Elizabeth bought him. He had likewise been spotted in France by Bobinski. Bel Ambre was by the French Derby winner Amber X, who was of the Teddy male line. He had useful form on the flat in France and Bobinski had seen him run well over hurdles and thought that he would improve, so Cazalet bought him on Queen Elizabeth's behalf.

Queen Elizabeth had her first winners of the new season at Folkestone in mid-October. Cazalet hoped for a second Folkestone treble for his principal owner, with Makaldar in the sponsored Martin Walter Dormobile Hurdle, Laffy in the Sevenoaks Chase and the novice hurdler

Colonius (W. Smith) at Worcester, 7 August 1976: he was Queen Elizabeth's
first runner and first winner of the 1976-77 season.

Queen's College (W. Smith) winning the Raglan Novices' Hurdle (Div. 1) at
Chepstow on 12 April 1977.

Tammuz (W. Smith) going
out at Cheltenham,
December 1978.

The winner Upton Grey
(W. Smith) leading Hollow
Away (R. Atkins) at the last
flight in the Speen Novices'
Hurdle (Div. II) at Newbury,
25 November 1978.

Irish Rover in the Penshurst Hurdle. Makaldar, having his first race of the season, did well to give over two stone to a fit Montecatini in the handicap hurdle. Mould, his broken leg sound again, as usual came the shortest way home. Makaldar after jumping well, led two out but bungled the last, then rallied and just got home by a head. Irish Rover, a five-year-old, thought to be by Vulgan, an outstanding sire of jumpers, out of Random Inn, winner of a bumper, never put a foot wrong in his division of the Penshurst Novices Hurdle but was hard pressed to beat Sir Charles Clore's Yellow Sovereign. Laffy, ridden by Rees, was an odds-on favourite to win the Sevenoaks Handicap Chase under top weight but failed to give twenty-one pounds to Cazalet's second string, Mrs R. Winn's Tar Baby, a well-bred Black Tarquin gelding, who had been given to his owner by her flat race trainer, Jeremy Tree. Tar Baby had shown his liking for Folkestone before, but it would be foolish to say that it was a popular result.

The grey Bel Ambre had shaped well over English hurdles for the first time at Ascot at the end of October. His next appearance was at the Sandown November meeting when he was favourite in a field over twenty strong in Division I of the Waterloo Novices Hurdle. Well ridden by Mould, Bel Ambre just got the better of a tight finish with Lord Rosebery's Tale Pitcher in a very fast time. Later in the afternoon, Mould rode the Fairlawne-trained Three No Trumps for Prince Rajsinh of Rajpipla in the Hinchley Wood long-distance hurdle. Having won a similar race at Kempton in October, Three No Trumps was a hot favourite. Mould brought Three No Trumps through to take the lead two hurdles from home, led at the last, and, without any doubt, had his race won. Mould, however, unfortunately dropped his hands just too soon, was caught in the last stride and beaten a short head by Grimsel, formerly trained by Cazalet but weeded out of the yard. The Prince, a sporting owner, took Three No Trumps's defeat very well. Cazalet on such occasions was a man of few words.

Cazalet had an ardent follower of his stable in a racing regular called Nat who was always touting for tips and liked to bet. Cazalet and his owners called him The Sweetie Man because he always produced sweets to sweeten up people in his search for information. As Three No Trumps was led away from the unsaddling enclosure, The Sweetie Man sidled up to one of the Cazalet owners: 'Oh, wasn't it awful. I saw that poor Prince and his face was pale blue.' The Sweetie Man looked decidedly white himself. At Sandown the next day, Mould rode a brilliant race to win the two-mile handicap chase on the Fairlawne-trained Blue Ensign and completed a riding double later in the day. All was forgiven, except by Nat, The Sweetie Man!

A week later at Cheltenham, Fairlawne brought off a notable hat-trick. Colonel Whitbread's tearaway Dunkirk won the Mackeson Gold Cup under top weight, ridden by Rees; Makaldar won the Mackeson Handicap Hurdle and Three No Trumps and Mould made amends for that narrow defeat at Sandown by winning the long-distance hurdle. Makaldar was receiving ten pounds from the Champion hurdler Kirriemuir in the Mackeson Handicap Hurdle and piquancy was given to the race by the fact that Mould, as usual, was on Makaldar and Rees rode Kirriemuir instead of Walwyn's injured stable jockey, Willie Robinson. There was not much between the two at the last but, with the weights in his favour, Makaldar stayed on the better up the hill. On that running, he was clearly not far off Champion Hurdle form.

Makaldar and Kirriemuir met at Cheltenham again a month later in the Cheltenham Trial Hurdle, this time at level weights with Robinson on Kirriemuir. Salmon Spray, who had fallen early in the Champion Hurdle in March, was also in the field, seeking revenge. Makaldar and Kirriemuir took each other on from the start, whilst Salmon Spray waited on the other two. Coming to the last, Makaldar had got the better of Kirriemuir, but when Salmon Spray came to challenge, Makaldar just failed to hold on, and Salmon Spray won by a neck. It was a fine race to watch.

Ten days later at Kempton Park on Boxing Day, Rees on Dunkirk went out to tackle the mighty Arkle in the King George VI Chase over three miles. Though there were four runners, the race was regarded as a match between Arkle and Dunkirk. At Ascot in October, Dunkirk, ridden by Dave Dick, had beaten Arkle's rival Mill House in a canter over two miles in exceptionally fast time. Dick was then hurt, so Rees rode Dunkirk to win the Mackeson Gold Cup and, with Dick still on the injured list, Rees, unfortunately for him, rode Dunkirk again at Kempton. At the last open ditch on the far side of the course, second time round, Rees felt Dunkirk falter and he died of a haemorrhage of the lungs, falling heavily, breaking his neck and in doing so, breaking Rees's right thigh. Cazalet had lost Mould with a broken leg for most of the previous season. Now he lost Rees likewise for the rest of the season and more.

Oedipe carried Queen Elizabeth's colours for the first time at the end of January in the Royal Windsor Centenary Chase to mark the opening of the present Windsor course. There had been racing previously in Windsor Great Park and at neighbouring Datchet since the days of Henry VIII. Mould had to put up three pounds' overweight on Oedipe, but Queen Elizabeth's new chaser went to the front half a mile out and won comfortably from the 1966 Grand National winner Anglo.

At the National Hunt meeting at Cheltenham, Oedipe appeared in the Kim Muir Memorial Challenge Cup for amateur riders. Although carrying top weight, he started favourite but could not give the weight to Jimmy Scot, ridden by John Lawrence. Makaldar ran disappointingly in the Champion Hurdle, and Sunbridge, John Lawrence up, was brought down at the water, when going well, in making his second attempt to win the National Hunt Chase. It was the centenary year of the National Hunt Committee and Queen Elizabeth, as patron of the Committee, was the guest of honour at a centenary dinner in London to mark the occasion.

The autumn of 1966 was the time for National Hunt Centenary Cups, each course putting on a special centenary race with varying conditions. Cheltenham had a special National Hunt Centenary Day at a one-day meeting at the end of October, to which Queen Elizabeth went. Cazalet saddled four fancied runners—Makaldar and Oedipe for Her Majesty and Gort and Old Pueblo for Dick Wilkins. Cheltenham's National Hunt Centenary Chase was thought to be at the mercy of the Irish-trained Flyingbolt who had won the National Hunt Two-Mile Champion Chase in a canter the previous March, with Gort then many lengths behind. Flyingbolt, however, had had training troubles and was never to reproduce his early brilliance. For a long way it looked as if Gort might win but in the end he was run out of it by Tibidabo from the stable of Fairlawne's former first jockey, Arthur Freeman. If Gort could not win for Fairlawne, then Queen Elizabeth felt that a horse trained by her former jockey was the next best result.

The sponsored T. W. W. Hurdle followed in which Makaldar had to meet at level weights Salmon Spray, winner of the 1966 Champion Hurdle, Sempervivum, the runner-up, Thames Trader, by then a light of other days, and Originator, bred by the Queen but sold as a two-year-old in 1963 to Tommy Robson, the North Country vet, trainer and rider, who had done well with several culls from Newmarket stables, including the Champion hurdler Magic Court. Originator, now trained by John Barclay at Lockerbie, was the only one in the T.W.W. Hurdle with winning form that autumn, though Makaldar had been narrowly beaten ten days before in a handicap hurdle at Newbury. The uphill finish suited the stamina and courage of Makaldar, and he won well from Originator, who was to win the Scottish Champion Hurdle at the end of the season.

Half an hour later, Oedipe appeared, carrying top weight in Pratt's Handicap Chase for amateur riders, ridden by Nick Gaselee, who had been riding out at Fairlawne since he was a boy. Gaselee had come close to winning the Kim Muir Cup on Oedipe at the National Hunt meeting and was now required to take on several horses with recent winning form including French March, trained by Tom Hanbury and ridden by his son Ben, now, like Gaselee, a successful trainer. 'Oedipe was a funny old monkey to ride,' recalled Gaselee. 'He had to be held up to the very last minute, and in this race he made a mistake coming down the hill at the third last. In a way it suited us because, but for that, he would have been in front too soon. French March led me at the second last, and I only struck the front going to the last to win from French March and The Fossa. With the Queen Mother there, it really was a very big thrill.'

Two days later, Gaselee went down to Plumpton to ride National Emblem of the Queen's breeding in the Cuckfield Novices' Chase. National Emblem had originally been in the Queen's name, but when he went in the wind and had to be hobdayed, the Queen decided not to persevere with him and gave him to his trainer O'Donoghue to train for himself. Also in the race was Queen Elizabeth's disappointing Sunbridge, at the age of nine still seeking his first victory. He was to be ridden by O'Donoghue's then head lad Dick Walker, who had come to Priory Stables from Fairlawne. 'I shall never forget the race,' said O'Donoghue. 'National Emblem was running in my name and colours and I said to Nick Gaselee beforehand that I hoped National Emblem would not beat Sunbridge, as I knew Queen Elizabeth would be so upset if this happened. Two fences from home the favourite Navy Lark fell, interfering badly with Sunbridge. National Emblem had a clear run, led at the last, and won by five lengths from Sunbridge. It was the one thing I did not want to happen! It was most awkward.' It was poor Sunbridge's twenty-fifth race for Queen Elizabeth and the last time in his career that he came close to winning a race. At the end of the season, he was taken out of training and went to Lady Abergavenny as one of the Eridge Hunt horses. National Emblem had more victories ahead of him.

In the race following Sunbridge's unlucky defeat, The Rip appeared, shouldering top weight in spite of his years in the Newhaven Handicap Chase. He had already finished second that autumn in the Whitelaw Gold Cup at Folkestone, and now he was just equal to giving away the weight to some moderate opponents. He was to go close to winning two more races later in the season, but this was, in fact, the thirteenth and last victory of Queen Elizabeth's great favourite.

Not long after his success at Plumpton, Cazalet had taken The Rip and two other horses by box from Fairlawne to Knole to work in the park. It was a misty morning, and, before working, Cazalet had to take down the chains which protected the gallop at intervals from other possible users. Three horses went up the gallop together at the start, Cazalet on The Rip in the middle, Mould on one side of him, Richard Dennard, who was to ride his first winner for Fairlawne later in the season, on the other. As they came towards the end of the gallop the three suddenly saw ahead of them, through the mist, a chain across the gallop, which should have been taken down. Mould just had time to alter course to the left, Dennard to the right but Cazalet and The Rip had no time to take avoiding action and both came a horrible purler. Cazalet was in his sixtieth year. His staff had seen him occasionally have a really unpleasant fall but he always made light of it. The Fairlawne team, including their guv'nor, worked hard and kept themselves very fit.

The Rip was rising twelve when he won his last race for Queen Elizabeth, and a mere chicken compared with Gay Record, who also, as it happened, won his last race for Queen Elizabeth at the end of October 1966. Ridden by John Lawrence, he had run well for a long way in a handicap chase for amateur riders at Fontwell at the beginning of October, and he now appeared in a three-mile handicap chase at Wye, ridden by Michael Scudamore, nearing the end of a highly successful career as a steeplechase jockey with sixteen consecutive appearances in the Grand National to his credit. Scudamore, now in his middle thirties, had three times come near to winning a race for Queen Elizabeth in the past: first on a chance ride at Nottingham on M'as-tu-vu twelve years before when he had taken the place of the injured Francis at the last moment and had been narrowly beaten by Bar Point, and then on two somewhat moderate animals, Manicola and Mandella, which O'Donoghue trained without success for a short time for Queen Elizabeth. With a Grand National to his credit on Oxo and a Cheltenham Gold Cup on Linwell, Scudamore had got up at cock-crow at his Herefordshire home and made the long journey down by train to Wye for his one ride of the afternoon on Gay Record.

'I remember well getting out of the train from London, and walking the last 300 yards of the Wye course on my way to the weighing room,' recalled Scudamore. 'I always liked to walk a part of the course, if possible, before racing. The going was definitely on the soft side at Wye that day and I thought that it was probably faster ground on the stands side of the 250 yards run-in from the last fence. I had ridden Gay Record half a dozen times before and I knew that he normally jumped well and was a good ride but, like many old horses, he was beginning to think slowly. Most people thought the race lay between two seven-year-olds, Montevideo II and Wilark Port Light, who were both half the age of Gay Record. More than half a mile from home at the open ditch last time round, I was riding Gay Record hard to keep in touch. As we came to the last, all seemed lost. I was third and the other two looked to be going better, but fortunately for me Wilark Port Light made a bad mistake. Josh Gifford on Montevideo went for the line the shortest way. I switched Gay Record across the course, seeking the better ground under the stand rails. It was my only chance, the gamble came off and I caught Montevideo in the last twenty yards and just beat him.

'I believe it was my 500th winner and, in fact, it was my last over fences, for the following week at Wolverhampton on a bend in a hurdle race I had a ghastly fall which ended my race-riding career. As I was slowly recovering in hospital, I had a very sympathetic letter from Sir Martin Gilliat on Queen Elizabeth's behalf, wishing me a speedy recovery and thanking me again for that exciting victory on Gay Record. It is a ride I shall never forget.'

In contrast to the victories of the gallant but elderly pair, Gay Record and The Rip, Cazalet took Charlot of Queen Elizabeth's own breeding to

Sandown at the beginning of November to run in Division I of the Toll House Hurdle for three-year-olds. By the Queen's top class horse Doutelle, who stood at stud at Sandringham, out of Queen Elizabeth's mare Nicola, Charlot had been reared at Sandringham. Then he had gone to Ireland for a spell when weaned and into training with Sir Cecil Boyd-Rochfort at Freemason Lodge at the end of his yearling days. But he had been big and backward, had setbacks in training and Boyd-Rochfort had been unable to run him. He had thus come to Fairlawne fully used to the life of a racing stable but without the advantage of racing experience in his three-year-old days on the flat, which all colts normally need. Cazalet was surprised and highly delighted that Charlot in his first racecourse appearance was up to winning and, in so doing, became Queen Elizabeth's first home-bred winner. Division II of the same event that day went to the future Champion hurdler Persian War. It would therefore be safe to say that Charlot's division of the Toll House Hurdle took less winning!

In the next race, Ballykine, with whom Cazalet and Fairgrieve had shown patience and skill, made all the running to win the November Novices' Chase. It was his fourth victory of the autumn, after appearing useless the previous season. Unsoundness and a proneness to break blood vessels had been Ballykine's undoing and unfortunately blood-vessel breaking started to recur later in the season. Mould had ridden both Charlot and Ballykine to victory and he proceeded to win the handicap hurdle which followed for an outside stable. He had brought off a hat-trick in the first three races of the day. In the next race, he was to ride Queen Elizabeth's promising six-year-old Irish Rover in the Pirbright Handicap Chase of two miles. Irish Rover was taking on more experienced chasers, but he had won his only previous race that autumn in a canter and was carrying a penalty for doing so. Few steeplechasing jockeys are given much chance to become swollen headed for long. Mould might have felt cock-a-hoop when he went into the parade ring in Queen Elizabeth's colours for the third time on Guy Fawkes Day that cold November afternoon. A quarter of an hour later, he returned to the weighing room very subdued indeed. Irish Rover had disgraced himself by falling at the very first fence in close view of the Sandown Saturday crowd. Fireworks were not required at Fairlawne that evening!

A month later, Queen Elizabeth was feeling very unwell and on medical advice entered Sister Agnes's in London for an investigation. The evening before she went into hospital, she first insisted on going to a reception, as previously arranged, given by the Women's Voluntary Service. Nobody there suspected for a moment that their principal guest was shortly to be facing the prospect of surgery and three days later, to the concern of the whole nation, Her Majesty underwent a major abdominal operation.

69 Irish Rover (D. Mould), winner of the Henry VIII Chase at Sandown on 17 December 1966, watched on television by Queen Elizabeth from her hospital bed.

Queen Elizabeth's spirit could not be kept down in spite of much discomfort. As luck would have it, she had five of her horses running at Sandown on Saturday 17 December a week after her operation, and Independent Television's World of Sport was due to cover part of the meeting, starting with the third race at 1.15 pm, with Eamonn Andrews as host to the programme, and John Rickman and Colonel Tony Cooke the commentators from the course. Someone pointed out that Queen Elizabeth had runners in the first four races of the afternoon and it might give her pleasure and help her to forget discomfort if I.T.V. could in some way put forward their broadcast to cover the second race—the Henry VIII Chase—at 12.45 pm. Sir Martin Gilliat and the rest of Her Majesty's staff at Clarence House thought that this would delight Queen Elizabeth, as her Irish Rover was a fancied runner in the Henry VIII Chase.

It was therefore arranged that the I.T.V. broadcast team at Sandown would come on the air half an hour early for Queen Elizabeth's benefit while the horses for the Henry VIII Chase were still in the parade ring. Irish Rover had run well in his previous race at Newbury but he had fallen at Sandown six weeks before, and horses have an unpleasant habit of remembering such things. Would he let down Queen Elizabeth again as she watched somewhat apprehensively from her hospital bed in London? Irish Rover had four opponents—Mr H. J. Joel's Sir Thopas, a future winner of the Imperial Cup, who had defeated Queen Elizabeth's Ballykine at Ascot in his previous race; Merry Stranger, who had made the long journey south from Ken Oliver's stable near Hawick in Roxburghshire; the West Country horse Wedding Dance, and Blue Note in the colours of Sir Nicholas Nuttall, who had two Grand Military Gold Cups to his credit on his chaser Stalbridge Park.

Irish Rover, a fast horse and a good one until halted by a liver complaint, was inclined to get very low at his fences. It had been his undoing at Sandown on Guy Fawkes Day, but fortunately for the nerves of his owner he had learnt his lesson, and it was Sir Thopas who was soon in trouble. Queen Elizabeth saw Sir Thopas make a bad mistake at Sandown's awkward downhill fence going away from the stands, and he blundered again at the next, getting rid of his jockey. After that, the race was a duel between Irish Rover and Merry Stranger, who led to the Pond fence and then started to weaken. Irish Rover in the end won with something in hand. He was Queen Elizabeth's 150th winner under National Hunt rules. Sir Martin Gilliat wrote appreciatively to thank Independent Television for the trouble they had taken on Queen Elizabeth's behalf.

The finish of the Henry VIII Chase had been uneventful. The two races which followed on the normal World of Sport broadcast must have been almost too exciting for Queen Elizabeth. Cazalet ran two in the long-distance handicap chase—Queen Elizabeth's Oedipe, who started favourite, and the six-year-old Different Class, owned by the film actor Mr Gregory Peck. Mould was on Different Class, Oedipe was ridden by Bill Rees, whose broken thigh had mended sufficiently well for him to be in action again after eleven months on the sidelines. Rees had not yet ridden a winner since his return and everyone was hoping that Oedipe would rise to the occasion, his owner included. Oedipe, as has been said, was a difficult horse to ride, as he had to be held up, and making up ground against the collar from the Pond fence at Sandown is bound to be unpredictable. Most of the field were in the hunt with a mile to go, and Oedipe was close up but under pressure two fences from home. From the last fence, the race lay between the stable companions but the post came too soon for Oedipe, who was beaten by a bare length. Sandown was Cazalet's favourite course and he always had plenty of runners there and quite often two strings to his bow in a race. On this occasion, it was not a policy which commended itself to the racing public in the special circumstances prevailing.

Everyone hoped that Queen Elizabeth's gallant Makaldar would make amends for Oedipe's narrow defeat by winning the Milburn Hurdle which followed. Antiar was also in the field, ridden by Rees, but he had been off the course for over a year with an injured hock and was in need of a race. Though Makaldar had a dozen opponents, the betting suggested that it was a three-horse race between Makaldar, his old rival Sempervivum, and the eight-year-old Beaver II, who had been a top class four-year-old hurdler but had been plagued by leg trouble for over two years. Ken Cundell, at his stable at Compton on the Berkshire Downs, had shown much patience with Beaver II and had got him sound again, and by the conditions of the race he got ten pounds from Makaldar and Sempervivum.

Makaldar needed a very strong gallop to bring his stamina into play. On his old form, Antiar would have been fully equal to the occasion, but he was no longer up to it, and in this race Makaldar had to do some of his own donkey work. Coming to the last hurdle, Makaldar had got the better of Sempervivum but Beaver was finishing very strongly. Makaldar ran on bravely under Mould's strong driving, but he was caught by Beaver in the last stride and beaten by a head. Queen Elizabeth from her hospital bed must have sunk back exhausted after such a dramatic afternoon of televised racing.

Later in the day, Cazalet rang up to report on the afternoon's happenings. Charlot had also run well for Queen Elizabeth in his division of the three-year-old hurdle, and Mrs A. S. Arnold's Sunny Weather, ridden by Mould, had won the Pond Handicap Chase for Fairlawne— Cazalet's 1,000th winner in twenty years since he had started to train again after the Second World War.

Ten days after his desperate duel with Beaver II at Sandown, Makaldar, with his big lop ears, was in action again in the National Hunt Centenary Cup Hurdle at the Boxing Day meeting at Kempton. Worcran, now a light of other days, was started as pacemaker but was always behind. Ill-suited by the sharp Kempton course, Makaldar was in trouble entering the straight and Saucy Kit from Yorkshire and Tudor Legend from Toby Balding's stable at Weyhill in Hampshire drew out with the race between them. Each already had a National Hunt Centenary Cup to his credit and Saucy Kit won his second Centenary Cup that day by a matter of inches. Makaldar, no doubt feeling his hard race at Sandown, was a disappointing fourth.

Queen Elizabeth was not going to be fit enough to come racing to see her horses run for at least a couple of months, so Cazalet enterprisingly suggested that he should send two promising young horses he had just acquired up to Clarence House for Her Majesty to inspect when she came out of hospital—with the possibility of buying one, or the other, or both. The two horses came from France and both were recommended by the diligent Bobinski. One was Retz, whom Bobinski spotted in a humble race for three-year-olds near Paris, and the other was Chaou II, whom Bobinski had seen run well over hurdles after winning a maiden race at St Cloud. Bill Braddon and Richard Dennard came up to London in charge of Retz and Chaou. No sooner had they arrived in the garden of Clarence House for Queen Elizabeth to inspect them when the pipe and drum band of the Scots Guards came marching up the Mall. The din was too much for Chaou II, who was not used to such strange noises in his native France! He caught Dennard off guard and broke loose. Flower beds and lawns were at risk and for a moment pandemonium reigned as the pipe and drum band drew nearer. However, peace was restored and Queen Elizabeth came out into the winter sunshine to inspect Chaou and Retz. She was undecided and asked Cazalet for his view. 'May I suggest, Your Majesty,' said Braddon, 'that there is only one answer. Buy them both,' and Queen Elizabeth decided to do so. Before spring was out, they had both won for her over hurdles. Chaou II was to prove an outstanding success, Retz a disappointment. After his early promise, he failed to train on and only won two more minor races in five more seasons at Fairlawne.

Two months after Chaou II and Retz were bought, at the beginning of March, poor Bill Rees was without a winner for over a year after his crash on the Fairlawne-trained Dunkirk. Cazalet had continued to put up Mould on most of the stables's fancied horses, and Rees had over fifty consecutive losers behind him since his return in November, many of them for outside stables. The tide turned momentarily when Rees went out to ride Oedipe in the Runnymede Handicap Chase at Windsor on March 1. Rees let others do the donkey work and the Grand National winner Anglo was in front for most of the last mile. Then Rees brought Oedipe to challenge and Queen Elizabeth's horse went away on the flat to win well. Rees slept soundly that night and went down to Fontwell the next day to ride Queen Elizabeth's Lochmore in the Petworth Hurdle. The horse had broken down over a year before after winning novice hurdles at Ascot and Lingfield. As a close relative of Lochroe, Lochmore's future had looked bright till leg trouble intervened. He was not going well at Fontwell when he fell awkwardly at the seventh flight, and Rees broke his right thigh in the same place as he had broken it on Dunkirk. Oedipe, in fact, was Rees's fifty-first and last winner for Queen Elizabeth. He no longer rode for Fairlawne when his thigh eventually mended a second time and he was back in the saddle.

The following day, Queen Elizabeth went racing again for the first time since her serious operation to see Makaldar have his preliminary race at Newbury before the Champion Hurdle. The going was soft and testing

and therefore to Makaldar's liking, but he had top weight in the Eastleigh Handicap Hurdle and had to give away nearly a stone or more to all his opponents. Worcran, ridden by Gaselee, was also in the field as a pacemaker, and still retained enough of his old ability to make much of the running to the bottom end of the course. 'Lying third coming into the straight,' reported John Lawrence in *The Daily Telegraph*, 'Mould found himself going so easily three flights from home that he was able to look round for danger. As he did so, Rosador appeared, darting past to take the lead, and for the first and only time in the race Makaldar had to be shaken up. The result was explosive. With a flourish of his long lop ears and a flawless leap at the last, the lean and angular seven-year-old fairly streaked away to win by four lengths. It is a long time since he had an easier victory and with so-called Champion Hurdle candidates trailing far behind, the message is pretty obvious. Cazalet says that Worcran will do duty again as pacemaker in the Champion Hurdle . . . so, granted a real end-to-end gallop, reasonable going and a fair share of luck, Makaldar is surely the one they all have to beat at Cheltenham.'

An hour later Charlot, likewise well-suited by the soft ground, won the March Hare Handicap Hurdle, unchallenged, and Cazalet as trainer and Mould as rider completed a treble when Dick Wilkins's Old Pueblo won his division of the novices' chase. Queen Elizabeth's first day at the races

70 Oedipe (W. Rees) jumping the water in the Runnymede Chase at Windsor which he won from the 1966 Grand National winner Anglo (H. Beasley). This was Rees's fifty-first and final victory for Queen Elizabeth, 1 March 1967.

71 Worcran (Mr N. Gaselee) who acted as pacemaker for Makaldar in the Eastleigh Hurdle, and in the 1967 Champion Hurdle, going to post.

72 Makaldar (D. Mould) clear at the last flight before winning Newbury's Eastleigh Hurdle impressively from Rosador (D. Nicholson) and Specify (J. Haine) on 3 March 1967.

since her operation could barely have gone off better. It gave pleasure to everyone.

The Champion Hurdle was to be run twelve days later. Cazalet and Mould were hoping fervently for soft ground for Makaldar, and the going was soft on the opening day of the National Hunt meeting. Unfortunately there was a strong drying wind that day and the going was much less testing the following afternoon when the Champion Hurdle field of twenty-three went to the post—one of the biggest fields in the history of the race. Makaldar was a clear favourite, Beaver II, Makaldar's conqueror at Sandown, the blinkered Johns-wort, who had beaten Makaldar's old rival Sempervivum at Wincanton, and the Irishman Talgo Abbess were fancied opponents. Saucy Kit, conqueror of Makaldar and Kirriemuir at Kempton, was at 100-6, for he had been on the easy list and a doubtful runner less than a fortnight before the race.

Worcran, Gaselee up, was again Makaldar's pacemaker, but in such a big field the pace was very strong from the start, and it was not till passing the stands that Worcran struck the front and made running as fast as he could going away into the country, with Johns-wort, Kirriemuir and Makaldar just behind. At half way Kirriemuir, Makaldar, Saucy Kit and the Irish pair Talgo Abbess and Interosian were among the leaders. With two to go, Beaver II and Talgo Abbess both looked dangerous with the 1961 St Leger winner Aurelius now improving. Rounding the bend towards the last flight, Saucy Kit and Talgo Abbess were clear, followed by Makaldar, Aurelius and Interosian. Saucy Kit was just ahead of Talgo Abbess at the last with Aurelius and Makaldar almost together three lengths behind. Aurelius and Makaldar in the long run-in both gained on Talgo Abbess but not noticeably on Saucy Kit. Close home, Aurelius started to hang badly to his left, interfering with Makaldar, who in turn squeezed Talgo Abbess.

Saucy Kit finished first four lengths in front of Aurelius, with Makaldar third, one length behind Aurelius, and the fading Talgo Abbess fourth. There was no doubt that Aurelius had failed to keep a straight course, and the stewards quickly disqualified him. But for interference, Makaldar would have finished much closer to Saucy Kit but, on the fast ground and as the race was run, he would not have beaten him. 'I was messed about and had trouble at the top of the hill,' reported Mould later, but the fact remained that Makaldar was always in the leading division and had the strong gallop he needed from the start. If the race had been run a couple of days earlier on soft ground, Mould believed he would have won on his favourite horse. Makaldar had had eight hard races in a row in the previous six months, of which he had won two and had been second four times. He certainly needed a rest, and he got it.

That spring saw the end of the steeplechasing days of three of Queen Elizabeth's favourites. In early March Laffy appeared in the Sussex

73   Saucy Kit (R. Edwards) leading after the last flight in the 1967 Champion Hurdle, from Talgo Abbess (F. Carroll). Makaldar (D. Mould) who finished third is half-hidden by Aurelius (D. Briscoe) No. 13, who was later disqualified for failing to keep a straight course.

Handicap Chase at Lingfield for the third year in succession and for the third year in succession he won it. It was his twelfth appearance on his favourite course and his eighth success on it—better figures even than those of Double Star at Lingfield. Laffy had run only in steeplechases for six successive seasons since coming from France. Bill Rees had ridden him in twenty-five steeplechases himself and it was sad that he was not fit to ride him in his twelfth and final victory. Mould, taking Rees's place, won fully extended from a good chaser in Honey End.

A fortnight later Honey End, due to finish second in Foinavon's Grand National on his next appearance in public, went to Folkestone and just succeeded in beating The Rip from whom he was receiving eight pounds. The Rip was a year older than Laffy and still, through Honey End, slightly his superior. Between them, The Rip and Laffy had carried Queen Elizabeth's colours on eighty-eight occasions, usually with much credit.

Gay Record similarly retired that spring, four months after his ninth and last victory, under Michael Scudamore's opportunism at Wye. After nine season's racing and in his fifteenth year he was clearly losing his zest. Having been discarded by Fairlawne, he had ended up by running in fifty-nine races and been placed in the first three in thirty-two of them. Hill-Dillon, who had found him in Ireland, Eldred Wilson, who had been so patient with him at Harpley Dams, Jack O'Donoghue, who had trained him for so long, and Collis Montgomery who had looked after him with so much devotion were all part of the Gay Record story and so were the jockeys who rode him to victory—Gene Kelly, 'Tumper' Lehane, Bobby Beasley, and Michael Scudamore and the others who came near to doing so. Queen Elizabeth gave Gay Record to Jack O'Donoghue and he remained at Priory Stables until O'Donoghue finally put him down in his twenty-second year. He is buried near Priory Stables with O'Donoghue's other favourites.

The Rip went to Edward Cazalet's barrister friend, Mr Richard Scott, who had come from Capetown to play Rugby football for Cambridge University, but had to forsake Rugby after entering the legal profession. The Rip went to his Buckinghamshire home to be hunted and point-to-pointed, and it was not long before he was out hunting with the Grafton. No doubt remembering his introduction to hounds with Eldred Wilson in Norfolk, The Rip took on the big ditches of the Grafton country with zest, thoroughly enjoying himself. He was not prepared to exert himself point-to-pointing, when the pressure was on. He was getting thick-winded. It must be said, however, that he and his Queen's Counsel were not beaten far in the Bar Point-to-Point. He ended his time sharing life with the Scott children and their ponies—in fact, as important a member of the Scott family as he had been of Fairlawne over eight racing seasons.

Laffy, like Queen Elizabeth's other French-bred chasers who had gone straight into racing stables as yearlings and had never seen hounds when young, did not take easily to hunting, so after a time he went to be used as a hack by Mrs G. Digby-Whitehead, a former supporter of the Bicester

74 Colonel T. G. Wilkinson's Stonehaven (P. Taaffe) and Mr Edward Courage's Certainement (J. Buckingham) well ahead of Makaldar (D. Mould) in Ascot's Black and White Gold Cup on 18 November 1967, which Makaldar still won.

who lived at Wing, near Leighton Buzzard. Queen Elizabeth looked in to see Laffy in his retirement, as she likes to do with her old favourites. Mrs Digby-Whitehead saw that Laffy always had company and she rode him regularly. 'Laffy's intelligence always delighted one,' she said years later. 'He was ready for me the moment he saw me and was always a perfect gentleman. For the first year, I had Cobb, my old groom, to help me and I once even allowed Laffy to be ridden by a twelve-year-old girl, accompanied by Cobb. At the end of three lovely years, I saw the decline start and I knew what was the kindest thing to do.'

Queen Elizabeth, for the second time, ended the 1966–67 season as third in the leading owners' list. If the going had been right for Makaldar in the Champion Hurdle and he had won that race, then Her Majesty would have been the leading owner, but such hypothetical thoughts do not count. Perhaps that day in Sister Agnes's watching Irish Rover, Oedipe, Makaldar and Antiar do battle, and that afternoon at Cheltenham when Makaldar so nearly won the Champion Hurdle were the occasions in the season Queen Elizabeth most clearly remembered.

To the disappointment of David Mould, it was decided soon after Makaldar's narrow defeat as a seven-year-old in the 1967 Champion Hurdle that the horse's attention in the following season would be turned to steeplechasing. Both Queen Elizabeth and Cazalet preferred steeple-chasing to hurdling and the custom at Fairlawne was that, unless a horse was particularly proficient at hurdling, he was put to chasing after one or two seasons. Makaldar had had four seasons' hurdling, so he had had much more than the normal Fairlawne ration. Mould could point out, however, that Hatton's Grace had gained the first of his three victories in the Champion Hurdle at the age of nine, that Free Fare, Our Hope and Solford had won it as nine-year-olds shortly before the Second World War and that Doorknocker, Winning Fair and Salmon Spray had all won it as eight-year-olds in more recent years. Furthermore, Mould did not think that Makaldar would ever make nearly as good a chaser as he had been a hurdler.

Makaldar ran for the first time over fences in a novices' chase at the 1967 Sandown November meeting. He jumped big and slowly and he was never in the hunt. 'He jumped like a desperado,' was Mould's brief, expressive comment. He clearly needed more schooling, and at the end of the following week he was one of three runners from Fairlawne in the Black and White Gold Cup Chase at Ascot—the favourite, Three No Trumps, was ridden by Nick Gaselee who had just won a three-mile chase on him; Makaldar was ridden by Mould, and the future Lord Soames's Sun Hat was ridden by the prevailing champion jockey, Josh Gifford. It was a very high class field of budding chasers with runners from both

The runner-up Special Cargo (W. Smith) leading Prince Eleigh (R. Linley) over the water in the Hopeful Chase at Newbury on 22 November 1979.

Queen Elizabeth presenting to Edward Courage, senior trustee of the Injured Jockeys Fund, the Wilkinson Sword award cheque for over £4200, at Newbury in November 1979. Left to right: Queen Elizabeth, Captain C. B. Toller, clerk of the course at Newbury, Joe Mercer, 1979 champion flat race jockey, Edward Courage and Geoffrey Summers, secretary of the Jockeys' Association of Great Britain.

Queen Elizabeth receiving the magnificent trophy from Mrs George Jackson after
Rhyme Royal had won the G.J. Hurdle at Kempton Park on Boxing Day 1979—
Queen Elizabeth's last winner of the 1970s.

Queen Elizabeth's first steeplechase winner of the 1980s: Isle of Man (W. Smith) wins at Windsor in February 1980.

Scotland and Ireland, Makaldar and Sun Hat being the only two who had not already won a steeplechase.

Each of the three from Fairlawne in turn looked the likely winner. Three No Trumps was going well just behind the leaders when he fell four fences from home. At the next fence, Sun Hat jumped to the front looking all over a winner, only to tire quickly and fall at the second last. A moment earlier, the Irish challenger Stonehaven, ridden by Pat Taaffe, had passed Sun Hat, coming to the last fence six lengths clear with the race at his mercy. Makaldar had jumped over-cautiously early on, but he was now really 'motoring', to use Mould's words, and in the run-in he surged past Stonehaven to win by two and a half lengths. Fifty yards beyond the post Makaldar stumbled and came down, but he and Mould were soon up again. The three Cazalet horses, in fact, were all on the floor at different stages—Makaldar fortunately when it did not matter! Sadly Queen Elizabeth was not at Ascot to see Makaldar win, being in mourning for her sister Lady Granville, who had just died. No doubt Her Majesty was able to see a replay of the race on television later.

Britain was in the grip of foot and mouth disease. Shortly after Ascot, three meetings had to be abandoned because of it, and there was no racing in the British Isles from the end of November until early in January. Cazalet enterprisingly sent a couple of Queen Elizabeth's French-bred hurdlers to run in France but without success. It was the first time Queen Elizabeth's colours had been carried there.

When racing restarted at Sandown after the six weeks' enforced break Cazalet met Nat, The Sweetie Man, looking decidedly pale. 'Well, Nat, we have been thinking of you during the long break and wondering what you have been doing,' said Peter Cazalet.

'I have been very fortunate,' said Nat, The Sweetie Man. 'I went to Huntley and Palmers and got £5 an hour for mending broken biscuits. Wasn't I lucky?'

Cazalet pondered. The Sweetie Man's activities were more varied than he had expected!

When racing restarted, few of Queen Elizabeth's horses shone. Her new horse, Three No Trumps, whom she had bought from Prince Rajsinh of Rajpipla in the autumn, failed in the Mildmay Memorial Chase at Sandown and also at Lingfield, jumping without confidence. He reverted therefore to hurdling, at which he had had much success for his previous owner. Makaldar failed twice over fences in the spring, but Chaou did well, winning two novice chases and nearly succeeding in the Mildmay Chase at Aintree. In a season much upset by foot and mouth disease, most owners had a frustrating time. In comparison with 1966–67, it was a disappointing season for Queen Elizabeth.

11

Escalus

AS THE 1968–69 season dawned, a new star was about to carry Queen Elizabeth's colours. Jim Fairgrieve, Cazalet's devoted right-hand man, had spent nearly all his early working life with horses in the Border country, first with Major A. D. Thomson of Nenthorn, Kelso, a brother of Mr Moffat Thomson of nearby Lambden, who had bred MacMoffat, second in the Grand Nationals of 1939 and 1940 in the colours of Captain L. Scott-Briggs. Fairgrieve had then moved on for ten years to Sir Jock Buchanan-Jardine, Master of the Dumfriesshire, with stables and a stud at Castle Milk near Lockerbie.

Fairgrieve, therefore, had many friends in the Borders, and in his holidays in the late 1950s he was apt to go north trying to spot horses. He had found Cupid's Charge and Kapeno, both big winners for Fairlawne, and now he found two for Queen Elizabeth, both bred in Northumberland by Mrs W. A. Benson of Newbrough Hall, Fourstones, which lies west of Hexham between Hadrian's Wall and the River Tyne. Mrs Benson was the daughter of Major W. P. Standish of Marwell Hall, Hampshire, an outstanding master of the Hambledon hounds in the first twenty years of the present century. Major Standish came of a North Country family, one of whose forbears, Sir Frank Standish, belongs to the small body of six men who have won both the Derby and the Oaks in the same season. Sir Frank won the Derbys of 1795, 1796 and 1799 with Spread Eagle, Didelot, and Archduke respectively, and in Didelot's year he also won the Oaks with Parisot.

Adela Benson was, therefore, entitled to be interested in horse-breeding and she started with a two-year-old filly, called Lucy Glitters, who had been condemned to the kennels but was given to her by a neighbour Mr Clive Straker who, with his elder brother Mr John Straker, was a leading amateur rider in the north after the war. Clive Straker had a mare called Leazes Flash named after a Straker home, The Leazes. The mare never ran but was mated in 1950 with Pheroc, a premium horse standing in Dumfriesshire, and Leazes Flash produced in 1951 Lucy Glitters who had a crooked near-fore and was only kept so as to run with another filly. She could barely walk and barely trot but Adela Benson noticed that when she was cantering she was a reasonable mover. When

she heard that Lucy Glitters was about to be sent to the kennels she asked the Strakers if she might have the mare to breed from. The Strakers thought she was being somewhat foolish but agreed.

Lucy Glitters lost her first foal at birth; her second foal, a filly, was of no account but Adela Benson had sent her that year to Melody Maker, an Orpen horse who was a useful handicapper in the north in the immediate post-war years and the winner of several races for Captain A. M. Keith. Melody Maker later stood at Captain Keith's home near Newbrough. The resulting foal Trumpet was bought by Verly Bewicke, had some ability

75 Escalus (D. Mould) going down to post at Cheltenham, March 1969.

but just failed to win over hurdles. The next foal Phemius, a full brother to Trumpet, was trained by Neville Crump at Middleham to win eleven races and was, in his prime, one of the best three-mile chasers in the north. Mrs Benson kept her last foal Singing Hinny, a full sister to Phemius and Trumpet, to breed from. Lucy Glitter's twisted foreleg had deteriorated and she had to be put down.

Thoroughbreds had not been bred previously at Newbrough, but it was limestone land and Mr Benson encouraged his wife's enterprise. He had bred the odd hunter before the Second World War and his father had bred Clydesdales with success. He had also been keen on racing since the day he had gone to a Newmarket autumn meeting in the early days of the Tote and had invested ten bob in the new-fangled Tote double. He was not well up in current form and in the first leg he had put in a horse owned by a Northumberland neighbour, Lord Allendale, and it had won. He had no idea what to put in the second leg, so he put in the mount of Sir Gordon Richards. That won, and Billy Benson quietly went to collect some £400 in ready money. He had come down to Newmarket by train on a 'race special' which, in those days, carried a fair sprinkling of toughs. He collected his money rather furtively and went back to London on the race special with his inside pockets bulging with notes, expecting to be attacked at any moment.

Billy Benson was a Northumberland Hussar and when he got to London, he made his way to the Cavalry Club, went to see the secretary and found a deputy he did not know. Slowly he produced from inside pockets wads of one pound notes and asked if they could be put in safe custody for the night. The secretary's deputy looked more and more suspiciously at the Northumbrian in his old mackintosh and called the hall porter. They finally decided that they were not dealing with a cat burglar.

Spurred on by her husband, Mrs Benson's ewe lamb Singing Hinny was shown as a three-year-old in the hunter class at the Royal Show, which was held that year at nearby Newcastle. She ended up reserve champion, but a few months later she looked a skeleton and no one could diagnose what was wrong. Three vets separately advised putting her down. One evening her bed was being made up by the Bensons' groom Joe Cleminson, who had fifty years' service behind him to the family, when the fork caught her leg. A vet gave her a shot of penicillin and from that moment she never looked back.

Singing Hinny had her first foal by a premium horse No Comment in 1963. Called Nullus in Verba, he was no more than a point-to-pointer. That year she went to Lord of Verona, a Dante horse, owned and bred by Lord Zetland from a family long in his Aske Stud in Yorkshire, and a winner at Royal Ascot as a three-year-old. Sold by Lord Zetland, Lord of Verona had gone up north and had become a useful hurdler and had then gone to stud, standing at Heckley High House near Alnwick and thus convenient to Newbrough. Singing Hinny was barren to him in 1964 but had a colt foal by him the following year.

Meanwhile, encouraged by Lucy Glitters and her foals, Adela Benson decided to seek a second mare in Ireland in 1960. She flew over, having arranged to meet Mr Dan Corrie of the Irish show jumping team on arrival. As her aeroplane passed over Hexham, her husband, unknown to her, was being carted to Hexham hospital after a fall out hunting. Corrie took Adela Benson to see various mares. The one she liked best and bought was a mare called Smile by Limekiln out of the Roidore mare Doremi, bred by Miss Dorothy Paget and the winner of a bumper for Miss Paget in the war. She was also the dam of the useful chaser Festival Hall and of Sir Guy Cunard's successful hunter chaser Calypso Mio. Adela Benson brought Smile back to Newbrough in foal to the miler My Smokey, who was out of Mr David Hely-Hutchinson's Goodwood Stakes winner Strathmore and, therefore, with plenty of stamina on the dam's side of his pedigree. Jim Fairgrieve took a liking to the My Smokey— Smile filly as a three-year-old and Peter Cazalet bought her for Lord Soames. Named Reefer, she proceeded to win steeplechases at Newbury and Ascot.

Three years after foaling Reefer, Smile foaled a bay colt by the Northumberland Plate winner New Brig, who stood at the Forth Stud in East Lothian. The resulting colt foal of 1964 was called Newbrough. The Lord of Verona—Singing Hinny foal was a year younger. After his success with Phemius, Crump was naturally interested in the Singing Hinny colt and was to have come to see him one day before Hexham races, but got delayed. A few days later Jim Fairgrieve came to see Reefer's half-brother, Newbrough, and the Singing Hinny colt and liked them both and in due course they were bought on Queen Elizabeth's behalf. The Lord of Verona colt was neatly named Escalus by Billy Benson, Escalus being Prince of Verona in *Romeo and Juliet*.

Escalus and Newbrough arrived at Fairlawne unbroken in the spring of 1968. Originally Fairgrieve used to deal with those horses who arrived unbroken. Now Richard Dennard, who was about to become second jockey to David Mould, was doing most of the making and breaking with considerable skill. Dennard had come to Cazalet as a schoolboy for a fortnight's trial in his Easter holidays from his home at Dover. He had already done some showing and show jumping. Jack Cook, who was to win the 1971 Grand National on Specify, was then the older lad in charge of the single lads in their quarters above the Fairlawne stables. Dennard, away from home on his own for the first time, found discipline very strict, but enjoyed his fortnight and joined Fairlawne on leaving school. He now had eight years' experience behind him, and was about to make his mark as a jockey. Shortly before the arrival of Escalus and Newbrough, he rode his first Royal winner on Woodman in a handicap hurdle at Folkestone.

Dennard found Escalus comparatively easy to break, Newbrough not so—but Newbrough had had an accident as a yearling in Northumberland and had been confined to his box longer than was good for him. It had left its mark. In appearance, he was a much bigger horse than Escalus and not with the same quality. A bay with a blaze, standing about 16 hands 1″ and bigger than he looked, Escalus was well made. 'A little topper,' in David Mould's estimation. 'Neat and rather resembling in my view the Champion hurdler Monksfield.'

Peter Cazalet, pleased with the way Escalus worked, decided to put him in at the deep end. He would make his first appearance at Ascot in early October in the Binfield Hurdle for three-year-olds, the probable favourite for which was Mrs L. Brotherton's Red Rum, who had just finished second in a similar race at Cheltenham. Bobby Renton had brought Red Rum down from Yorkshire to run in the race but had to withdraw him at the last moment. In his absence, Ron Smyth's Mustalgo was made favourite; he had been racing hard during the flat racing season. Coltan, the other fancied runner, was already the winner of two hurdles in the north. John Lawrence reporting on the race for *The Daily Telegraph* had his eyes on Escalus. 'The standard of jumping in this hurdle was pretty low. Escalus, a fine handsome three-year-old, had been jumping noticeably better than most and, as he drew away from Coltan at the second last, it looked long odds-on that the Ascot jumping season would open with a royal triumph. But this was Escalus's first appearance on a racecourse and not surprisingly in this heavy ground he landed over the last a tired horse. Mustalgo was still some way behind but, aided by Stan Mellor, he was lifted bodily into the lead a few yards from the post.' Mould had ridden a well-judged waiting race on Escalus and naturally was not hard on him on his first appearance on the racecourse.

The following week in mid-October, Newbrough, ridden by Richard Dennard, still claiming a three pounds' allowance, appeared for the first time on a racecourse at Folkestone in the Marden Novices Hurdle. Dennard always had a high regard for Newbrough and thought he was a horse of great potential and in his first race he stayed on well to beat Cosber, a hot favourite, trained by Ryan Price. An hour later, Mould won the novices' chase on Queen Elizabeth's six-year-old Woodman, who had won three hurdle races for Queen Elizabeth in the previous season. Woodman had been bred in Kent by Grenville Underwood, who won the 1957 Champion Hurdle on the versatile Merry Deal. Woodman's dam, the Fastnet mare Kirghiz, was to breed three years later the useful chasing mare Katie Fare.

Cazalet hoped that Three No Trumps would complete a second Folkestone treble for Queen Elizabeth in the long-distance handicap hurdle, but top weight and soft ground just beat him.

Queen Elizabeth came to Newbury at the end of October to see Escalus

76 Woodman (R. Dennard) winning the Eastbourne Hurdle at Folkestone, April 1968.

reappear in the Hedge Hoppers Hurdle, which he was fully expected to win, but he pulled hard from the start, would not settle, jumped indifferently and was beaten a long way from home. The race was won by his Ascot conqueror Mustalgo who, at the altered weights, was the one horse Escalus should certainly have been expected to beat. Fortunately Chaou II, in the sponsored Sports Medicine Chase, beat Makaldar's old Ascot rival Stonehaven on merit. It was Chaou's second success of the season and Queen Elizabeth's sixth winner. She had made a much better start than in 1967.

At the end of the month, Queen Elizabeth went to Smithfield Market to celebrate its centenary and was presented with a baron of Aberdeen Angus beef. It was not this gift which she remembered but the appearance of a retired octogenarian meat porter, Billy O'Brien, racing enthusiast and accordion player who, when she appeared, struck up on his accordion the old song: 'If you were the only girl in the world'—and all the porters joined in.

At Folkestone on Guy Fawkes Day there were plenty of fireworks—two sustained objections, an enquiry into the running of one of Queen Elizabeth's horses, a double for Queen Elizabeth, and four successive winners for Cazalet as trainer and Mould as rider. Cazalet and Mould started their four-timer by winning the handicap hurdle with Dick

Wilkins's Old Pueblo. Queen Elizabeth's first winner was the penalised Woodman in the Channel Tunnel Novices' Chase. Woodman, an odds-on favourite, and Ryan Price's Brilliant Knight, the second favourite, came to the last fence together. Brilliant Knight blundered, interfering with Woodman, and then went on to finish first. Mould objected to Brilliant Knight for 'crossing and taking my ground' and was awarded the race. The third of the Fairlawne winners was Mr F. C. Penney's Willow Moss in Division I of the November Hurdle for three-year-olds. The fourth—and Queen Elizabeth's second—was Escalus in Division II of the November Hurdle. As Escalus had refused to settle at Newbury, he ran at Folkestone in a citation bit, and he settled well, Mould letting others do the donkey work. Mould then brought Escalus from behind two flights from home to beat the joint favourite Rabble Rouser with ease.

Peter Cazalet, cock-a-hoop at four winners in a row, and standing by the victorious Escalus in the unsaddling enclosure, smiled warmly at the cricketer Ronny Aird, one of the stable owners, as Aird made his way to the weighing room. 'See you at Fairlawne, Ronny, I hope?' said Cazalet, cheerfully. 'Maybe I shall see you before then,' replied Ronny Aird, not so cheerfully. A few minutes later Cazalet was up before the stewards, of which Aird was normally one, to explain the difference in the running of Escalus at Newbury and at Folkestone. The citation bit, enabling Mould to settle Escalus at Folkestone, was quickly accepted by the stewards as the correct explanation. Aird, an admirable secretary of the M.C.C. for a long time, had met Cazalet much sooner than Cazalet expected!

The following day at Newbury, after winning a novice hurdle for Queen Elizabeth on her disappointing four-year-old Stubbs, Mould was top of the jockeys' table, but at the end of the afternoon he had a spare ride in a novice hurdle, broke his collar bone when the horse fell and was off for a fortnight. Mould's injury gave Dennard his chance and he seized it with both hands, winning eight races for Fairlawne in the next ten days. His winners included two for Queen Elizabeth. He landed the odds in a two-mile chase at Newbury on Chaou II, and won a division of the Toll House Hurdle at Sandown on Escalus, who was pulled out again only four days after his victory at Folkestone, and beat much stronger opposition. At Windsor, Dennard was only just beaten in a novice chase on Queen Elizabeth's grey, Bel Ambre.

On Saturday 16 November, Dennard went to Cheltenham to ride Mould's favourite Makaldar in the Mackeson Gold Cup which, as usual, brought out a field of experienced chasers, most of them with recent winning form. Makaldar had had a preliminary race at Sandown the previous week when he had finished second. In the Mackeson Gold Cup, Jupiter Boy, trained by Rimell, the future Grand National winner Specify and Makaldar came to the last fence with the race between them. Makaldar met it wrong, blundered and came almost to a standstill, and was passed by Specify, Moonduster, and Playlord. Jupiter Boy just held on to win, Makaldar being placed fifth. 'I was tucked in behind Eddie Harty on Jupiter Boy,' reported Dennard. 'On the way I had gone up to the other two, I would definitely have won if I had jumped the last well. They were stopping and I was not. Makaldar went straight through the fence, scrambled over it and came almost to a complete stop. I am afraid that Makaldar was never a top class chaser. He was long limbed and he could not put himself right quickly at fences.' So near and yet so far from victory!

Mould was back in action a few days later and Queen Elizabeth came to Ascot hoping that Makaldar would win the Black and White Gold Cup for the second time, but he did not run so well as at Cheltenham, and Her Majesty presented the cup to Mr Edward Courage of Edgcote, owner, breeder and trainer of the winner Spanish Steps, a son of his great race mare Tiberetta, second, third and fourth in three successive Grand Nationals. Queen Elizabeth had a disappointing meeting for Antiar, Charlot and Stubbs over hurdles and Three No Trumps over fences all ran well without winning. It was a misty day and, with the National Hunt course lying beyond the flat race course, the racing seemed rather remote. 'Racing at Ascot in the winter is like being at the seaside when the tide is out,' observed a somewhat short-sighted and petulant punter!

On the eve of Queen Elizabeth's visit to Fairlawne for the Lingfield December meeting, Her Majesty dined at Gray's Inn as guest of the Inns of Court. Not feeling hungry but wanting to avoid hurting the chef's feelings, she quietly put her partridge on the plate of her host, Sir Dingle Foot. Not so quietly, he demolished a brace. Some said he did so from a sense of courtly duty; others that he did not notice the extra helping. Opinion at the Bar—not for the first time—was divided. History does not relate on which side of the fence sat those eminent barristers Mr Edward Cazalet and Mr Richard Scott, then the new owner of The Rip.

At Lingfield Escalus won, the others failed and with frost washing out most of the Boxing Day meetings, the racing of 1968 ended quietly—but on a sad note for Queen Elizabeth when Three No Trumps was brought down by another runner in a steeplechase at Sandown and killed instantly. A couple of months previously, he had won for Queen Elizabeth over fences at Sandown but he had been rather disappointing as a chaser compared with his ability as a hurdler. It was a sad end to a brave horse.

Queen Elizabeth came racing at Windsor in the New Year, hoping to see Charlot and Bel Ambre win the two divisions of the Montem Novices' Chase. Charlot had so far won four hurdle races and was appearing over fences for the first time. At the first fence, Abdication fell plumb in front of him and he escaped disaster by inches. It was disconcerting for a young horse, to put it mildly, and Charlot proceeded to jump the next few fences

77 Charlot (D. Mould), winner of the Montem Novices' Chase at Windsor on 25 January 1969—Queen Elizabeth's first home-bred winner.

with elaborate care and was soon at the tail end of his field. Mould was determined to give him time to recover his shaken confidence and only began making up ground with half a mile to go. In the end Charlot won easily, thanks to Mould's patience and skill, but it was his last victory for Queen Elizabeth. He broke down the following season.

Bel Ambre was disappointing in Division II. He had already run and been placed in four novice chases and seemed to lack fight in a finish. Cazalet was to recommend to Queen Elizabeth a change of scene for Bel Ambre. He had only won one race in three years after doing well in his first season. At the end of the 1968–69 season, he was to go north to join the Army and flower again.

Following the same four-year-old programme as Makaldar, Escalus went up north at the beginning of March to run in the Victor Ludorum Hurdle at Haydock Park. He had won four of his eight races and on form was of similar ability to Mr B. P. Jenks's Coral Diver and the Winter-trained Soloning, who had just beaten him in a desperate finish at Newbury. Sticky going was against Escalus at Haydock and Coral Diver was too good for him. Ten days after getting back to Fairlawne from Haydock Park, he was off again to run in the *Daily Express* Triumph

Hurdle at the National Hunt meeting at Cheltenham, but in heavy going he did not reproduce Haydock form, and ran like a horse over the top and in need of a rest. He had certainly earned it.

Newbrough, the other Benson-bred horse by contrast, had an easy first season. He appeared at Folkestone for the first time over fences at the end of March and, in spite of making a hash of the last fence, he just won. As bad luck would have it, he was started again in another novice chase at Folkestone on April Fool's Day, fell at half way, jumped the racecourse rails, and was never completely sound again. It wrecked his racing career.

As May came in, Queen Elizabeth with twenty-two winners to her credit during the season, went down to Devon to open the modernised stands at Newton Abbot, a course Lord Mildmay had always strongly supported. Her consistent Woodman was to represent her in the Lord Mildmay Cup. Woodman had won two novice chases at the beginning of the season and had been runner-up in the two handicap chases in which he had run subsequently. He seemed to have a good chance in the Lord Mildmay Cup but the going was soft and Woodman for the first time in a race fell. Unfortunately he fell awkwardly, breaking a shoulder, and had to be put down. Poor Queen Elizabeth had lost two good chasers in Three No Trumps and Woodman in the same season. It hurt.

On a happier note before the season finished, Peter and Zara Cazalet's son Victor was appointed to captain the Eton College cricket XI, which his father had narrowly failed to do. Queen Elizabeth went to Lord's to see part of the traditional match between Eton and Harrow, and to support her principal trainer. At the same time, the engagement was announced of David Mould to the show jumping star Marion Coates. The wedding was to take place in Hampshire after the new season had started.

Marion Mould did not have to wait long before she realised what it was like to be married to a steeplechase jockey. Two days after their September wedding, Mould had a spare ride on the novice hurdler San Michele at the Folkestone meeting. San Michele hit the rails after jumping the fifth flight of hurdles, the newly married jockey breaking three toes as a result. Although in great pain, Mould continued in the race and was only just beaten.

It was a dry autumn and Fairlawne had few runners. The exception was the chaser Dark Highway, owned by Cazalet's close friend Ronny Aird. Dark Highway liked the firm going and ran up a sequence of five victories on the ground he liked—to the delight of Nat, The Sweetie Man, highly worried at the unusual lack of Fairlawne autumn runners. Ridden by Dennard, Dark Highway won races at Fontwell and at Plumpton in September and then went up to Worcester at the beginning of October to run in an amateur riders' race. Nick Gaselee, as a serving soldier, could no longer get down to Fairlawne regularly to ride out and his place as

Cazalet's chief amateur rider had just been taken by David Evatt, who lived not far away in Sussex and already had a lot of point-to-point winners to his name. Evatt's father, Major Derek Evatt of the Sussex Yeomanry, had done well in military races in Austria after the war and his mother Dorothy Evatt had been a leading point-to-point rider in Sussex since pre-war days.

Evatt had been over to school Dark Highway and Cazalet had said to him firmly: 'There is one golden rule here which I will enforce. You will never talk outside the yard about any of the horses. If you break that rule, you are out.' Cazalet's instructions before the race were equally firm: 'Hands and heels only, please, in a finish. No flourishing of sticks, it is apt to stop them.' Evatt went up to Worcester in some trepidation. Dark Highway's opponents included Captain A. H. Parker-Bowles's The Fossa, and Popham Down ridden by Peter Cundell. Dark Highway was five lengths up at the last but in the run-in was stopping fast. An hour afterwards he was beginning to cough. The race had come just in time.

At Folkestone the next day, Ronny Aird met a highly excited Nat, The Sweetie Man. 'Well done, Ron,' said Nat. 'I was in a betting shop and told them all he would win. I listened to the race and said, "He'll soon be in front. Ronny will be in front in a minute, and then they'll never catch him." Then I heard Dark Highway take the lead. "What did I tell you," I said, "Ronny's in front, now they'll never catch him. Can I collect my money now," I said. I killed 'em.' Whereupon Ronny Aird found a number of sweets thrust upon him, and retired to the stewards' room to continue his duties—and to the surprise of his fellow stewards to distribute the sweets of Nat, The Sweetie Man. Fortunately, perhaps, the going was still firm and runners were few at Folkestone that day! Queen Elizabeth and the other Fairlawne owners followed the antics of Nat, The Sweetie Man, with much enjoyment.

Three weeks later at Sandown, the going was positively hard when Queen Elizabeth's home-bred chaser Inch Arran, running over fences for the first time, gained a bloodless victory over a solitary opponent in the Mitre Novices' Chase. The going was still firm when Cazalet took Escalus up to Nottingham in the final week of October to run in the Bulwell Hurdle against older experienced in-form opponents in Tudor Legend and Gay Kildare. Escalus was the only four-year-old in the field. Mould, fit again with his broken toes mended, waited with him and came to beat his elders with ease. Escalus had had a satisfactory preliminary race for the Ackermann Skeaping Trophy, a valuable weight-for-age hurdle at Sandown ten days later. The ground was still firm, but not hard enough to deter a field of ten for the big prize. The favourite was Mugatpura who had won the valuable 'Fighting Fifth' hurdle at Newcastle as well as four other hurdles already that autumn, and clearly liked the firm going. Clever Scot, a stable companion of the Champion Hurdle winner Persian War, trained by Colin Davies near Chepstow, Major E. M. W. Cliff-McCulloch's Celtic Gold from the north, Rabble Rouser, an old adversary of Escalus, Tikitas, a novice bred and trained by Edward Courage and the Winter-trained State Visitor were other opponents.

Although Escalus had sweated up in the parade ring before his victory at Nottingham, he had settled well in the race, and he did so again at Sandown. Clever Scot, a front runner, was soon clear, with Mould and Escalus tucked in on the rails in fourth place. In the back straight below the railway, Mould moved Escalus up into second place. Four flights from home Clever Scot made a mistake, and Escalus, jumping quickly and economically, had his race won at the second last flight. He won in the end unextended from Clever Scot, Celtic Gold and Mugatpura. Before receiving the trophy, Queen Elizabeth went over to Fairgrieve to thank Cazalet's head lad for discovering Escalus for her in Northumberland and later wrote an appreciative letter to his breeder, Adela Benson, about her horse. Escalus to most eyes had won like a top class hurdler. Queen Elizabeth was getting near her second century of winners.

Her Majesty went to Cheltenham a week later to see the gallant Makaldar make his second attempt to win the Mackeson Gold Cup. The going was now good, and it was a high class field. Makaldar had not been disgraced in a preliminary race at Worcester the previous week. Ridden by Mould, he looked a possible winner two fences from the finish of the Mackeson, but weakened going to the last fence and finished third to the future Grand National winner Gay Trip and Titus Oates, who was to win the King George VI Chase at Kempton the following month. It was no disgrace to be beaten by such high class chasers.

When Sir Cecil Boyd-Rochfort retired as a trainer at the end of a reign of forty-five years at Freemason Lodge, the Queen made over to her mother two of her horses in training—the staying Zaloba and Castle Yard, winner of the 1968 Zetland Gold Cup. Now rather more than a year later, they were attempting to win their novice hurdles. At Fontwell in the last week in November both had their third runs over hurdles. Castle Yard, ridden by Mould, won Division I of the Middleton Optional Selling Novices Hurdle with ease as a horse of his class on the flat was entitled to do. It was Queen Elizabeth's 199th winner under National Hunt rules. Zaloba for a long way in Division II looked as if he was going to be the 200th. Dennard kept him covered up in the middle of his field, going easily and well. Round the final bend Zaloba went to the front but, once there, his enthusiasm evaporated. He made a mistake at the second last flight and was beaten into third place.

The week had started badly for David Mould when he was had up before the Folkestone stewards for an incident when riding Queen Elizabeth's novice hurdler Master Daniel in the Hawkhurst Hurdle. As a result of the enquiry, the Folkestone stewards reported Mould to the stewards of the Jockey Club and the official notice in *The Racing Calendar*, announcing the findings of the Jockey Club enquiry read: 'After hearing the evidence and viewing the camera patrol film, the stewards were satisfied that Mould struck Mr Peter Upson with his whip after the penultimate flight of hurdles in the Hawkhurst Hurdle at Folkestone on November 24, and suspended Mould from December 3 to December 31.' Upson was riding the five-year-old Preston Gubbalds, who eventually finished fifth. It was sad that Mould suddenly lost his head, and it was not in keeping with his character, for when jockeys were down on their luck through injury Mould was always one to help keep up their spirits and to go to see them in hospital.

Mould with three broken toes two days after marriage and with a four weeks' suspension three months after marriage, suffered dearly for his momentary lapse. In addition to Castle Yard, Zaloba and Master Daniel, Queen Elizabeth had two or three other promising novice hurdlers that autumn, including Black Magic and Steel Drum. On the first day of Mould's suspension, Cazalet and Dennard went to Worcester for Dennard to ride Queen Elizabeth's novices Master Daniel and Steel Drum and Sir Martin Gilliat's Charles Le Bel in different divisions of the Hindlip Novices Hurdle. Master Daniel, after the promise shown at Folkestone, was a hot favourite in Division I. Dennard was leaving nothing to chance, took up the running approaching the second last and was luckily well clear coming to the last. Master Daniel proceeded to hit it hard, but Dennard sat admirably tight and all was well. The only sadness was that Queen Elizabeth had a London engagement at the British Theatre Centre and could not be present to see Master Daniel gain her 200th victory under National Hunt rules.

Master Daniel had been bred by Mr and Mrs E. Davies of the Stone House Farm Stud near Leominster in Herefordshire, had changed hands and had been offered for sale as a three-year-old by Dr Geoffrey John, then farming at Babcary in Somerset. He was bought as a store by Mr Ian Pattullo, a neighbour of Cazalet and owner and breeder of Mulbarton, on whom Gaselee had won the Foxhunters' Chase at Cheltenham in 1967. Alex King, who had left Fairlawne to go as stud manager to Ian Pattullo, later told Fairgrieve of Master Daniel's promise. Fairgrieve had been to see Master Daniel run close up third in a novice hurdle in the spring of 1969 before Cazalet bought him on Queen Elizabeth's behalf.

Master Daniel had won the first race of the day when winning at Worcester. Sir Martin Gilliat's Charles Le Bel appeared in Division II of the same event an hour and a half later and looked a possible winner two flights from home, but he then weakened. Mould was to win on Charles Le Bel at Sandown a month later. Divison III went to Captain E. J. Edwards-Heathcote's novice Bula, who was to go through the season unbeaten. In Division IV was Queen Elizabeth's Steel Drum, who was

78   Master Daniel (R.
Dennard) winning the
Hindlip Hurdle at
Worcester on 3 December
1969—Queen Elizabeth's
200th victory under N.H.
rules.

out of a mare with the masculine name of Tommie, who happened to be a
half-sister to Mrs Hodgson's useful chaser Double Choice. Cazalet was
hopeful that Steel Drum would have similar ability. He was lying second
in his race at Worcester and going well when he came a purler three flights
from home. It was not till the end of March in a humble race at Plumpton
that Steel Drum managed to win a novice hurdle at the seventh attempt.
He was no world beater.

   A few days after Master Daniel's victory, the following poem appeared
in the *Sporting Life* under the name of its book reviewer John Bliss, then
concealing the name of Sir David Llewellyn, brother of Sir Rhys

Llewellyn and Colonel Sir Harry Llewellyn, all three of them keen supporters of racing.

To the Queen Mother on her 200th winner

> Ma'm, if you'd never won a race
> The Turf would still be blessed in you
> Who, with the worst of luck to face,
> Still come serenely smiling through.
> And that is why in happier hours
> When you stand in the winner's place,
> We count your wins, like you, as ours.

Peter Cazalet later recited the poem at a party given to celebrate Queen Elizabeth's two hundred winners, and Sir Martin Gilliat wrote on Queen Elizabeth's behalf to John Bliss to thank him for the poem and to say how very touched Queen Elizabeth was by it.

Ten days after Master Daniel's victory at Worcester, Escalus returned to the fray at Sandown. He had earned golden opinions when winning the Ackermann Skeaping Trophy at Sandown in November and he was now to take on the Champion hurdler Persian War in the Gold Bond Hurdle at weight-for-age. Ken Oliver's versatile Even Keel, the recent winner Tanlic trained by Denys Smith, and Le Vermontois, winner of the 1966 Schweppes Gold Trophy, were also in the field. Persian War was having his first race of the season but he already had two Champion Hurdles under his belt. The champion had not run since falling over French hurdles in the Prix La Barka at Auteuil in June. Escalus, taking a strong hold and outjumping his opponents, went to the front down the back straight after Brogan on Even Keel had made the early running. Two flights from home there was little to choose between Escalus, Even Keel and Persian War. Even Keel and Persian War both made a mistake at it, and Escalus came to the final flight in front, took it in his stride and went away to win by five lengths from Persian War.

Only a week later at Ascot, on a foggy afternoon, Escalus was in action again to win the Copper Horse Hurdle for four-year-olds from three opponents, and at Kempton on Boxing Day he appeared in the Christmas Hurdle, having his third race in less than a fortnight. In this he had to meet his old rival Coral Diver, who had proved his match in the previous season. Escalus, pulling hard, nearly slipped his field on the sharp Kempton course but Coral Diver came from behind to wear him down in the run-in and to beat him narrowly. The going was not so fast as in those Sandown victories earlier.

David Mould returned to the fray at the beginning of January 1970 and immediately made his presence felt at the Sandown January meeting by winning on Charles Le Bel on the first day and on Makaldar on the second.

79 Escalus (R. Dennard) out clear, winning the Gold Bond Hurdle at Sandown on 13 December 1970. The Champion hurdler Persian War was second.

80 A few minutes later Queen Elizabeth receiving the trophy from Mrs Mark Maunsell on behalf of Benson and Hedges, the sponsors.

Makaldar ran some of his best races at Sandown. The uphill finish seemed to suit his stamina and dogged determination. Two novice chasers Doughty Cottage and Fair Nicola were more fancied than him in the Londesborough Chase. Makaldar was now running in a hood and beginning to feel he had done enough. It was, in fact, his forty-eighth race in Queen Elizabeth's colours—and few had been easy ones.

Mould spent most of the Londesborough Chase chasing Doughty Cottage and trying to keep in close touch. In the end at the last fence there was little to choose between Makaldar and Spartae, the two old gentlemen of the party. Fortunately for the supporters of Makaldar, Spartae made a mistake, and Mould conjured the old strong run from Makaldar to take the lead near the finish. It was Makaldar's fifteenth and last victory for Queen Elizabeth—thirteen of them over hurdles and only two over fences, though there were two near misses in the Mackeson Gold Cup.

Richard Head, now training with success at Lambourn, was at Fairlawne for a short period doing his two and, like David Mould, loved Makaldar. Head summed him up thus: 'He was everything that a racehorse should be, a marvellous sleepy temperament like an old pet, the courage of a lion and the constitution of an ox.' What more can be said?

Would Escalus go one better than Makaldar in the Champion Hurdle? Escalus's two best performances so far had been on fast going at Sandown. He appeared at Sandown again at the beginning of February in the Oteley Hurdle, ridden by Dennard in place of the injured Mould. The conditions of the race greatly favoured Ryan Price's Major Rose, winner of the 1968 Cesarewitch and two years before narrowly beaten by Persian War in the Schweppes Gold Cup. Escalus was meeting Major Rose on seventeen pounds' worse terms than weight-for-age and the going was soft. On such terms, if Major Rose had kept his form, he looked reasonably certain to win and, in fact, he did. Escalus, however, finished only fourth behind not only Major Rose but the twelve-year-old Sempervivum and the novice Dutch Bells. On soft going, it was not form good enough to win a Champion Hurdle. At Ascot in heavy going less than a fortnight later, Escalus was beaten by Viroy, another of Price's hurdlers in the Big Ben Handicap Hurdle. Cazalet now gave Escalus a month off racing and produced him at Wye at the beginning of March to win a race against minor opposition so as to restore his morale.

Just as Makaldar needed soft ground to give him his best chance in the Champion Hurdle and failed to get it, so Escalus needed the fast conditions on which he had twice shone at Sandown. Unfortunately on Champion Hurdle day the going was yielding and all in favour of the stayers Persian War and Major Rose, and against Escalus who was amongst the 25-1 outsiders in the field of fourteen. Celtic Gold, whom he had beaten easily at Sandown in the autumn, his old rival Coral Diver and Normandy, winner of the Sweeps Hurdle at Fairyhouse, were all much

more fancied than Queen Elizabeth's horse. Mould felt that Escalus's only chance was to hold him up as he had done successfully in the Ackermann Skeaping Trophy. After jumping the second last flight in the Champion Hurdle, the race lay between Persian War, Major Rose, Escalus, Coral Diver, and Ken Oliver's 1969 Champion Hurdle runner-up Drumikill who was the first to weaken. Persian War led at the last from Major Rose and Escalus and that is the way they finished, Escalus being beaten three lengths by the winner, but turning the tables on his old rival Coral Diver who was fourth. Mould reported later: 'I had every chance. He was not quite good enough on the yielding going.' Nevertheless he had finished first of the five-year-olds in the race. It was reasonable to hope that he would do better still in the years ahead.

Queen Elizabeth's supporting cast also won races in the second half of the season. Master Daniel, having broken his duck at Worcester, won two long-distance hurdles at Kempton; Zaloba also improved in the New Year, winning novice hurdles at Fontwell and Plumpton and at the Plumpton Easter meeting Stubbs and Steel Drum both won. In Scotland, the talented but chicken-hearted Tangle gelding, Hibiscus, a failure at Fairlawne who had been sent to J. McMurchie in Dumfriesshire to be hacked about and hunted to try to encourage his enthusiasm eventually consented to win a novice chase at Ayr, ridden by Brian Fletcher, a great jockey at Aintree.

The grey Chaou II, who had been disappointing early on, found his

81   Escalus (D. Mould) being led in after running third to Persian War and Major Rose in the 1970 Champion Hurdle at Cheltenham.

form in the spring. 'Chaou II may not be the most predictable horse in training,' reported John Lawrence in *The Daily Telegraph*, 'but those who cast aspersions on his courage must always be prepared to eat their words at short notice. At Worcester today, he won his thirteenth race, battling home from the last fence to catch and beat Rainbow Valley by a head. It almost looked as if he had heard about the theft of his owner's binoculars at Folkestone, where he had won previously, and was loyally bent on making it up to her with a Royal Worcester dinner service, which went to the winner of today's race. David Mould had a big hand in the matter, riding one of his most powerful finishes. Mould also lost treasures when his home was raided on the night of the Jockeys' Show Jumping Championship, including the silver cigarette box given by Queen Elizabeth as a wedding present to him and his wife Marion.' It must be added that not only did the Folkestone race committee give Queen Elizabeth new binoculars to replace the ones she lost, but a number of Her Majesty's admirers also gave her binoculars as presents. For her part, Queen Elizabeth sent another cigarette box to the Moulds to replace the one the thieves had stolen.

At the Grand Military meeting at Sandown, the grey Bel Ambre came back suddenly into Queen Elizabeth's racing life. As Colonel-in-Chief of the 9th/12th Royal Lancers, she had loaned him in the late summer of 1969 to the regiment, then stationed at Catterick, hoping that Bel Ambre might make good as a hunter and point-to-pointer. Captain P. M. L. Hibbert-Foy, then in charge of the regimental stables but now a Jockey Club stewards' secretary, went down to Fairlawne to see Bel Ambre and to arrange for his move to the north. 'Out hunting, we found him a bit unpredictable,' recalled Hibbert-Foy. 'Some days fairly reasonable, some days not. So, as he was fit, we asked permission to put him into training.'

It so happened that Nigel Wright, a subaltern in the regiment and a son of a real racing enthusiast, Captain Stephen Wright, a 9th Lancer, who had won Cheltenham's 1953 United Hunts' Challenge Cup at the age of forty-five on Tiger Tim III, was riding out regularly with 'Jumbo' Wilkinson at Middleham. Wilkinson had taken on Jack Fawcus's Middleham stable when he had been killed in a car crash in 1967. He had been apprenticed to Fawcus, and—after his military service in the Royal Horse Artillery—had returned to Fawcus to become one of the best jump jockeys in the north. As Jack Fawcus and Stephen Wright had been close friends as prisoners of war together, it was natural that Nigel Wright should wish to ride out for 'Jumbo' Wilkinson, then seeking to establish himself as a trainer.

'Bel Ambre arrived with me towards the end of January,' recalled Wilkinson. 'We were frozen up for most of the next few weeks. I soon found that the horse did not like going out in the string and needed a lot of humouring. Nigel Wright, who rode exceptionally well, came over every possible morning to ride out. He usually hacked him about on his own, and I found that the horse did not like schooling. Queen Elizabeth's wish was that he should run, if possible, in the Grand Military Gold Cup at Sandown in the middle of March. I was not able to give him a preliminary race in the north beforehand owing mainly to the weather, so we took him over a couple of times to work on Redcar sands and sharpen him up, and he went down to run in the Grand Military, unfancied but fresh and well.'

A small syndicate of officers in the 9th/12th—including four racing enthusiasts, Captain Hibbert-Foy, in whose name the horse ran, Nigel Wright, and the Enderby brothers, Major Charles Enderby and Captain Daniel Enderby—banded together to pay Bel Ambre's training bills, which 'Jumbo' Wilkinson, admiring the venture, kept exceptionally low.

In a field of ten, the 1970 Grand Military was thought to rest between Charles Dickens, then a good novice, ridden by Colonel Piers Bengough, Ballyverine, ridden by his owner Captain G. Vere Nicoll, on whom he had

82 Queen Elizabeth presenting the 1970 Grand Military Gold Cup to Colonel P. Bengough after he had won it on his own horse, Charles Dickens. Bel Ambre was fourth in the race.

won the race in 1968, Risky Nap, a hunter chaser from Kelso, and The Fossa, now elderly but the most experienced chaser in the field, ridden by his owner Captain Andrew Parker-Bowles. Nigel Wright had already won over the Sandown course and had ridden in a previous Grand Military. 'We always ran Bel Ambre in open blinkers to get him to concentrate,' recalled Wright, 'and the plan was to have him well up with the leaders from the start, and never to give him the chance to drop himself out, and it happened to work. Bel Ambre proceeded to jump like a buck and made much of the running on the second circuit until he began to tire going to the Pond fence second time round, when Charles Dickens, who won, The Fossa and Ballyverine passed me in turn, and we were fourth.'

Queen Elizabeth was highly pleased that Bel Ambre had run so well, and delighted to hear a week later that Bel Ambre had gone up to Newcastle to win the Whalton Chase from a big field of novices, again ridden by Nigel Wright. I suspect that with this success the regimental syndicate paid their training expenses for the year. Bel Ambre won at a long price and 'Jumbo' Wilkinson remembers the occasion with very great pleasure!

There were two celebration parties in the first half of 1970. In February, Queen Elizabeth acted as hostess at a dinner-dance given by Dick Wilkins to celebrate Her Majesty's 200th winner, at which were present the racing people associated with her successes and a number of friends from other walks of life. After dinner Queen Elizabeth was talking to two of her former jockeys—Dick Francis and Bill Rees—when a well known actor, who shall be nameless, came up to the table and asked Queen Elizabeth if he might have the honour of dancing with her. Queen Elizabeth, who particularly enjoyed racing talk on such occasions, replied that she was in the middle of talking to two of her former jockeys and would prefer to dance later in the evening. Dancing with Queen Elizabeth later in the evening, the actor, seeking perhaps to ingratiate himself, asked Her Majesty where the lovely dress she was wearing came from. 'Didn't you know I made it myself?' said Queen Elizabeth with her usual charm. The actor wondered if it was his duty to try to change the conversation or to remain mute. He was not easily non-plussed!

There was another happy occasion at the beginning of June when the Queen gave a party at Windsor Castle to celebrate the seventieth birthdays of her mother Queen Elizabeth, her uncle the Duke of Gloucester, her Master of the Horse the Duke of Beaufort and her cousin Admiral of the Fleet Lord Mountbatten of Burma. Queen Elizabeth the Queen Mother was the youngest of the four. She was not to celebrate her seventieth birthday till August 4.

Kenneth Rose, a skilled chronicler in the *Sunday Telegraph* for many years, probing into the secret of Queen Elizabeth's popularity on the eve of her seventieth birthday put it like this: 'In her gestures, her smiles, her

83 Bel Ambre (Mr N. Wright), led by his lad Joe Wright, returning to the unsaddling enclosure after winning the Whalton Chase at Newcastle on 21 March 1970. Bel Ambre's trainer, 'Jumbo' Wilkinson and his wife follow.

ability to radiate a sense of intimately-shared enjoyment, Queen Elizabeth is enchantment itself. She takes an intense and genuine interest in the lives and problems of others so that all who meet her feel in retrospect that never before have they sparkled to such advantage. . . . By the calm inspiration of her love, she has sustained one Monarch through the stress of war and beyond: by laying before another a matchless example of dedication to duty, she has proved herself a Queen Mother in every sense.' It was a very moving tribute, and all who had met Queen Elizabeth at Fairlawne and at Priory Stables at Reigate felt that it was fair comment.

Last Years at Fairlawne

THE NEW season of 1970–71 was to be a season of contrasts. The five-year-old Escalus, who looked a champion hurdler of the future, was to fall ill and die during an operation—a dreadful disappointment and sadness to all concerned. On the other hand, promising horses of Queen Elizabeth's own breeding were beginning to come into training and were going to play an increasing role in the 1970s, whilst in Black Magic from Ireland and Game Spirit from England Queen Elizabeth had two exceptionally promising young horses.

Queen Elizabeth first started to take an interest in breeding her own jumping stock in the late 1950s when she bought the 1952 King Hal mare Queen of the Isle as a five-year-old at the same time as her full brother King of the Isle, who was one year her senior. A lightly-framed bay mare with a good action, Queen of the Isle was very excitable in training at Fairlawne and failed to win under National Hunt rules, but made her mark in no small way as a brood-mare. About the same time as Queen Elizabeth bought Queen of the Isle, she bought another King Hal mare Queen of the Sea and two mares from Mr Sidney McGregor—Nicola, a Nicolaus mare, and Honeypot Lane, a Lancewood mare. McGregor at his Lillington stud in Warwickshire had bred the 1932 Derby winner April the Fifth with his friend Mr G. S. L. Whitelaw, both McGregor and 'Grimey' Whitelaw being supporters also of National Hunt racing. Eldred Wilson, a friend of Sidney McGregor, from whom he had bought his hunter chaser Essandem, believed in the McGregor lines of blood and had also bought from him the mare Nolana, who came of the same female line as Nicola.

Queen Elizabeth was naturally also keen to have a Manicou mare, bearing in mind the affection she had both for Manicou and for Manicou's son The Rip, so in 1958 she bought as a yearling the Manicou filly Mandella from her breeder Mr C. W. Godden of the Gables Stud Farm at Rotherfield in Sussex where Manicou stood. After spending three years at Mooresfort in County Tipperary, the home of the Queen's former Manager of the Royal Studs, Captain Charles Moore, Mandella had gone for a short time to Fairlawne and then for further handling to Roy Trigg in Sussex. She was a powerfully built mare but was very excitable and she

went as a six-year-old to O'Donoghue, who just failed to win a novice hurdle with her at Sandown as a seven-year-old. She had the speed and looks to suggest that she might make a useful brood-mare.

The three of her own breeding Queen Elizabeth had in training at the beginning of the 1970–71 season were the six-year-old Inch Arran, a grey gelding by the Sandringham-based Colonist II out of Queen of the Isle, the six-year-old Colonsay Isle, a gelding by Colonist II out of Queen of the Sea, and the four-year-old Mascara, a brown filly by the Queen's Doncaster Cup winner Atlas out of Nicola, dam of Charlot. Mascara was in training with John Oxx in Ireland for flat racing and won a race over a distance of ground in the autumn of her four-year-old days, and also ran well in the Irish Cesarewitch.

Brigadier A. D. R. Wingfield, who had succeeded Captain Moore as Manager of the Royal Studs, started handling some of Queen Elizabeth's young jumping stock at the beginning of the 1960s at his home at Brownstown Park near Navan in County Meath. Nicola's first foal

84 Inch Arran (R. Dennard), owned and bred by Queen Elizabeth.

Manicola, a Manicou colt, arrived at Brownstown Park as a weaned foal in 1960 and was broken as a three-year-old but he made a noise, was hobdayed and then went into training with O'Donoghue. After a second operation on his wind at Newmarket, he ran a few times but to no avail, and Queen Elizabeth gave him to Brigadier Wingfield as a hunter. Nicola's second living foal was the brown Doutelle colt Charlot.

At the same time as he had Manicola, Wingfield also had at Brownstown Park Queen of the Sea's second foal, Carragheen, a chestnut filly by the stayer Bitter Sweet. Cazalet normally did not like training fillies. He considered in a big string that they were inclined to upset both colts and geldings, and as a result only had the odd one at a time at Fairlawne. Carragheen therefore went into training with O'Donoghue. She was a small thick-set mare, a good jumper with a nice temperament but she had not the speed to win races, and it was decided to sell her. As it happened Sea Brief, her first foal by the Counsel horse Lucky Brief, who stood in Yorkshire, became in due course one of the best chasers in Ireland, winning the Leopardstown Chase twice for Anne, Duchess of Westminster, and finishing second in the Irish Grand National. There was nothing at the time to suggest that Carragheen might make a good brood-mare and it certainly seemed sensible to weed her out.

Honeypot Lane, after producing three fillies in a row at the start of her life as a brood-mare, was also sold. Queen of the Isle also started with two fillies. She wisely was kept in the stud. Her first foal, Boulay Bay by Lord Allendale's Goodwood Cup winner Tenterhooks, went briefly into training at Fairlawne and was discarded. Her second foal, La Vik, a full sister to Boulay Bay, was sold in Ireland before going into training and won a couple of races as a five-year-old in 1968.

The 1964 progeny of Queen of the Isle and of Queen of the Sea both went in the autumn of 1964 as weaned foals from Sandringham to Brownstown Park—Inch Arran, a dark grey, and Colonsay Isle, a strawberry roan. They were gelded as yearlings the following spring and in the autumn of 1965 they left Brownstown Park to make way for another batch of weaned foals from Sandringham belonging to the Queen and Queen Elizabeth. Inch Arran and Colonsay Isle were moved to Eileen, Countess of Mount Charles's stud at Ashfield nearby. 'I led Inch Arran and one of my men led the "pink horse", Colonsay Isle, to Ashfield,' recalled Brigadier Wingfield, 'and I remember Inch Arran carted me all over the place on our one and a half mile walk. Inch Arran was very big and strong from the start, but at that time Lady Mount Charles and I both liked the "pink horse" the better.'

Colonsay Isle and Inch Arran both left Ashfield as three-year-olds to return to England and both went in due course to Bob McCreery's Moreton Paddocks Stud at Moreton Morrell in Warwickshire to be broken. Colonsay Isle arrived in May 1967, Inch Arran a year later. At the

time of Colonsay Isle's arrival, Queen Elizabeth also had with McCreery another promising young horse, Black Magic, who had arrived as a two-year-old from Ireland. Colonsay Isle was ready to go to Fairlawne three months later; Black Magic stayed much longer.

Black Magic was by Mr William Woodward's 1948 St Leger winner Black Tarquin out of the Flamenco mare Ballyrory, a winner herself of a steeplechase and of point-to-points in Ireland and hunted by her breeder Mrs Marshall Parkhill for a couple of seasons from their then home at Butlerstown in County Waterford. Mrs Parkhill, as Master of the Wicklow hounds, had hunted hounds from Ballyrory's dam Fuse, unbeaten in point-to-points and dam of the Grand Sefton winner Polished Steel.

On breeding, therefore, Black Magic was entitled to jump. Marshall Parkhill sold him as a two-year-old to Jack White of Clonsilla through whom Peter Cazalet had bought likely jumpers before, and from there, the horse went straight to McCreery. Black Magic, a hard bright bay, arrived at Moreton Morrell early in 1966 and stayed two and a half years. Long before he left to go to Fairlawne, Bob McCreery had fallen in love with him. 'I reckoned Black Magic was a most marvellous young horse,'

85 The spectacular chaser Black Magic (R. Dennard) going down to post at Ascot.

recalled McCreery, 'the sort of fine-looking chaser Lord Bicester liked to have after the war, 17 hands, magnificent limbs, light on his feet, marvellously balanced and a terrific jumper. I used to hack him round the farm and he never needed a lead and would absolutely fly anything he was asked to jump. He was also very high metalled, very much on his toes, interested in everything and intelligent.

'I remember in September 1968, I took Black Magic as a four-year-old up to Leicestershire to have some cubbing with the Quorn to give him experience. We had a yard in the Quorn country at Grimston and I took him to a well-known meet at Welby Osiers. I can only remember two things about that day. I lowered the ramp of our horse box at the meet and a cloud of steam came out. Black Magic had hardly ever been in a horse box before. Soon afterwards, before we moved off, he backed smartly and sat on the boot of a car with a terrible grinding noise, and I thought that someone was going to have to pay a fortune in damages! Black Magic then plunged round and sat on the front of the car. I expected the people inside to burst out fuming, as they were entitled to do, but Jeanette, my wife, was near and luckily she said loud and clear to the terrified people inside the car: "That is the Queen Mother's horse. He is rather a fine horse, isn't he?" and when they heard it was the Queen Mother's horse, they never even complained!

'I remember having a very uncomfortable day on Black Magic. He was too valuable to go out hunting properly. The idea was to get him used to people. I left him for three weeks with a friend, George Rich, living at Gaddesby in the middle of the Quorn country, to continue his education.' George Rich had an equally high opinion of him—'a bottomless horse, with a tremendous gallop in him, big, strong and powerful.'

Soon after Black Magic came back from Leicestershire, Bob McCreery took him to Newbury to show him to Peter Cazalet. Queen Elizabeth, on her way to engagements in the Midlands, had looked in to see Black Magic, Inch Arran and company two or three times, so knew what McCreery thought of them. Colonsay Isle, smaller and neater than Inch Arran and more forward, had his first race as a three-year-old, but did nothing. Inch Arran did not run till he was a four-year-old; the huge Black Magic did not run till near the end of his five-year-old days and then won first time out over hurdles at Kempton. That season, Inch Arran had a couple of novice chases to his name, the 'pink horse' had been second in a novice chase. On bare form, there seemed to be nothing remarkable about any of them.

Meanwhile Game Spirit, two years younger than the other three, had spent all his early days in England. His dam Castile had been bought by Lord Cadogan in Ireland from Mr R. J. Powell of Nenagh in County Tipperary as an unbroken three-year-old in 1959, and was put into training with Bewicke but continued to grow and, in Lord Cadogan's words, was so slow that she could not keep herself warm and was sold in 1962, having been tailed off and pulled up in the only two novice chases in which she ran that season. Her future looked black but she was bought at the Ascot Sales for some 300 guineas by Captain Michael Lumsden, a 12th Lancer, as a potential hunter and point-to-pointer.

Captain Lumsden was son of an outstanding soldier, General Herbert Lumsden, who commanded the 10th Corps at El Alamein, and in his younger days had won the 1926 Grand Military Gold Cup on his own horse Foxtrot. 'I remember very well buying Castile at the Ascot Sales,' recalled Lumsden. 'I could only afford a cheap horse and her form was so bad under rules that Guy Cunard turned her down. My wife and I were living near Hungerford at the time and I bought her to hunt with the Old Berkshire and the Craven. I hoped to ride her in a couple of point-to-points that year. I had a walk-over at an army meeting and I won the member's race at the Craven. The only other runner fell at half way, so I had to complete the second half of the course alone, so the form was difficult to assess! She was a bold mare and quite good out hunting.

'We moved up to Shropshire in 1966 and I then decided to breed from Castile, who was by Cacador out of a Steel Point mare, who was the dam of a couple of winners. I sent Castile to George Maundrell's Blacklands Stud near Calne in Wiltshire where the stayer Romany Air and the Big Game horse Game Rights were both standing. As Game Right's fee was the cheaper of the two, I asked that Castile should be covered by Game Rights but when Castile came back there was a certificate with her to say that she was certified in foal to Romany Air. I wrote and asked what had happened and Maundrell sent me another covering certificate, stating that Game Rights was the sire of my foal. Nevertheless, I always felt certain that my foal was really by Romany Air. Nearly all Romany Airs had a prominent bump on their forehead, which this foal had.

'The foal which was to be known as Game Spirit was terribly small but he grew a lot between one and two. I remember one day our groom came down to say that Castile's offspring had jumped out of his paddock but he was none the worse. Sadly, in retrospect, I decided to sell Castile and her two-year-old Game Spirit and I sent them both down to the Ascot Sales in September, 1968.'

It so happened that Mr Gordon Cook, a permit holder, then farming at Godsfield Manor near Alresford in Hampshire, was at the sale and took a great liking to Game Spirit. Cook's father, Tom Cook, a noted coursing man, had been a patron of 'Sonny' Hall in pre-war days and his grandfather Sir Alan Gordon-Smith trained with Jack Jarvis, owned the Goodwood Cup winner Fearless Fox, and in post-war days had the good chasers Kami and Cloncarrig with Tom Masson. Gordon Cook had been asked to look out for a likely young horse to do well in the show ring by Miss Olga Bhandari who was farming near Angmering in Sussex. He recommended Game Spirit, and Roy Trigg, on Miss Bhandari's behalf, bought the two-year-old for 300 guineas.

Six months later Cook went over to see Game Spirit again at Miss Bhandari's and thought that he had done extremely well. Miss Bhandari had more horses at the time than she wanted and she was quite prepared to part with him. 'I fell in love with Game Spirit when I saw him again,' said Gordon Cook, 'and I bought him in June 1969 on the spot for £450, sending my horse box over to collect him the next day. He was now a big fine upstanding horse of about 16 hands 1″, a good mover and a terrific outlook—"the look of eagles", as the Americans would say. We regarded him as unbroken. He was the quietest horse to break in my whole experience. My half-sister was staying with us at the time and I remember we had just started driving Game Spirit in long reins. I asked her to give a hand, but she said she had not the faintest idea what to do. I told her not to worry, Game Spirit knew what to do!

'Soon after I had bought Game Spirit, I was so pleased with him that I decided to show him at the Alton Show nearby. We took three young horses to the show. We only had one double bridle and we had to swop round. We were late getting there and Game Spirit in the three-year-old class was very late getting into the ring. Mr Harry Dufosee of Stalbridge, Dorset—breeder of Stalbridge Colonist—was judging the hunters-in-hand and consented to see the late arrival. Not only did he put Game Spirit top of the class, but eventually made him champion of the young hunters.'

Dufosee, a fine judge of a horse, and a dedicated supporter of steeplechasing, remarked years later that when Game Spirit came into the ring at Alton that day and the rug and the bandages were removed, he saw what he thought was one of the nicest young horses he had ever seen at the many shows at which he had judged. 'He is,' he added, 'by Game Rights, who stamps his horses so much alike, the real show hunter types, and I have never understood why Game Rights got such a perfect example of a high class three-mile chaser.' I think the answer was, as Captain Lumsden suggested, that Game Spirit was in fact by Romany Air, a much better racehorse than Game Rights and trained by Reg Day at Newmarket to win the 1955 Jockey Club Cup and other races for stayers.

When autumn came, Gordon Cook took Game Spirit out with the H.H. a few times and started to school him over baby hurdles. 'The first time I knew he was a racehorse in the making,' said Cook, 'was when I worked him with Arctic Well, a mare I then trained who had won hunter chases and had run well in the Foxhunters' at Cheltenham. I saddled Arctic Well to win a three-mile amateur riders' chase at Kempton in February 1970, and not long afterwards I took Arctic Well and Game Spirit to work above Stockbridge with horses of another permit holder Richard Read. Arctic Well and Game Spirit jumped off at the bottom and went a sharp gallop. Game Spirit was only getting about ten pounds from the mare but he laid up with her all the way. I then intended to give Game Spirit a run over hurdles in the spring but the ground was hard and I decided not to risk him.

'I saw George Smith, the handicapper, who lived not far away at West Meon, and I told him of Game Spirit's promise. He came over to see him and so did Tom Masson, with whom I used to ride out, and they both liked him a lot. I offered the horse to Fulke Walwyn but he had no owner with cash available at the time, but George Smith mentioned him to Queen Elizabeth and as a result Cazalet came over to see him. Charlie Guest, brother of the jump jockey Joe Guest, used to ride work for me and he came over to ride him when Cazalet came. I trotted him and cantered him and popped him over a couple of flights of baby hurdles and Peter Cazalet was very impressed. We heard a couple of days later that Queen Elizabeth was interested in buying him. He then passed a very thorough examination from the vet, and I delivered him to Fairlawne in April 1970.'

At the start of the new season, therefore, in addition to the five-year-old Escalus, Queen Elizabeth had some very promising young horses in the six-year-olds Black Magic, Colonsay Isle and Inch Arran, the four-year-old Game Spirit, and the three-year-old Playagain, whom Jim Fairgrieve had found in the north. Playagain, like Escalus, was by Lord of Verona and a full brother to Playlord, winner of the 1969 Scottish Grand National, and at the time one of the best chasers in the north.

For the first time for many years, Queen Elizabeth went racing at Perth in September to see Hibiscus run, but, after leading at the last fence in a two-mile handicap chase, he pulled out nothing when tackled. In the south, Cazalet had Inch Arran, Master Daniel and Stubbs ready to do battle early at Folkestone, Plumpton and Wye. Master Daniel, admirably consistent in the previous season, started by winning a handicap hurdle and then a novices' chase at Folkestone in September, and Inch Arran won handicap chases unchallenged first at Plumpton and then at Wye.

It was a dry October and Cazalet had entered Escalus in the valuable 'Fighting Fifth' Hurdle at Newcastle at the end of October, in which the Champion hurdler Persian War, who had had a preliminary race was favourite, and Mugatapura, who had won the event in 1969, was fancied to win the race again on the firm ground in which he revelled. A third fancied runner was Rimell's Inishmaan, narrowly beaten at Cheltenham in March in the *Daily Express* Triumph Hurdle and thoroughly fit, having won an amateur riders' race at Epsom in August over the Derby course, with a subsequent race over hurdles. Escalus went north without the advantage of a preliminary race. Mould had been hurt two days before, so Cazalet and Dennard flew up together by aeroplane.

By the conditions of the 'Fighting Fifth' hurdle, Escalus received only three pounds from Persian War, now with three Champion Hurdles to his

86 Escalus (D. Mould) and Sharavogue (A. Branford) locked in battle in the 1970 Ackermann Skeaping Trophy at Sandown on 7 November 1970. The winner was Moyne Royal. Escalus won this race in 1969.

credit, and had to give four pounds to the front runner Even Keel, and four pounds more than weight-for-age to Inishmaan. It was a desperately exciting race, Even Keel leading until after the second last flight of hurdles with Escalus poised, sitting on his tail. Dennard then sent Escalus past Even Keel but as he came to the last in the lead, Biddlecombe and Inishmaan were at their quarters, going ominously well. In a tense duel to the line Inishmaan got up to defeat Escalus by a head. Even Keel was four lengths away in third place and Persian War was fourth. Cazalet was very disappointed. Like any keen competitive person, he minded very much being narrowly beaten in a big race—particularly if it was one of Queen Elizabeth's horses.

Escalus was considered to have run a good trial for the Champion Hurdle but hopes did not remain high for long. At Sandown only ten days later Escalus and Inishmaan met again in the Ackermann Skeaping Trophy Hurdle, Escalus seeking a repeat of his previous year's victory. He was meeting Inishmaan on four pounds better terms than in the 'Fighting Fifth' Hurdle and turned the tables on him but both were beaten by the handicap hurdler Moyne Royal. Escalus had had a very long journey north and it was hoped that he had not got over his hard race at Newcastle when failing at Sandown.

Three weeks later at Newbury, he met his old rival Coral Diver, who had finished just behind him in the Champion Hurdle. In this race, poor Escalus finished twenty lengths behind Coral Diver. The sparkle had suddenly gone. There was clearly something wrong. Tests showed that he was suffering from anaemia. Three weeks later he failed again at Ascot in a race he would have certainly have won at his best.

A month later, he was badly cast in his box, colic perhaps being the indirect cause. He was clearly in great pain soon afterwards. The symptoms suggested a twisted gut and Fairgrieve, in Cazalet's temporary absence, took him by horse box to the Veterinary College at South Mimms in Hertfordshire for an emergency operation, but he died under an anaesthetic. A May foal, he was still strictly four months short of his sixth birthday when he died, although technically, of course, a six-year-old since, for the sake of simplicity, the age of all racehorses is reckoned from the first of January in their year of foaling. 'As bold as brass at his best, and just as good as Makaldar,' was Mould's summing up. If he had kept his form, he would have had to tackle Bula in the Champion Hurdle of 1971. Bula would have been a very difficult horse to master, but if Escalus had made normal improvement from five to six he would not have been easily beaten.

Fortunately in the autumn, the six-year-olds Inch Arran and Black Magic—and to a lesser extent Colonsay Isle—began to show the great ability Bob McCreery felt they possessed. They started inauspiciously when Cazalet sent Colonsay Isle and Black Magic up to Worcester to run in two divisions of the novices' chase in the third week of October. Colonsay Isle ran in the first division, blundered at the third fence and got rid of his rider. Black Magic went straight through the first fence and got rid of his rider, too. A fortnight later, however, at Folkestone, Black Magic, Dennard up, having learnt his lesson, made every yard of the running in a novices' chase, finishing many lengths clear of the runner-up, and the following week Colonsay Isle, Dennard up, won a novices' chase at Plumpton by a whisker in the last stride. He then followed it up by going to Lingfield and winning the Wilderwick Chase much more impressively from a useful field of novices, including Mrs John Rogerson's Cuckolder, who was to win the Great Yorkshire Chase at Doncaster and other good three-mile chases before he was finished.

Queen Elizabeth, back from her beloved Scotland, went racing at Windsor in mid-November. Following course alterations, the fences had been remade, were stiffer than they had been in the past and there was a lot of grief. Cazalet had four Windsor runners. Mould was at Cheltenham riding Colonel Whitbread's Cloudsmere in the Mackeson Gold Cup, so Dennard was on the Windsor four—Game Spirit, Black Magic, Castle Yard and Don't Weaken, a chaser found by Fairgrieve and originally bought as a possible point-to-pointer for Lord Abergavenny's nephew

87   Colonsay Isle (R. Dennard) winning the Wilderwick Chase at Lingfield on 24 November 1970.

but found to be unsuitable for hunting. Game Spirit, making his first appearance on the racecourse, hit the second hurdle hard and finished at the tail end of his field in the four-year-old hurdle. Don't Weaken looked the probable winner of the Saxon House Handicap Chase when he fell two fences from home; Black Magic, with his victory at Folkestone fresh in mind, fell within sight of victory when leading in Division I of the Holyport Novices Chase and Castle Yard fell in Division II of the same event when disputing the lead at the last fence, and looking reasonably certain to win.

Queen Elizabeth wrote an amusing and sympathetic letter to console her principal trainer the following day: 'I feel that after the anguish of yesterday at Windsor, I must send you one line of commiseration over the perfectly extraordinary combination of slips and falls. This, coupled with the relentless driving rain, the soggy going and the revered trainer heading rapidly for pneumonia, made the day a never-to-be-forgotten one of pure hell. I cannot help feeling that it must be a long time before anything so dreadful happens again! . . . Yours hopefully (remembering Tobruk and other reverses). . . .'

Fortunately the Revered Trainer did avoid another bout of pneumonia, but he did have cause to remember Tobruk and other reverses in the weeks ahead. He took Queen Elizabeth's new young horse Playagain, to make his first appearance on the racecourse in a three-year-old hurdle at Folkestone ten days later. Playagain jumped the second last, hit it and stopped. He had broken a bone in a hind leg and there was no alternative but to put him down. Fairgrieve had found him at the home of his breeder Mr Neil Pringle near Alnwick in Northumberland, a promising young horse knocked down right at the start of his racing life.

The next week, Cazalet, not perhaps sufficiently mindful of the fact that his three Fairlawne chasers had all fallen at Windsor's rebuilt fences at the previous meeting, took three of Queen Elizabeth's chasers to Windsor on the last day of November. Fortunately Queen Elizabeth could not come. The day started all right when Inch Arran, ridden by Dennard, made every yard of the running to win the two mile Round Oak Handicap Chase after making mistakes. It was noticeable, however, that four of the field of nine handicap chasers failed to get over the first fence. Queen Elizabeth's other two runners were in the two divisions of the novices' chase—Castle Yard, who had already fallen at Windsor, in the first, Colonsay Isle in the second.

A fortnight before at Windsor, Castle Yard had fallen at the last fence when looking the winner. He now fell at the second fence. He was a small horse and not the cut of a chaser and he did not enjoy jumping fences. His fall was not unduly significant, but it was significant that only four of the fourteen novice chasers completed the course over Windor's remade fences. There were also fourteen novice chasers in Division II, of which Colonsay Isle was favourite after his impressive victory at Lingfield a week before.

Let Richard Dennard, who rode Colonsay Isle, take up the story. 'Colonsay Isle had been rather harum-scarum when schooling at Fairlawne, but he seemed to have learnt his lesson when winning at Plumpton, and for the first time he had jumped really well when winning at Lingfield the week before. We all felt very bucked to think that Queen Elizabeth had another good chaser in the making—particularly his lad Guy Francis, who rode well and who had come near to winning on the horse earlier in the year, and was devoted to him. I had walked the course at the previous meeting and we thought the remade fences were stiffer than they had been, but you can't really tell till you start jumping them. After the grief in Castle Yard's race, I think we were wondering what was in store for us in Colonsay Isle's race. I do not really remember what happened but I know Colonsay Isle was one of the leaders at the first fence, hit it and was one of those who fell like ninepins. Colonsay Isle picked himself up and went on with a swinger—a broken leg—and I knew he had had it. It was a ghastly moment for us all but particularly for Guy Francis.' Again, only four of the field of fourteen completed the course; after this débâcle, the Windsor fences were modified.

Colonsay Isle was the first horse of her own breeding Queen Elizabeth had lost in this way and perhaps the worst racing blow she had had. She had bought Colonsay Isle's dam, she had been largely responsible for Colonsay Isle's sire, Colonist II, coming to Sandringham, she had planned for Colonsay Isle to go to Wingfield in Ireland and to McCreery in Warwickshire, she had been down to Fairlawne to see him work and to mark his progress and, just as he was beginning to come good, it was all finished. Now many people were hurt and sad—not only at Fairlawne but at Sandringham, at the two studs he had been in in Ireland, and at McCreery's stud in Warwickshire. Owners of steeplechasers have, at times, to be stoical and philosophical. Steeplechasing is apt to be a much more unpredictable sport than flat racing and things must sometimes go wrong, but when they go right, then they do seem to be doubly worth while.

On the Saturday before Christmas, Queen Elizabeth had Inch Arran running at Ascot and the Queen brought Prince Edward and Prince Andrew racing for the first time and Princess Margaret brought her children. Inch Arran, with four victories in chases to his credit during the autumn, was tackling a field of seasoned handicap chasers for the first time in the Dunkirk Chase. Winter, Turnell and Scudamore, as trainers, all had fancied runners in the field, but Inch Arran, ridden by Dennard, led throughout, jumping fast and well. It was a spectacular victory and showed that in Inch Arran Queen Elizabeth had bred her first high-class chaser. It seemed to make up in a trice for much of the sadness over the loss of Inch Arran's former sparring partner, Colonsay Isle.

On New Year's Day at Sandown, Black Magic appeared in a handicap chase for the first time with two successes in novice chases and a couple of falls as well in his autumn record. 'Black Magic must be a somewhat nerve-racking partner but no doubt Richard Dennard is prepared to put up with some nervous strain in return for the sort of ride he got at Sandown today,' reported John Lawrence. 'Apart from one nasty moment at the water, Black Magic never really looked like paying for his boldness and none of his opponents ever got near enough to feel his slipstream.' Guy Francis did Black Magic as well as Colonsay Isle. He felt in a much happier frame of mind after the race.

It was a day full of interest for Queen Elizabeth and Fairlawne. Game Spirit ran well to finish third in a big field in Division I of the Metropolitan Hurdle, and St Patrick's Blue, bred at Sandringham and the winner of a couple of big handicaps for the Queen on the flat, but now in different ownership, won Division II. Fairlawne had a double, for Dick Wilkins's Old Pueblo, well-ridden by Evatt, won the amateur riders' three-mile chase.

Cazalet had second thoughts about one of his declared runners and decided to withdraw it, although there had been no overnight change in the going. In such circumstances, the stewards almost automatically impose a fine on the trainer concerned for not running the horse without a very clear reason for the change of plan. In their view, Cazalet's explanation for not running the horse was not adequate and he was fined £30. One of the stewards came up to join the Royal party later in the afternoon and found both Queen Elizabeth and Cazalet present. Queen Elizabeth turned to the newly arrived steward with a friendly smile: 'We are thinking how we can raise the money to pay the fine,' said Queen Elizabeth. The steward had come up hoping vaguely for a cup of tea. He thought it politic to change his mind and beat a retreat at the appropriate moment, and ordered himself a double whisky and soda elsewhere to restore his equanimity!

A fortnight later at Ascot, Black Magic reappeared in the Mar Lodge Handicap Chase, carrying a penalty for his success at Sandown. Most people considered the outcome of the race depended on whether Black Magic got round or not, and he did so to no mean tune. 'The jumpers toiling in the wake of Black Magic at Ascot might well have imagined there was something supernatural in the way Queen Elizabeth's seven-year-old kept widening the gap between himself and his pursuers,' ran the *Sunday Telegraph* report. 'He jumped every fence beautifully and, although slowing up a trifle after jumping the last, he trotted up. . . . Trainer Peter Cazalet is not the Turf's most effusive character and when he said, "Black Magic did not make a mistake at any stage," it was rather like nominating Black Magic for an Oscar.'

The second half of January 1971 was very wet and Queen Elizabeth's old stayer Zaloba, now running in a hood, appeared in the mud at Folkestone in the last week of January in a long-distance handicap hurdle—probably not enjoying it over much. Mould was still on the side lines with a broken pelvis after a bad fall at Wye in mid-December and Dennard rode Zaloba. It was a humble race but the nearest I have seen to a triple deadheat. Zaloba crossed the finishing line almost at one with Ally and Cheapside, bred by Mrs Peter Hastings, widow of the Queen's former trainer. David Nicholson had had to put up two pounds' overweight on Ally, whom he also trained. Richard Dennard thought Zaloba had just hung on to win; Cazalet thought Cheapside had got up to beat Zaloba.

Nicholson steered Ally into the winners' enclosure; he did not think that he had won but neither Dennard nor Ron Atkins on Cheapside wished to do so. The camera showed that Ally had been beaten perhaps by six inches. The judge, Mr J. M. Phillpotts, took six minutes to decide that Zaloba in the centre and Cheapside were definitely inseparable. It was Zaloba's last victory—three over hurdles and two on the flat. Later in the season he split a pastern and later on Queen Elizabeth gave him to Mr Michael Oswald, Manager of the Royal Studs, to hunt.

Black Magic went to Sandown in February to win the Scilly Isles Chase unchallenged and to make his opponents look—in the words of a wag—'downright scilly'. Colonel W. Whetherly's Jabeg, the unbeaten winner of a string of novice chases that season, followed Black Magic home but could never close with him, nor could the Ascot winner Moon Storm. Black Magic went to the National Hunt meeting at Cheltenham with a great chance in the Arkle Challenge Trophy for novices—if he stood up. He had won his last four races in brilliant style but people were beginning to realise that the way to beat him was to take him on from the start and, hopefully, cause him to blunder at an early fence. For the first time, Black Magic was sweating in the paddock before his race at Cheltenham and had not travelled well to the course. He nearly fell at both of the first two fences, setting a furious pace, with others vying with him, and then came to grief irretrievably at the third. It was most disappointing, but he had won five of his eight races and had justified all the kind things Bob McCreery had said about him. Inch Arran also retired for the season in March as the winner of six of his eight races.

Queen Elizabeth's last and twenty-third winner of the season came when Game Spirit won a novices' hurdle at Newbury towards the end of March. He had previously gained his first success for Queen Elizabeth appropriately enough on Grand Military Gold Cup day at Sandown, which Her Majesty always supported, if possible. Not expected to win, Game Spirit had run on up the hill under pressure to hold the challenge of Lord Rosebery's odds-on favourite, Trumpeter. Game Spirit's two victories at the end of the season boded well for the future.

Meanwhile in the north, Queen Elizabeth's Bel Ambre, loaned to the 9th/12th Royal Lancers, was continuing to improve. The number of officers in the Bel Ambre syndicate had also increased. Queen Elizabeth, as Colonel-in-Chief, had been up to inspect her regiment and 'Jumbo' Wilkinson had brought Bel Ambre over from Middleham to Catterick Camp for Queen Elizabeth to inspect, too. The happy relationship between Bel Ambre and Nigel Wright continued and he rode out daily whenever possible. Richard Head, who had looked after Bel Ambre for a time at Fairlawne, had found him highly-strung and a handful to do. 'Jumbo' Wilkinson had a good lad to do him in Joe Wright. As it was so muddling to have two Wrights dealing with Bel Ambre, Nigel Wright was allowed to keep his identity but Joe Wright became known as Joe Bloggs in the Wilkinson stable!

Bel Ambre with his fired forelegs wanted some give in the ground, so he was turned out from May to August and did not reappear until mid-November 1970 when he ran well in a hurdle race at Carlisle. He then went up to Newcastle for the Gosforth Park Amateur Cup, which attracted some of the best amateur riders in the north, including Alan Mactaggart, Charles Macmillan, Robin Greig and Jimmy Walton. Among them, Nigel Wright was virtually unknown. Bel Ambre opened as the extreme outsider at 33-1 in a field of seven and started at 14-1. The race was over Bel Ambre's ideal distance of two-and-a-half miles and he won on merit. 'He liked a good galloping track, preferably left-handed,' recalled Wright. 'He had a real turn of foot and an extra gear up to two-and-a-half miles. Beyond that he did not stay.' Wilkinson and the regimental syndicate had brought off something of a coup in the Newcastle race.

When Bel Ambre came down from Yorkshire to run in his second Grand Military Gold Cup, it was realised that he did not get the trip. Captain Hamish Lochore, a Scots Grey, attached at the time to the 9th/12th Lancers, also brought his hunter chaser Napoleon Brandy II, which he had been training himself, down for the race. On form, Napoleon Brandy II had no chance, and Lochore, really an 'eventing' man, had to put up six pounds overweight. Bel Ambre again jumped well, made all the running but faded from the Pond fence. Lochore, bringing Napoleon Brandy II from behind and riding like a man inspired, nearly brought off one of the biggest surprises in the history of the race, only going under by a head to the odds-on favourite, Charles Dickens.

A spring horse, Bel Ambre then went back to his proper distance of two-and-a-half miles and Queen Elizabeth was delighted to hear that Bel Ambre and Nigel Wright had finished the season with a hat-trick—another victory at Newcastle and two races appropriately won at Hexham on home ground for the Enderby brothers, where their father, Colonel Samuel Enderby, a Northumberland Fusilier, had been starter for over twenty years. When the regiment left Catterick for Germany, Captain Hibbert-Foy, managing the Bel Ambre regimental syndicate, was able to distribute a substantial pay-out to members, after having paid all racing expenses. Queen Elizabeth's idea had certainly borne fruit.

When autumn came, Black Magic, Inch Arran and Game Spirit looked to be Queen Elizabeth's chief hopes for the new season of 1971–72. In his first race at Ascot in October, Black Magic had to take on the Australian champion Crisp, who had arrived in England late in 1970 and had electrified the steeplechasing world by running away with the National Hunt Two-Mile Champion Chase at Cheltenham six months later. Crisp had not run since, nor had Black Magic since coming to grief over the same Cheltenham course on the following day. Others in the Ascot field were The Dikler, who had been third in the Cheltenham Gold Cup, and a good handicap chaser in Master Eye, who already had two races to his credit that autumn. Black Magic in the Ascot race led to the fifth fence where he blundered badly and, though he completed the course behind Crisp, he was the last to finish.

88   Black Magic (R. Dennard) defeating the Australian champion Crisp in the Sandown Park Pattern Chase on 6 November 1971. Crisp's head is just visible.

Ten days later, it was decided that Black Magic would take on Crisp again at level weights in the Sandown Park Pattern Chase over two miles with New Romney and the Cheltenham Gold Cup horse The Laird also in the field. This time everything went right for Black Magic. He jumped superbly throughout, made every yard of the running and won all out by two lengths from Crisp. Sir Chester Manifold's Australian champion, who was to give the most marvellous display of jumping when just beaten by Red Rum in the 1973 Grand National, did make a definite mistake at the first fence on the far side of the course, and on the form Black Magic showed then, that was asking for trouble. Black Magic's time that day of 3 minutes 51.60 seconds was, I think, at that time a record for the course, although Tingle Creek, another brilliant front runner, has beaten it since.

It was a marvellous duel between the two and the crowd rose to Black Magic and Crisp as it rises on all special occasions when something of breath-taking excitement has been seen. Sadly Queen Elizabeth could not be present. 'I jumped out of the gate and went all the way,' said Richard Dennard, 'especially at the first when I had to go with Black Magic and eat the fence. I cannot explain to you the thrill of riding him that day. He put in one enormous leap and we went back and measured it. From where he had taken off to where he landed was thirty-two feet. Crisp got to within three lengths of me at the last, but Black Magic kept galloping on.'

A fortnight later, Black Magic was in action again in the Black and White Whisky Gold Cup. It was his third race in three and a half weeks and for a horse who took a lot out of himself both in his races and when working solo at home, the Ascot race possibly came too soon. At any rate, the superlative brilliance he showed at Sandown was missing at Ascot. An old rival in Jabeg took him on from the start. Black Magic led to the open ditch before the water, then Jabeg passed him, and Black Magic was in trouble before the final bend into the straight and could only finish third behind Jabeg and the Irishman, Colebridge. It was the last good race Black Magic ever ran. The dreaded navicular disease was beginning to rear its ugly head. He ran twice more at Sandown—once in December and once in the first week of January, but the sparkle had gone. He was pulled up in the December race and was last of four in January. Soon after his failure in January, a course of penicillin was tried. In August a foot was X-rayed and a few days later he went to Newmarket for treatment for four months. He returned to Fairlawne in time for Christmas 1972 not significantly better. He was never completely sound again. He had run his last race.

Fortunately Inch Arran had plenty of racing ahead of him. He reappeared at the beginning of November 1971 and had a tremendous duel at Newbury with Osbaldeston, a full brother to Sonny Somers. Richard Dennard on Inch Arran made practically all the running, was two lengths clear at the last but only held on by a head. In a couple more strides Osbaldeston would have won. Inch Arran, in returning a time of 3 minutes 59.40 seconds for the two miles 150 yards course was breaking the Newbury time record set up by Thataway over ten years before.

It was a tough race to have at the beginning of a new season and, partly as a result, the handicapper got his mark clearly on Inch Arran. New Romney, who had been no match for Black Magic in his great duel with Crisp at Sandown, found Inch Arran a different kettle of fish and beat him at Newbury. Inch Arran then finished second in four handicaps. His most disappointing defeat was in the Cheltenham Grand Annual at the National Hunt meeting when Tudor Dance just wore him down.

Victory came again in the last race of the season at Folkestone in the Kent Amateur Riders' Handicap Chase when Inch Arran, ridden by David Evatt, made all the running. Evatt rode him out quite often at Fairlawne. 'Though he pulled like hell, he was my favourite,' said Evatt. 'He was so human. I used to say to him, "Hang on, Inky, I have not got my reins yet", and the old horse used to stop. When I was ready, he used to go swinging up the hill as if saying, "Now sit and suffer, boy". When I won on him at Folkestone, and it was right at the end of the season, he jumped superbly, and made it all.'

Dennard usually rode Black Magic and Inch Arran in their races, with courage and dash. Mould rode Game Spirit—and, without any doubt, superlatively well. Game Spirit for most of his time at Fairlawne was done by Sam Manktelow, a man of Kent, born on the estate of Lord Camden, and apprenticed initially to Sam Darling at Newmarket. When weight beat him, he joined Whiteman at Fairlawne in 1934 and—with the exception of the war years—he stayed there for the rest of his working life. Manktelow had had Manicou, Rose Park and other stars. I think Game Spirit was his favourite. 'He was a beautiful mover, he went on any ground, he liked a nice long rein, he loved racing and gave it all, and like my other top class horses, Manicou and Rose Park, he had different gears. He was no one pacer,' summed up Manktelow.

Game Spirit won his first novice chase over the same two-mile course at the same Sandown meeting on the day before Black Magic beat Crisp. Black Magic's time for the course was 3 minutes 51.60 seconds, Game Spirit's time 4 minutes 4 seconds, but the latter was not fully extended in beating two opponents. Game Spirit next won at Newbury in February over three miles. Handa Island, bred by Anne, Duchess of Westminster, and named after a bird island near her estate in Scotland, was backed to beat Game Spirit, but could not extend him. At Lingfield at the beginning of March, he was hard pressed to give weight and a beating to the more experienced Moon Storm. He won in spite of making mistakes and showed for the first time on the racecourse that Queen Elizabeth had named him well. At Sandown at the Grand Military meeting, Game Spirit completed a hat trick in the Beech Open Chase.

Mould felt that he had done enough for his first year over fences. Cazalet thought one more race would not come amiss and he was saddled for the valuable Heinz Chase at Ascot on the day of Well To Do's Grand National, in which Mould and Dennard were both riding. Evatt had the ride on Game Spirit, who was pitted against much better chasers than he had met before. Game Spirit was going extremely well lying about fourth and one off the rails when he took off too soon at the open ditch before the water. 'We were going lickety split in a good challenging position, with the leader only three or four lengths ahead of me,' reported Evatt. 'Game Spirit had been foot perfect up to then and he took off a length too soon. It was inexperience. I got up off the floor and the horse got up and went on. I got a lift back to the paddock, saw that Game Spirit was caught and all right and dashed off with my father to ride in the last race at the Crawley and Horsham Point-to-Point, which I managed to win, but it did not, of course, begin to make up for Game Spirit's fall. That for me was a tragedy.'

At the Grand Military meeting, Queen Elizabeth saw Bel Ambre competing in his third Grand Military Gold Cup. When the 9th/12th Lancers left England, the Queen's Dragoon Guards, of which Queen Elizabeth is also Colonel-in-Chief, came to Catterick in their place and took on Bel Ambre who, as a result of his hat-trick at the end of the 1970-71 season, had gone up to the top of the handicap. Captain William Crosbie Dawson, whose father had been in the Queen's Bays, took the place of Nigel Wright. Twenty officers in the regiment formed a syndicate and the horse ran in Crosbie Dawson's name and colours. Crosbie Dawson, at the age of sixteen, had got leave from school and had won the Vine and Craven Members' race on one of the family horses but he had had no experience, like Wright, of riding under rules. He finished second twice in races at Hexham in the autumn, but the horse had clearly shown by now that he did not stay beyond two-and-a-half miles and he was not fancied in the Grand Military. He fell at the last fence on the far side of the Sandown course. Crosbie Dawson had bad concussion as a result, and he was not able to ride Bel Ambre a fortnight later when he won over two miles at Hexham. Bel Ambre paid most of the syndicate's bills by winning again at Hexham towards the end of April. A year later, Bel Ambre was to take part in his fourth successive Grand Military Gold Cup, and Crosbie Dawson was to finish fifth on him. At the age of twelve, he was ready to leave the racing scene and to turn to hunting in Yorkshire, which he came to enjoy in his old age.

On Easter Monday, with Mould and Dennard not available, Evatt rode Royal Marine, Soldo and Queen Elizabeth's new horse, Just Lit, for Fairlawne at Plumpton. Royal Marine did no good, Mrs B. Moresby's Soldo, who had been a National horse, was past his best and was pulled up in the Abergavenny Challenge Cup. Just Lit remained. He was a hard puller and would not settle. 'Is it worth trying a rubber bit in his mouth, a steel bit doesn't seem much good,' said Mould helpfully. Cazalet was apprehensive. His instructions to Evatt in the parade ring were clear: 'Just take him down to the start very slowly in a hack canter, and take him down last.' Just Lit arrived safely at the starting gate, much to the relief of Cazalet who muttered to Fairgrieve, 'Thank God for that, at least Evatt has arrived there in one piece.' And Evatt remained in one piece throughout the race. He tried to tuck Just Lit in and keep him covered up, but when he pulled him to one side going into the first hurdle, to give him an inch of daylight, that was too much for Just Lit. He went shooting past his field, took the lead, and when he had shot his bolt Evatt pulled him up. Miraculously perhaps Just Lit was to win a novices' chase three years later. He was not Her Majesty's most attractive horse.

Fortunately, another of Queen Elizabeth's newcomers was of a different calibre. A chestnut four-year-old rejoicing in the misleading name of Greystoke Pillar, he nearly made a winning début on the racecourse in February and then won two novice hurdles at Lingfield in quick succession. Fairgrieve had found him in Cumberland and he had been bought on Queen Elizabeth's behalf from his breeder Mr D. Batey, who farmed near Penrith and owned his dam Residence, a useful chasing mare in the 1950s. Greystoke Pillar got his name from the fact that his sire Straight Cut stood at Tommy Robson's then home at Greystoke near Penrith. Robson had trained Straight Cut to win the Cumberland Plate and Kempton's 1956 Heathorn Hurdle, when Robson rode him to victory himself.

As the 1971–72 season ended, Peter Cazalet was feeling ill. He had a swelling on his left arm near a birthmark and sought medical advice, but it was too late. He had cancer in the arm and tests showed that it had spread. Zara Cazalet naturally knew and he told his son Edward and said, furthermore, that he was going to fight to the last against the disease. But during his last season of 1972–73 he looked and felt increasingly ill. He was only up to riding a pony, and he decreased the number of horses in training.

Fortunately with Queen Elizabeth's horses, things went well. Inch Arran covered himself with glory by bringing off an autumn and spring double at Aintree; Game Spirit went from strength to strength; Chaou II returned to winning form after being fired and after surviving a horsebox crash which landed Fairlawne's long-serving horse box driver, 'Curly' Skinner, in hospital for many weeks. What was exciting for Queen Elizabeth also was that two more of her home-bred horses struck winning form—Colonius and Colonello, both sons of Colonist II.

In October 1972, Inch Arran went up to Aintree for the first time with no preliminary race under him to take part in the B.P. Chase, a new race over the last two miles five furlongs of the Grand National course, over which the Becher Chase used to be run at the old Liverpool Autumn meeting. Favourite for the race was Gay Trip, winner of the 1970 Grand National and second to Well To Do in the 1972 Grand National seven months before the running of the B.P. Chase. In the field were the locally trained Glenzier Lad, Tazu, who carried the colours of Major Cliff-McCulloch, and The Pooka who had run well in the 1972 Grand National.

Richard Dennard, with memories of a great ride on the Fairlawne-trained Beau Bob in the 1971 Grand National, was no stranger to Aintree and was soon making running on Inch Arran. Queen Elizabeth's chaser took a strong hold as usual, jumping a bit to his right as he went away from the stands. The Pooka was an early casualty and soon after Valentine's the race lay between Inch Arran, Gay Trip and Tazu. Gay Trip, who had been held up in his work, was the first beaten. Tazu looked the winner at the second last, but hit the last fence hard and in the long run-in Inch Arran, battling on bravely, slowly forged ahead to win by one and a half lengths. It was certainly a Red Letter Day for Dennard for it was the 100th winner of his career and his first at Aintree. Inch Arran's time of 5 minutes 20.40 seconds was the best for the distance at Aintree and nearly three seconds faster than Silver Dome's time in winning the 1964 Becher Chase eight years before.

Inch Arran and Black Magic always worked at Fairlawne away from the string, and Inch Arran had been trained specifically for the race. 'We jumped off and went,' reported Dennard later. 'I was clear going to the first and as The Chair loomed up, I was very apprehensive—as I think I was entitled to be on Inch Arran's record. All I had was steering, nothing else. He didn't make a single mistake and I took the same line as I had done on Beau Bob in the National—the middle of the inner. To go round the National course is something in itself. To go round it as Inch Arran went round it was like riding with the gods. There was no doubt about it.'

Four weeks later at Newbury poor Dennard was brought down to earth with a bump, for Inch Arran disgraced himself in a two-mile chase and fell at the last fence on the far side of the course. However, at Kempton at the Boxing Day meeting, Inch Arran was in favour again, defeating his old rival New Romney after a long duel. Dennard shone on him, as he shone, too, on the hurdler Padlocked, who won a division of the three-year-old hurdle. Padlocked was owned in partnership by Sir Martin Gilliat, Dick Wilkins and Major and Mrs Derek Wigan.

Towards the end of November Queen Elizabeth had her last Fairlawne double. Chaou II had come back to racing after an absence of twenty months and had only just failed to win on his reappearance at Windsor. Then at Fontwell, ten days later, he won the Whitelaw Challenge Cup after a long duel with the National horse Fair Vulgan. The handicap hurdle, which followed, was won comfortably by Greystoke Pillar. Queen Elizabeth's National Hunt score had risen with this double to 250. In

December, Chaou II carried a penalty to victory in the Ewell Chase at Kempton. It was his seventeenth success for Queen Elizabeth and, as it happened, his last. It was almost exactly six years since he had taken fright

89   Chaou II (D. Mould) defeating Lady Thomson's Prince Tino (T. G. Davies) in the Ewell Chase at Kempton—his 17th and last victory for Queen Elizabeth—on 1 December 1972.

at the noise of a band in the gardens of Clarence House. He had not hit the headlines like Manicou and Devon Loch, Double Star and The Rip, Makaldar and Escalus, but he had gone on winning in an admirable way—and in the six years which spanned his racing days in England, Queen Elizabeth herself had won over one hundred races.

That season, Game Spirit was to look Chaou's natural successor. He started by winning handicaps at Ascot and at Windsor in January and then, after two reverses, he ended the season with a hat-trick—at Lingfield, at Folkestone and finally at Newbury where he carried a penalty to beat Edward Courage's top class two miler Royal Relief, twice winner of the National Hunt Two-Mile Champion Chase. Game Spirit's victory at Folkestone gave Queen Elizabeth particular pleasure for it was in the inaugural running of the Whitbread Fremlins Elephant Chase exactly twelve years before that The Rip, ridden, like Game Spirit, by Mould, had first shown real promise.

In mid-March at Lingfield, Chaou II had his final race before going to Aintree to take his chance in the Grand National. He had broken down in the spring of 1971 when he was intended for the National and now at Lingfield in the spring of 1973 this attractive dappled grey broke down again. Mould had thought that he would run well in the 1973 National but there had been a question mark over his complete soundness for four or five weeks and such horses rarely win a National. Cazalet in his last Grand National was now without a runner in a race he had sought so often to win. However, he sent two horses north to run at the meeting—Queen Elizabeth's Inch Arran in the Topham Trophy and Greystoke Pillar in the B.P. Shield Handicap Hurdle. Cazalet himself was now too ill to go north and Fairgrieve was in charge of Queen Elizabeth's runners. Dennard had broken a collar bone badly in a fall on Queen Elizabeth's novice chaser Kelso Brig ten days before Liverpool and was not fit to ride.

On firm going, which suited Inch Arran, the Topham Trophy as usual brought out a high class field of two-and-a-half mile chasers on the first day of the Grand National meeting. The Cheltenham winners Vulgan Town, successful in the Mildmay of Flete Challenge Cup, and The Chisler, winner of the National Hunt Handicap Chase, were the two most fancied, French Colonist, who had won four races off the reel, was third favourite and others fancied in the field of fourteen were Inch Arran and Champers Galore, who had beaten Game Spirit at Kempton. The Topham Trophy was the second race of the day and timed to start at five minutes past three o'clock. Jim Fairgrieve had declared Mould to ride Inch Arran but as the runners prepared to go out for the first race timed to start at 2.30, there was still no sign of Mould, and Fairgrieve, desperate with anxiety, sought and obtained the stewards' permission to substitute Lord Oaksey—the former John Lawrence—for Mould if the latter did not arrive in time. Lord Oaksey had just succeeded his father, the 1st Lord Oaksey, formerly

Lord Justice Lawrence, who had presided with distinction at the Nuremberg trial of war criminals. John Oaksey's report in *The Daily Telegraph* graphically tells the story of Peter Cazalet's last big winner at the place where he wanted winners most of all. 'David Mould came within thirty hectic seconds of missing the ride of a lifetime at Aintree today when Inch Arran won the Topham Trophy for Queen Elizabeth. And the same brief space was all that stood between your correspondent and an entirely undeserved opportunity to fulfil a long-held ambition in the Royal colours. Just half an hour before the Topham Trophy, Fairgrieve obtained the stewards' permission to substitute me for the still missing Mould.

'The clerk of the scales, Mr G. W. Gregory, advised a 2.45 p.m. deadline and I was changed, standing ready to weigh out, when with a timing the United States cavalry never bettered, David Mould made his entrance. His brother's brand new Jaguar had boiled on the motorway and, by the look of them, its passengers were close to the same high temperature on arrival at the course! But once aboard Inch Arran, David Mould reverted to his usual ice-cool self and the Royal grey rewarded him with a clear round as flawless as any his wife Marion ever achieved in Stroller's heyday.

'French Colonist took a real liberty with The Chair and Myritus was just in front when he fell at the fence before Becher's. But Inch Arran was always up there sailing merrily along and measuring every fence with the accuracy of a metronome. Quintus, owned and trained by Edward Courage, looked a big danger just before the last, and Norwegian Flag made up a lot of ground after it. But, having been through so much, David Mould was even more determined than usual and, though very tired, his gallant companion did the rest.' It was Mould's 106th and last winner for Her Majesty.

Queen Elizabeth, watching on television at Clarence House, and the Cazalets, watching at Fairlawne, fortunately for their peace of mind, knew nothing of the high drama at Aintree until Fairgrieve and Mould filled in details later in the day. Mould, who had barely sat on Inch Arran before the Topham, reported briefly to Cazalet: 'He gave me a super ride—the best I have ever had at Aintree. I made practically all the running, being headed going to Becher's, and once again at Valentine's and there was not much between Quintus and me over the last four fences. I think Inch Arran remembered his previous victory in the B.P. Chase in the autumn and he was not so headstrong as usual and more careful. He was, in fact, foot perfect.' Inch Arran again broke the time record for the $2\frac{3}{4}$-mile-course—a furlong further than the distance of his autumn race six months before.

Dennard, who had always schooled Inch Arran, watched the race also on television and rued the broken collar bone Kelso Brig had given him at

Plumpton. He had ridden Inch Arran in thirty of his thirty-four races for Fairlawne and it was sad for him that he should not complete Inch Arran's Aintree double. Nevertheless, it had been injuries to Mould which had given Dennard his chance to shine as Cazalet's second jockey in the first place—an opportunity Dennard had grasped with both hands.

A few days after Inch Arran's success in the Topham Trophy, Sir Martin Gilliat arranged for the race to be televised again at Clarence House, so that Queen Elizabeth and Peter and Zara Cazalet could go through the race again together. Inch Arran was the 250th winner Cazalet had trained for Her Majesty and it was, in fact, the last. It was best, I think, that Cazalet's last winner for Queen Elizabeth should be a big one. Inch Arran was almost certainly the best Sandringham-bred horse Cazalet had trained.

Two other home-bred horses won over hurdles for Queen Elizabeth in Cazalet's final season. Colonius, a half-brother by Colonist II to Inch Arran, won at Newbury in November, and Colonello, the second foal of the Manicou mare Mandella, won at Plumpton in January—Mould's 100th Royal winner. Edward Cazalet took his father racing for the last time to an April meeting at Plumpton. As he was not up to saddling his own horses, nor giving a leg up to a jockey, the great trainer watched the racing quietly down the course from his car. Fairlawne had its last three runners at this Plumpton Easter meeting. The offending Kelso Brig, 'a morning glory', was beaten by inches in the Falmer Novices' Chase, and Colonius was beaten by a length in the four-year-old hurdle.

Fairgrieve's stable diary for the first four months of 1973 gives glimpses of things to come. Apart from the fifteen horses Queen Elizabeth had in training, his other owners had under a dozen horses left. At the beginning of the year, Newbrough, who had never come sound again, left the yard with two more of Queen Elizabeth's horses who had never made the grade. Roman Meeting, a very promising Quorum filly out of Tiberetta, given by Edward Courage to Queen Elizabeth as a seventieth birthday present, met with an accident in training, never ran, and was sent back to Sandringham where, in due course, I think, she will prove a great asset to Queen Elizabeth's stud. Into training came Isle of Man, who was to give Queen Elizabeth so much pleasure in the future. Isle of Man, like The Rip, was by Manicou and out of Inch Arran's dam, Queen of the Isle.

By the beginning of May, practically all the horses were turned out. On 29 May at the age of sixty-five, Peter Cazalet succumbed to cancer. Fairlawne as a training stable was at an end. Since he had started training again after the Second World War, Cazalet had turned out over 1,100 winners—nearly a quarter of them for his principal owner Queen Elizabeth. Cazalet was buried in the family grave at Shipbourne nearly a hundred years after his forbears had first come to live in Kent. Of his staff, most of whom had been with him for many years, Jim Fairgrieve, I think,

90 Queen Elizabeth presenting a special award to John Hole for the best turned out horse of the day at Kempton in 1973 — over forty years after Hole had joined Fairlawne in 1932.

felt his death more than anyone. 'He was my idea of a real man,' said Fairgrieve. 'Honest, upright, god-fearing, courteous and kind when it was merited, and outspoken, to say the least, when he was annoyed. . . . I held him in high esteem, admired and respected him and envied his character.' Cazalet, in short, was the driving force in a well run and happy ship.

Nearly four weeks after the funeral on Monday 25 June, Queen Elizabeth, at her own wish, came down alone to Fairlawne to say good-bye to all the men she had got to know during her twenty-four years as an owner there. She saw each one of the staff separately in an office in part of the stable block. She had chosen parting presents for each of them according to what she thought they would appreciate. Everyone had looked forward tremendously to Queen Elizabeth's visits to the yard and now they were going to cease.

For the rest of the week, those of the horses still at Fairlawne left day by day. Queen Elizabeth's main lot went last of all to Lambourn to her principal new trainer Fulke Walwyn, a man with an outstanding record as a trainer of steeplechasers for the previous quarter of a century. To Walwyn's Saxon House yard went Inch Arran, his full-brother Colonius and his half-brother Isle of Man, Game Spirit, Colonello, Greystoke Pillar and the unsound Black Magic. Kelso Brig went to Richard Head at Upper Lambourn, and a newcomer, Earl's Castle, to Ken Oliver near Hawick in

Roxburghshire. Colonello was to go on from Lambourn to Jack O'Donoghue, who was already training his full sister Mertensia.

Fairgrieve's entry in his diary of 29 June after the last horse had gone and the yard was silent again for the first time for over a quarter of century was to the point:

THE END OF FAIRLAWNE TRAINING STABLE.

Edward Cazalet, with his knowledge of horses, could have continued the stable with skill but he was already a successful barrister, with a wife and children to support. Death duties meant that he could not go on living at Fairlawne as his father and his step-mother had lived there, and as he himself would have wished to have done. So all was sold, except for houses in Shipbourne, where Peter Cazalet's staff still lived. Edward Cazalet saw that they were not worried and not disturbed.

Jim Fairgrieve, who had worked so single-mindedly for his guv'nor, went back to the Borders, Edward Cazalet building him a bungalow in the village of Birgham near Kelso, from where he still goes out to give electrical treatment to horses with sprains and strains. He of the staff felt the demise of Fairlawne more than anyone. His verse, I think, explains his feelings:

> The sound of the stable is silent
>   Now the horses have all gone away,
> The sun may be high in the heavens
>   But the cloud over Fairlawne is grey.
> No more will the dawn be awakened
>   By the whinny of impatient steeds,
> As I open the door of the feed house
>   And give them their first morning feed.
> No more will the sound of the hoof beats
>   Resound through the fog in the park,
> No more will we go to the race meets—
>   The future looks gloomy and dark.
> So lock up the door of the stable,
>   Start walking, never look back.
> Bite your lip just as hard as you're able,
>   If you don't, then you're quite sure to crack.

13

Transition

QUEEN ELIZABETH'S new principal trainer Fulke Walwyn was less than four years younger than Cazalet and both had started to train in 1939 after having to give up race-riding through injury. Fulke's father, Colonel F. J. Walwyn, a Royal Welch Fusilier, whose home was near Raglan, south-west of Monmouth, had become joint-master of the Monmouthshire Foxhounds in 1921 after retiring from the army, when Fulke and his twin sister Helen were only ten years of age. From then on, Fulke was heavily involved in riding and hunting and in his late teens in point-to-pointing.

Walwyn's first ride under National Hunt rules was at the now defunct Cardiff meeting not far from his home on a five-year-old called Alpine Hut in April 1930, in the £82 Glanely Novices' Chase. He was the only amateur riding in the race and his opponents included Billy Stott, then the champion jockey, Tommy Cullinan, who had won the 1930 Grand National a month before on Shaun Goilin, Danny Morgan, who was to win the 1936 Cheltenham Gold Cup on Morse Code and Eric Foster who had been a leading National Hunt rider in the mid-1920s and rode Lord Westmorland's Royal Chancellor in the first Cheltenham Gold Cup of 1924. 'I was as green as grass,' recalled Walwyn. 'I had not been in the jockeys' room before and I didn't know any of the jockeys.' Nevertheless, the nineteen-year-old Walwyn won his first race under rules from five experienced professionals—and he did not look back.

After Sandhurst, Walwyn joined the 9th Lancers, a cavalry regiment with a great tradition of race-riding since General Sir David Campbell as a subaltern had won the 1896 Grand National on The Soarer. Walwyn's contemporary and close friend in the 9th Lancers was the Irishman Frank Furlong, son of Major Noel Furlong, who had left his home in County Cork to settle in England after the then equivalent of the I.R.A. had made life too threatening and unpleasant for his family. Noel Furlong, a great racing enthusiast, had started to train and breed a few horses after coming to live in Leicestershire and, after nearly winning the Grand National of 1933 with Really True, had won it in 1935 with Reynoldstown, ridden by his son Frank.

The Colonel of the 9th Lancers was good to Walwyn and Furlong and allowed them to take their leave day by day to go racing and ride as amateurs. At the end of the 1932–33 season, Fulke Walwyn was the leading amateur rider ahead of another Welshman Evan Williams, who was about to turn professional and to win the 1937 Grand National on Royal Mail. Three cavalry soldiers were the three leading amateurs the following year—Walwyn, Peter Payne-Gallwey, who was to come to train at Upper Lambourn after the Second World War, and Sir Peter Grant-Lawson. When Walwyn went out at Aintree to ride Reynoldstown in the 1936 Grand National, in place of his friend Frank Furlong, he had already ridden in over a hundred races during the season and had determined to leave the army and turn professional.

It was in the 1936 Grand National that the Fairlawne-trained Davy Jones, Anthony Mildmay up, came to the last fence with a clear lead but rudderless—the buckle of the reins had parted after the second last fence—and Davy Jones had run out. Walwyn and Reynoldstown were then left to jump the last fence on their own and to win comfortably from Ego, ridden by the future Sir Harry Llewellyn, Bachelor Prince, ridden by Jack Fawcus who had just turned professional, and Crown Prince, ridden by Mr R. Strutt—the present Lord Belper. It was the last time amateurs were to dominate a Grand National finish.

When Walwyn turned professional, he was dogged by bad falls but nine months after winning the Grand National he finished second, as a professional, on Miss Dorothy Paget's great chaser Golden Miller in the Becher Chase at the 1937 Liverpool Autumn meeting. He was the only man able to get Golden Miller round Aintree once the famous chaser had taken a firm dislike to the course. This was to stand him in good stead, for when he started training again at Lambourn after the war, Miss Paget soon asked him to train her horses, then the most powerful string of steeplechasers in the country.

In 1939, when Walwyn had first taken out a licence to train, he had his horses at Delamere House, Lambourn, from which yard Marcus Marsh had sent out Windsor Lad to win the 1934 Derby for the Maharaja of Rajpipla, but in 1944 he bought the Saxon House yard between Lambourn and Upper Lambourn from the well-known trainer Ted Gwilt, who had won the 1937 Champion Hurdle with Free Fare. The Paget horses began to arrive in the 1946–47 season and in the next eight years, Walwyn won well over 350 races for her, but she was a very exacting owner. Mont Tremblant was the particular Paget star; he won the 1952 Cheltenham Gold Cup as a six-year-old and was then second under top weight in the 1953 Grand National to Early Mist.

Since those Paget days in the first half of the 1950s, Fulke Walwyn has never looked back. He has always had a full stable of horses and one star after another has been trained at Saxon House—Madame K. Hennessy's Mandarin who, I suspect, was the biggest favourite of all, winning the first

91 The string leaving the yard at Saxon House, Lambourn.

Hennessy Gold Cup in 1957, the Cheltenham Gold Cup and the Grand Steeplechase de Paris; Taxidermist, on whom John Lawrence excelled; the giant Mill House; the Grand National winner Team Spirit; and the hurdlers Anzio, Kirriemuir and Secret Service. The chasers Charlie Potheen and The Dikler were the stars of the stable when Queen Elizabeth decided to join.

When Cazalet died, no doubt many trainers hoped that they would have the honour to train for Queen Elizabeth. When it was announced that Fulke Walwyn was to take Cazalet's place, it was felt that the appointment had gone to the man with the most consistently successful jumping stable since the end of the Second World War, and that the honour had been well and truly earned.

Nevertheless for Queen Elizabeth it was a very big change. When she went to Fairlawne, she was going to a country house which she had known since she was a girl, with its own gallops in the park and on neighbouring parts of the estate. In contrast, Saxon House, although a most attractive yard kept spick and span by Walwyn, was on the edge of Upper Lambourn with half a dozen training stables within less than a mile. The gallops a mile away up on the downs were used both by Walwyn and other Lambourn trainers. From the training point of view, the facilities at Saxon House were definitely superior to Fairlawne, but no one can train at a place like Fairlawne for a quarter of a century and not miss it greatly when the stable suddenly dies.

92 Fulke Walwyn on Lambourn Downs watching his string.

After Cazalet's death, Queen Elizabeth was not in fact to race again on the same scale. She still had sixteen horses in training at Fairlawne at the beginning of 1973. A year later, the number was down to ten and it has remained roughly at that level or slightly less ever since. Of the seven horses Walwyn received from Fairlawne, the unsound Black Magic was clearly no longer trainable and soon left the yard, Colonello soon left to join his full sister Mertensia with Jack O'Donoghue, who hoped that a spell of hunting would calm the horse, as it had done Gay Record. Game Spirit, Greystoke Pillar and the three sons of Queen Elizabeth's most successful brood-mare, Queen of the Isle, remained — Inch Arran, a nine-year-old at the start of the new 1973–74 season, the six-year-old Isle of Man and the four-year-old Colonius.

The Queen had passed on to Queen Elizabeth the five-year-old Tammuz, who had been trained at Kingsclere on the Hampshire Downs by Ian Balding to win a two-mile maiden race at York in the autumn of his three-year-old days. Balding thought Tammuz would make a useful staying handicapper as a four-year-old and so did Harry Jessop, the old Yorkshireman who looked after him and had looked after horses of the Queen's at Kingsclere since the days of Kitimat in the mid 1960s. Unfortunately, Tammuz broke down before the beginning of his four-year-old season, was pin-fired, went back to the Royal Stud at Hampton Court to recover and arrived at Saxon House a year later. By Lord Porchester's Two Thousand Guineas runner-up Tamerlane out of the

Queen's outstanding brood-mare Highlight, Tammuz was a half-brother to the Queen's One Thousand Guineas winner Highclere. With such top class breeding, Tammuz appeared to be strangely deficient in speed on the flat. He was to come into his own as a hurdler.

The men who were usually to ride Queen Elizabeth's horses in her first season at Saxon House were both Englishmen—Terry Biddlecombe from Gloucestershire, then in his final season as a jockey, and the Warwickshire-born Aly Branford from the Atherstone country, who spent the whole of his racing life attached to Walwyn's stable. Biddlecombe had been champion jockey three times in the 1960s and with his cheerful smile, determination to win, and evident enjoyment of life, was a great asset to steeplechasing in general and in particular to the stable to which he was attached. Unfortunately, he had had to waste hard throughout his time as a steeplechase jockey and had had to endure a succession of broken bones and other injuries, and had already said that the 1973–74 season was to be his final one when he went out on an October day to ride Colonius at Chepstow—Queen Elizabeth's first runner from Saxon House.

Colonius was one of a big field of four-year-old hurdlers in Chepstow's Free Handicap Hurdle. The firm going suited him but he was not quite good enough and could only finish third. At Newbury three weeks later, he was second in the Wyld Court and Tom Masson Trophy Hurdle, and that was the nearest Colonius got to winning a race in his first season at Saxon House.

Walwyn took both Colonius and Game Spirit to Cheltenham at the beginning of November, Colonius to run without distinction in a handicap hurdle, Game Spirit to make his first appearance of the season in the Mackeson Gold Cup over his best distance of two and a half miles. Game Spirit was the only horse in the field without a previous race to his name that autumn. He had ended his days at Fairlawne with a hat-trick, ridden on each occasion by Mould and he was now well up in the handicap. With Biddlecombe *hors de combat*, Walwyn engaged Mould for Game Spirit, which seemed a wise move as he knew the horse's every attribute. The two best-backed horses both came from Irish stables—the American-bred Inkslinger from Dan Moore's stable on the Curragh and Skymas trained by Brian Lusk in the north in County Antrim. Skymas had defeated Inkslinger in a handicap chase at Punchestown three weeks before, receiving fifteen pounds from Inkslinger, whilst at Cheltenham, in spite of a penalty, Skymas was receiving six pounds more from Inkslinger. Skymas, near the end of the previous season, had only just been beaten in the Irish Grand National and it looked as if the handicapper had made a mistake and taken too much of a chance with him. Such, sadly for Queen Elizabeth, proved to be the case, for though Game Spirit jumped well throughout and was with Skymas two fences from home, the weight told up the hill from the final fence and Game Spirit was beaten half a length by Skymas, giving the Irish-trained winner fifteen pounds. The honours of the race clearly went to Game Spirit, the prize to the lightly weighted Skymas.

The following week at the Ascot November meeting, two of Queen Elizabeth's novice hurdlers both appeared for the first time over hurdles in different divisions of the Bingley Hurdle—Isle of Man as a six-year-old, Tammuz as a five-year-old. Isle of Man had spent most of his early days with Brigadier Wingfield at his stud in Ireland. 'He came to me as a weaned foal from Sandringham,' recalled Wingfield, 'and he remained with me till 1972. He was fairly "down on his joints" with me and I thought that it was quite likely that he would not stand training. Luckily I was wrong.' Isle of Man went back to England, first to the Royal Stud at Hampton Court and then to Windsor Castle where the Queen and the Crown Equerry Colonel Sir John Miller both took a personal interest in him. A big, loose-framed horse, it was realised that if Isle of Man was not given plenty of time, he would go to pieces and would not stand training. After being broken by Roger Oliver, the stud groom at Windsor, and handled with sympathy and patience, he eventually went to Fairlawne early in his six-year-old days and was now appearing on the racecourse for the first time.

With Biddlecombe on the sidelines, Isle of Man was ridden by Aly Branford who had come to the fore after winning the 1968 Massey Ferguson Gold Cup on the Walwyn-trained Tassilo. Branford had come into racing indirectly through Harry Brown, the leading amateur rider after the First World War, who finished second in the 1921 Grand National on The Bore in spite of a broken collar bone. Harry Brown trained in Branford's village near Atherstone and his daughter Cynthia ran the pony club. 'Harry Brown's gallops were modelled on Ascot racecourse,' recalled Branford. 'He was a splendid chap and came to the pony club sometimes and encouraged us. I was the only one in my family who was keen on horses. I rode a lot in gymkhanas and did a little showing, and Cynthia Brown wrote to Walwyn to know if he would take me on. I was seven stone at the age of fifteen and therefore on the heavy side, but I was given a month's trial. Then I signed on for a five-year apprenticeship and at Saxon House I remained.'

Queen Elizabeth was present to see Isle of Man's first race on a cold day in mid-November. Her grand-daughter Princess Anne had been married in Westminster Abbey two days before to Captain Mark Phillips, and the Royal Family were much in the thoughts of everyone, for the wedding had been seen by millions of people on television in many parts of the world. Although Isle of Man had been showing a lot of ability at home, Branford was under strict orders not to touch him with the whip under any circumstances. He was not expected to win and surprised everyone by leading at the last flight of hurdles and only being caught in the last thirty yards by the hard-ridden Fervor from the stable of Winter. 'One smack with the whip and I would have won,' reported Branford to Queen Elizabeth. 'He has a superb action and seems to eat the ground.' Branford proceeded to win the next two races for Walwyn's stable. Isle of Man had just failed to land the first leg of what would have been a hat-trick for Saxon House.

At the end of the afternoon, Tammuz appeared in Division II of the same event. He had been working better than Isle of Man and was the more fancied. A heavy-shouldered gelding, he had had the advantage of five races on the flat, and so, unlike Isle of Man, had a greater knowledge of what was required of him. Two hurdles from home Tammuz looked the likely winner, but he made a mistake and his chance went with it. In the end he was a respectable third, and it was clear that both he and Isle of Man had the ability to win over hurdles shortly.

A week later at Newbury, Game Spirit and Inch Arran both made their second appearances of the season. Although only a nine-year-old, Inch Arran ran without sparkle and finished last of three in a two-mile handicap chase. He had had a hint of leg trouble after winning the Topham Trophy and he was never to reproduce with Walwyn the brilliance he had shown in his last season at Fairlawne.

Game Spirit, however, was all the better for his race at Cheltenham and in the Clanfield Chase of two-and-a-half miles, he had to take on again Mr H. J. Joel's Helmsman and Coolera Prince whom he had run against in the Mackeson Gold Cup. 'I reported to Queen Elizabeth before the race that Game Spirit had schooled well with me over six fences two days beforehand,' said Branford. 'I had never ridden him before and obviously I wanted a feel before the race. Coolera Prince made much of the running and then I won as I pleased. I was never off the bridle and I remember thinking that if they were all like Game Spirit that day, the job would be much more straightforward.' A racing scribe reported that 'Game Spirit had cool, relaxed handling from Branford and turned in a flawless round.' Appropriately, I think, Game Spirit was Walwyn's—and Branford's—first winner for Queen Elizabeth. It seemed right to start off with a victory of one of Her Majesty's special favourites. Biddlecombe was not to ride a winner for Queen Elizabeth until late December.

At the beginning of December Queen Elizabeth had four runners at the Lingfield December meeting which she had supported so strongly in the days of Fairlawne. Branford up, Tammuz ran disappointingly to finish third in a novice hurdle, and Greystoke Pillar, starting a hot favourite, was a moderate fifth in a handicap hurdle. 'He was not my favourite horse,' recalled Branford. 'There was always something wrong with his back and he used to flatten every hurdle.' O'Donoghue saddled at the meeting Queen Elizabeth's four-year-old home-bred filly Mertensia, but this

daughter of Colonist II had not the ability to win a race and went back to the Sandringham Stud, where she died young.

Queen Elizabeth's fourth runner was Kelso Brig, who had been sent to Richard Head, then in his early days as a racehorse trainer. After serving in the Life Guards, Head had retired from the army in 1966 and had learnt his trade as a trainer first at Fairlawne, then with Alec Head at Chantilly in France, and finally with Walwyn at Saxon House. He had then started to train on his own account at Upper Lambourn in 1968. Queen Elizabeth had thought that Kelso Brig, a rather difficult customer, might benefit from individual attention in a small string—as Gay Record had done with O'Donoghue. Her Majesty had met Head at Fairlawne, and wished to encourage his enterprise. In fact, Kelso Brig showed a clear dislike of jumping fences and was not persevered with at the end of the season.

A week before Christmas, Walwyn took Tammuz up to Warwick for his third race over hurdles, with Biddlecombe to ride him. Favourite for the race was Mr Straight, who was penalised for winning a novice hurdle at Newbury in November. 'I knew Tammuz had a lot of ability and was a brilliant jumper,' recalled Biddlecombe, relaxing in the sitting-room of his Gloucestershire home, overlooking the Welsh hills, where he spends his time making and breaking horses amongst other activities. 'I had

93 Game Spirit (A. Branford) jumps the water in the Clanfield Chase at Newbury on 23 November 1973, on his way to victory— Walwyn's first winner for Queen Elizabeth.

schooled Tammuz and I had schooled Isle of Man and I considered that Tammuz had the more class as a two-mile hurdler. They had different ways of jumping. Tammuz was very immaculate and Isle of Man rather extravagant. When he was on the bridle, Isle of Man was brilliant in the way he stood off. Once unbalanced, he was inclined to gallop straight on and lose his hind legs. Basically that year, Isle of Man was a big, weak, young horse who thoroughly enjoyed galloping.

'On Tammuz in the Warwick race, I took up the running from Mr Straight two hurdles out and I was ten lengths clear at the last. But unfortunately for me Tammuz jumped the last hurdle very casually, hit the top hard and stumbled on landing. He proceeded to do the splits, his tummy hitting the ground and I had no chance of staying on board. Instead of winning by ten lengths or more, I was on the deck and Mr Straight was left to come home alone. I must own I was rather glad the race was not on television and the Queen Mother was not watching from afar!'

At the Boxing Day meeting at Kempton, the tide turned for Biddlecombe on Isle of Man, one of a field of twenty-two in the Yule Tide Hurdle. Biddlecombe had finished second on Isle of Man in a long distance novices' hurdle at Cheltenham three weeks' before when Queen Elizabeth's hurdler clearly failed to stay the three miles. The sharp Kempton two miles suited the front-running Isle of Man much better, and he led from start to finish. Queen Elizabeth was not well and was unable to come to the Boxing Day meeting as she liked to do. Biddlecombe reported

94   Inch Arran (R. Barry), in action at Newbury, November 1973.

to Walwyn that Isle of Man hurdled superbly until he began to tire and had then hit the last two hurdles hard. Isle of Man could not put himself right over hurdles when extended, whilst Tammuz could do so, was Biddlecombe's opinion.

Ten days later at Sandown, in yielding going, Biddlecombe brought off his only double for Queen Elizabeth, winning novice hurdles on Tammuz and Isle of Man, Tammuz recording a time nearly a second faster. 'Tammuz hurdled brilliantly,' reported Biddlecombe. 'I held him up, we led approaching the last, and I won on the bridle.' Tammuz was sound after the race but he had a leg again soon afterwards. As he had already been fired, it was decided that the only thing to do was to try the split tendon operation which was uncommon at the time. Walwyn's vet, 'Spike' Kirby, did Tammuz and results were to show that the operation was a great success. He was not to run again till nearly a year later.

Isle of Man was much harder pressed in winning his Sandown race after being badly hampered when a horse ran out after jumping the second flight of hurdles. 'I had to push him hard in a driving finish,' reported Biddlecombe. 'He was a horse who did not win on the bridle. Being a long-striding horse, he had to be kept balanced.' Isle of Man won in fact by two-and-a-half lengths from a useful novice in Sasha, owned by Mr D. W. Cherry, a strong supporter of Sandringham's local meeting, Fakenham.

Isle of Man was to complete a novice hurdle hat-trick for Queen

95   Isle of Man (T. Biddlecombe), hard-driven, on his way to victory in his division of the Metropolitan Hurdle at Sandown on 4 January 1974.

Elizabeth. The third leg was at Sandown at the beginning of February when he battled on really well to get the better of Single Spur—Biddlecombe on Isle of Man, Biddlecombe's brother-in-law Bob Davies on Single Spur. Isle of Man's winning run ended in the Sun Alliance Novices' Hurdle at the National Hunt meeting at Cheltenham. The race was over two and a half miles and he did not get the trip in soft ground. He clearly showed that he was better at two miles, but he had been first or second in five of his six races—a highly successful first season.

Nevertheless, Game Spirit, in spite of the doings of Isle of Man and Tammuz, remained Queen Elizabeth's star performer. Through injury, Biddlecombe had missed riding Game Spirit in his first two races of the season. He was not to do so again. At Newbury at the Old Year meeting in the Weyhill Handicap Chase he gave a beating of more than a stone to two useful handicap chasers in Soloning, trained by Winter, and Potentate from Gifford's stable. Soloning, a small horse, could not carry a lot of weight but on the right handicap mark he took a lot of beating. Potentate was to win his next race at Sandown, thus showing Game Spirit in a good light.

Three weeks later, in the Royal Windsor Handicap Chase, Game Spirit was asked to tackle three miles in yielding going and failed to give nearly two stone to a useful staying mare Credo's Daughter, ridden by Charlie Goldsworthy, a Welshman attached to Jack O'Donoghue's stable. It was not much of a gallop and Game Spirit jumped rather deliberately in the yielding going and the weight began to tell approaching the second last. In the Wincanton Challenge Cup at the end of January, Game Spirit's solitary opponent was a virtual novice called Crystal Gazer. It was long odds on Game Spirit winning in a canter, but the race was run on the heavy ground he disliked and Biddlecombe reported ruefully, 'His jumping was absolutely awful, up and down on the loose ground he hated. He won easily enough in the end, but he was certainly not at his best.'

Game Spirit had now won three of his last four races. He returned to Windsor towards the end of February to run appropriately in the Fairlawne Chase over three miles, a condition race in which he met Credo's Daughter on two stone better terms than in January. He had no difficulty in turning the tables. 'On the better ground, he jumped like a bird and made all,' reported Biddlecombe. Game Spirit on the form he was showing clearly had to take his chance in the Cheltenham Gold Cup in which Walwyn had three intended runners—Game Spirit, The Dikler, winner of the 1973 Cheltenham Gold Cup, and Charlie Potheen, a great front runner. The Dikler was usually ridden by Ron Barry. Biddlecombe had to decide whether to ride the brilliant but erratic Charlie Potheen or the more reliable Game Spirit. Granted good or fast ground Biddlecombe was inclined to favour Game Spirit.

The field for the Cheltenham Gold Cup of 1974 numbered seven with

96   Game Spirit (T. Biddlecombe) and French Colonist (C. Read)
in the Royal Windsor Chase
on 19 January 1974.

97 Game Spirit (T. Biddlecombe) in the Cheltenham Gold Cup, 14 March 1974.

Pendil, who had been much too good for The Dikler three months before in the King George VI Chase at Kempton, an odds-on favourite. Although the going was soft and against the prospects of Game Spirit, Biddlecombe chose to ride Queen Elizabeth's chaser. It was Biddlecombe's very last day as a steeplechase jockey after eighteen years of race-riding and over nine hundred winners to his credit. As a Gloucestershire man, Cheltenham was his home course. Biddlecombe has told how he and his brother Tony used to go racing together at Cheltenham as young boys, jumping in over a fence on to the course. The two brothers would position themselves near a fence a long way from the stands. The Blond Bombshell, Terry Biddlecombe's descriptive nickname, had won the Cheltenham Gold Cup of 1967 on Woodland Venture—the race which gave him the most pleasure amongst all his victories. Everyone hoped that he would go out in a blaze of glory on Queen Elizabeth's Game Spirit. Terry Biddlecombe had a tremendous will to win. If Game Spirit was good enough, his rider was dead game, too. Biddlecombe had survived a long series of injuries and now he was being forced to call it a day. Apart from Pendil and the Walwyn trio, there were also in the Gold Cup field the Irish-trained pair, Captain Christy and Inkslinger and the rank outsider High Ken, who had no apparent chance on form but whose presence in the field was to have an important bearing on the outcome of the race.

'On good ground, Game Spirit could be brilliant,' recalled Biddlecombe. 'He was one of the best jumpers I rode. He used to love to stand off. On false ground, however, if he made a mistake he would be deliberate, balloon the fence and take his time. Though I really wanted faster ground for Game Spirit, I thought I would take a lot of beating in the Gold Cup. Charlie Potheen, ridden by Bill Smith, made the running throughout the first circuit. I was on the inner—normally the only place to be going round Cheltenham—going extremely well in close company with Inkslinger, Pendil and High Ken, with The Dikler and Captain Christy the back markers. Inkslinger fell towards the end of the first circuit and Charlie Potheen still led going away from the stands for the second time. At the bottom end of the course High Ken took over from Charlie Potheen, and Pendil and I moved up. I was going just as well as Pendil when High Ken fell three fences from home bringing down Pendil and nearly bringing me down too. Game Spirit had been jumping brilliantly and I was cruising going down the hill, when he suddenly weakened and died in my hands. At the time I thought it was lack of stamina and that he did not get more than two and a half miles but, with hindsight, I think it must have been his heart or his lungs. Captain Christy and The Dikler now went away from me with the race between them, Captain Christy winning. Game Spirit was absolutely exhausted when he jumped the last fence, and I was easy on him when all chance of winning had gone. I was third and Charlie Potheen, the only other to finish, was fourth. It was nice to finish third for the Queen Mother in my last race in her colours, but of course I longed, like Old Harry, to win.' Sadly the fairytale ending to a great riding career did not happen.

At the end of Cheltenham week, Colonello appeared for the first time over fences at Lingfield. Walwyn had reported to Queen Elizabeth soon after Colonello had arrived at Saxon House that he was very wild—that during his first school, he had finished up in a hedge at the end of the paddock. He doubted if he was worth persevering with. Remembering Gay Record, Colonello had then been sent, at Queen Elizabeth's suggestion, to O'Donoghue at Reigate. 'Colonello was very excitable when he arrived,' recalled Jack O'Donoghue. 'He was liable to go haywire and gallop through jumps so we started hunting him with the Surrey Union, as we had done Gay Record. Squadron Leader Nigel Carter used to come and ride out with me and he took Colonello hunting. The first few times he nearly went mad, but he then started to settle down and we were able to run him for the first time at Lingfield in the middle of March in the Shaun Spadah Chase over two miles. Ridden by Charlie Goldsworthy, he ran really well, took up the running on the far side of the course, led at the last and was only caught and beaten by a neck on the post.'

Not only has Queen Elizabeth always liked to support the Grand Military meeting at Sandown at the beginning of March, but she has also supported the Royal Artillery meeting at Sandown at the end of March and has always liked to have a runner at this meeting. O'Donoghue produced Queen Elizabeth's Colonist II mare Colonia of Eldred

98 Colonello (C. Goldsworthy) winning the Novices' Chase at the Royal Artillery meeting at Sandown on 26 March 1974.

Wilson's breeding on three occasions to try to win the Novices' Chase at the Royal Artillery meeting. Nicholson was second on Colonia once in this race and Mellor was third but she was an unlucky mare and went back to stud at Sandringham without winning a race. Where Colonia had failed, however, Colonello was to succeed. His second race over fences was in this same event at Sandown. He had strong opposition from Lord Vestey's well-bred Battle Hymn and two other recent winners, but Goldsworthy was able to get Colonello to settle and come from behind to get the better of Battle Hymn. It looked as if O'Donoghue's skill with a really difficult horse was going to pay big dividends.

A fortnight later, O'Donoghue took Colonello down to Wye to carry a penalty in another novices' chase. Colonello was in the lead, going well, when he overjumped at the first fence in the home straight and the horse behind struck into him and brought him down. Colonello punctured a lung and broke three ribs, amongst other injuries. There was no alternative but to put him down. Following O'Donoghue's hard work to get Colonello to mend his ways, this was a cruel blow both to his owner and to his trainer and in fact to all at his trainer's stable at Reigate.

Later in the week, Walwyn took Queen Elizabeth's Greystoke Pillar to Ludlow to run in a novices' chase for the first time. Walwyn believed in very thorough schooling of a novice before letting him run over fences in public. Branford always schooled Greystoke Pillar and always did so on his own. Greystoke Pillar liked the top of the ground, jumped well at Ludlow and won with something to spare. A week later at Cheltenham, he was beaten into second place, but finished the season by winning his second novice chase at Fontwell. Queen Elizabeth had two other April winners—Inch Arran at Cheltenham and Earl's Castle in the north.

With the retirement of Biddlecombe, Walwyn needed a successor and chose Bill Smith, a Hampshire Hog by adoption, who had made his home near the cricket ground on which the men of Hambledon used to play the rest of England and repair afterwards to The Bat and Ball for liquid refreshment. After winning point-to-points both at the Hambledon and the H.H. (Hampshire Hunt) meetings, Smith had ridden his first winner under National Hunt rules in 1968, and had turned professional the following year. He had come to the fore after winning a succession of big races on the Champion Hurdler Comedy of Errors and two National Hunt Two-Mile Champion Chases on Edward Courage's Royal Relief.

Bill Smith's first ride for Queen Elizabeth had been on the grey mare Colonia, but he had yet to ride a royal winner when he joined Walwyn. It came sooner than expected when he won the Gratwicke Blagrave Memorial Challenge Cup at the Cheltenham April meeting on Inch Arran who, throughout the season, had looked a light of other days. Inch Arran after making the running had been passed by the mare Eyecatcher and by Henry Morgan from 'Frenchie' Nicholson's Prestbury stable only a mile from the stands. The race then seemed to lie between these two but Eyecatcher fell three fences from home, leaving Henry Morgan out clear on his own. He then proceeded to fall at the last fence, leaving Inch Arran in turn on his own, to come home a totally unexpected winner. It was clearly time to retire Inch Arran and Queen Elizabeth lent him to a friend to go hunting, much to the enjoyment of both Inch Arran and the recipient of Queen Elizabeth's kindly thought.

Queen Elizabeth's first winner after the demise of the Fairlawne stable had been in the north and the fourteenth and last winner in the 1973–74 season was also in the north. When Cazalet died, Queen Elizabeth decided to have another horse in training in Scotland and had sent the four-year-old Earl's Castle to be trained by Kenneth and Rhona Oliver just north of the Border at Hassendean Bank near Hawick. Kenneth Oliver—'The Benigh Bishop' to many friends—had been a good amateur rider and had won the 1950 Scottish Grand National on his own mare Sanvina, but he has also been a leading auctioneer in the north for a long time and it is his wife Rhona who is responsible for the day-to-day running of the Oliver stable, with help and advice from her husband in the limited time he is able to give to it amongst many activities.

Rhona Oliver, a 'natural' with animals, as someone has put it, is the daughter of Major P. C. E. Wilkinson, a Royal Scots Fusilier, who was farming at Whitehaugh near Hawick in the late 1930s. In 1943 he bought for 22 guineas an unbroken seven-year-old mare called Swinnie at Hawick Auction Mart. In due course, Swinnie produced a foal called Wyndburgh who was hunted and point-to-pointed by Rhona Wilkinson before she trained Wyndburgh—her father holding the permit—not only to run second in the 1957 Grand National but also to win the Grand Sefton in the following autumn and other races. When Kenneth Oliver and Rhona Wilkinson married in 1958, they started a public stable a year or so later at Hassendean Bank, from where Wyndburgh was to finish second in two more Grand Nationals.

When Earl's Castle arrived at the Olivers' stable, Wyndburgh was still holding court. Earl's Castle had been found in Cumberland by Jim Fairgrieve, now settled near Kelso within easy distance of the Olivers. Queen Elizabeth's young horse was out of a mare called Castle Inn, bred by a leading Cumbrian farmer Mr R. N. Tinniswood, who had owned a brilliant National Hunt performer in Cockbridge of his own breeding in the 1950s. Tinniswood sold Castle Inn to another Cumbrian, Mr Robert Johnston of Sandwich, near Penrith, who, as a permit holder, trained Castle Inn to win over hurdles. He then mated her with the premium stallion Rubor, Earl's Castle being the result.

The Olivers produced Earl's Castle to win a novices' hurdle first time out at the 1973 Ayr October meeting, ridden by Ron Barry, but he did not win again till the following April, when he just got home in a novices' chase at Hexham, Ron Barry's strong finish just turning the scale. Earl's Castle had a very hard race that day and it appeared to leave its mark for in the following season he did not race with zest, won one minor steeplechase at Sedgefield in November and was sold at the end of the season. Of Queen Elizabeth's successes in the 1973–74 season two were trained by the Olivers in Scotland, one by O'Donoghue in Surrey and the remainder by Walwyn at Lambourn.

Peter Cazalet's death and the end of Fairlawne had been a great blow to Queen Elizabeth, and racing was not going to be quite the same for her for a long time, but Walwyn's expertise and the successes of O'Donoghue with Colonello, and the Olivers with Earl's Castle, had made the transition much easier than it might have been. Also, as Lambourn was only just off the motorway, Saxon House was as easy to reach from London or from Windsor as Fairlawne, so if Queen Elizabeth wanted to see her horses at Saxon House she could easily do so. She soon knew she would be assured of a warm welcome not only from Fulke Walwyn and his wife Cath but from the whole of their staff. Stablemen like to have racing enthusiasts around them. It makes all the difference when one knows one's work in good weather and in bad is fully appreciated.

14

Sandringham To The Fore

QUEEN ELIZABETH started the new season of 1974–75 with ten horses in training with Walwyn and Earl's Castle still with the Olivers. The five newcomers to Saxon House were the home-bred Colman, a full-brother to the ill-fated Colonello, Present Arms, Sandringham-bred, who had broken down whilst in training with Major R. Hern at West Ilsley, Sunyboy a stayer of note who had been bought from Lady Beaverbrook after being trained by Dick Hern to run second in the Irish St Leger, and Drumhead and Just Lit, two young horses who had broken down whilst in training at Fairlawne and were now sound again. With one exception, the eleven horses Queen Elizabeth had in training were to win during the season—a very remarkable percentage for any racing owner with more than half a dozen horses in training.

Walwyn had discovered that the home-bred Colonius was a far better horse on firm going than when there was any give in the ground, so he brought him out early at Warwick in September and, Bill Smith up, he made every yard of the running to win a novices' chase after hitting the first fence hard. The going was soft by the time he appeared again, so Walwyn put him by till the spring and it was May before he next ran.

Colman was a bright chestnut with a big white blaze and four white socks and jumped like a stag, but he was not much bigger than a circus pony and looked too small to make a chaser. Walwyn had him out early at Fontwell in August before the horses with more scope appeared on the scene and he was close up fourth in a novice hurdle; he was third at Hereford in September and won at Towcester in October—Bill Smith's third winner for Queen Elizabeth. Colman went on running over hurdles for two more seasons but, disappointingly, he did not win again and eventually went to Princess Anne as a possible event horse.

Game Spirit had not been on the racecourse since his third in the 1974 Cheltenham Gold Cup. After a seven months' absence, he reappeared at the mixed meeting at Newbury at the end of October to take on the brilliant Pendil over two-and-a-half miles in the Hermitage Chase. Game Spirit was a horse who always used to run well first time out. He was better when he was fresh, running on good ground and he was at his best on a flat left-handed course like Newbury. By the conditions of the

Hermitage Chase, Game Spirit was only due to receive four pounds from Pendil, who started at long odds-on in a field of four. Smith was *hors de combat* and Branford rode Game Spirit. He had won on Queen Elizabeth's horse at Newbury a year before and Game Spirit went well for him. 'My orders,' recalled Branford, 'were to be there or thereabouts but not to make running if I could help it, as we considered Pendil was a better horse if held up for a late run. In fact, Richard Pitman on Pendil decided to make the running, and in the last mile the race was virtually a match between the two of us. Pendil produced an almighty leap at the downhill fence at the bottom end of the course, and at the first fence in the home straight with four to go he was two or three lengths clear of me. I remember thinking: Is Pendil going to go right away from me and win as he pleases? Then, after jumping the open ditch three from home, Pendil started to come back to me, and we jumped the last together. Pendil, I think, jumped it just the better. We may have ballooned it slightly but it was ding-dong up the run-in. It was a very exciting race to ride in and the thought of perhaps beating Pendil gave me a helluva thrill. I was under strict orders not to touch Game Spirit and it is possible that this may have cost me the race. I do not know. Pendil beat me by half a length.'

As with the duel between Black Magic and Crisp at Sandown, the duel between Pendil and Game Spirit at Newbury was a marvellous race to watch. Although Branford lost on Game Spirit, I thought that he rode like a man inspired and gave nothing away.

A week later at Sandown, Queen Elizabeth was present to see her three runners perform on the opening day of the November meeting—Isle of Man running in a novices' chase for the first time and the novice hurdlers, the northern-bred Drumhead and the Sandringham-bred Present Arms, running in the two divisions of the Waterloo Hurdle. Drumhead had been discovered in Cumberland by Jim Fairgrieve, at the same time as Earl's Castle, at Robert Johnston's attractive home near Penrith. Drumhead was by Drumbeg out of a mare called Kergore, closely related to the 1962 Irish Grand National winner Kerforo, an outstanding chasing mare. Drumbeg was a useful handicapper by Dumbarnie who had won half a dozen races in the north. Drumhead had two runs with Cazalet early in 1973 but then had leg trouble and went to the Royal Stud at Hampton Court. He had a split tendon operation and a year off before going to Saxon House. A thick-set horse, Drumhead looked a chaser in the making with plenty of scope and had been working well prior to running at Sandown. He looked a possible winner two flights from home in his division of the Waterloo Hurdle, but weakened suddenly going to the last flight and shortly afterwards broke down on both forelegs. His racing was at an end.

Branford won the two-mile handicap chase which followed Drumhead's race on the Walwyn-trained Black Andrew and an hour later appeared on Isle of Man in the November Novices' Chase over the same distance. 'Isle of Man jumped brilliantly,' reported Branford, 'though inclined to jump slightly to his left. Gay Kindersley's promising seven-year-old Thurday Christian kept with me for a bit, but Isle of Man did not make one mistake. It was an absolute dream ride. The only thing I was frightened of was that he would overjump, but he didn't.' Walwyn was full of praise after the race. 'He is the best novice I have schooled since the Cheltenham Gold Cup winner Mill House,' said he with emphasis. 'He is a very exciting horse, and has always been a fantastic jumper at home.' For a man with such exceptional knowledge of high class chasers, that was praise indeed.

At the end of the day, Branford completed a double for Queen Elizabeth and a treble for Walwyn by winning Division II of the Waterloo Hurdle on Present Arms, a liver chestnut by the Derby Winner Relko out of the Queen's good mare Amicable, herself winner of the Lingfield Oaks Trial and dam of three top class fillies in Amphora, Example and Expansive. If Present Arms had been a good-legged horse, it is probable that he would have won the Gold Vase at Ascot for the Queen as a four-year-old, for which he was being trained by Hern. He broke down beforehand, was fired and came to Saxon House a year later. 'He felt like a real racehorse with the right temperament,' reported Branford. 'He hurdled brilliantly. His only fault was that he was a bit too keen. I was cantering at the second last. He started to tire up the hill in the long run-in but he still won well from the Cheltenham winner Mister Fantasy, ridden by the American George Sloan.'

A week later, Game Spirit, none the worse for his gallant failure against Pendil, went to Cheltenham to make his second attempt to win the Mackeson Gold Cup. He was now at the top of the handicap, sharing top weight with the American horse Soothsayer. The going, however, was yielding and all against Game Spirit, who had shot his bolt two fences from home. Bill Smith after fracturing a shoulder and cracking a pelvis in a fall the previous month was only just fit enough to ride Game Spirit at Cheltenham.

At Ascot a week later, Smith brought off his first double for Queen Elizabeth. The day started badly, for Present Arms, starting an odds-on favourite in Division I of the Bingley Novices' Hurdle was pocketed between two horses going to the second last flight of hurdles, had nowhere to land and was brought down. He was going well and would probably have won, though he was carrying a ten pounds' penalty in soft going.

In the Hurst Park Novices' Chase which followed, Isle of Man frightened away most of the opposition after his spectacular display at Sandown and only Lord Howard de Walden's home-bred Calzado, already the winner of two novice chases, was fancied against him—and Calzado could not really extend Isle of Man, who led throughout. At the

99 Game Spirit (W. Smith) going out to run in the Mackeson Gold Cup at Cheltenham on 9 November 1974.

end of the afternoon, the Mourne horse Sunyboy, a half-brother to the Gimcrack Stakes winner Double Jump, appeared for the second time over hurdles. Well suited by the testing conditions, he came right away from the opposition to win impressively. The following day, the Ascot course was waterlogged and racing was impossible—a pointer to the fact that the ground was testing when Isle of Man and Sunyboy landed Queen Elizabeth's second double of the season.

After winning so easily at Ascot, Walwyn took Sunyboy up to Wolverhampton to take part in the second running of the Reynoldstown Pattern Hurdle, named after the great chaser on which Walwyn had won the Grand National. The distance of the race was two-and-a-half miles which was clearly in favour of Sunyboy's proven stamina, and he started an odds-on favourite, but he did not have much in hand over the subsequent Ascot winner Moonstone Lad. The form suggested that he would not be in the top class as a two-mile hurdler but might well take a lot of beating in long-distance hurdles. Stamina was definitely his strong suit as Hern had discovered on the flat. Sunyboy's Wolverhampton victory was his owner's 280th winner.

In the next six weeks, Queen Elizabeth had mixed luck with her racing. Greystoke Pillar, having run well in two chases in September and October, went to Ludlow at the end of November to take on one solitary opponent, Some Surprise, to whom he was giving two stone in a two-mile handicap chase. At the second fence, Some Surprise fell and brought down Greystoke Pillar. Some Surprise's jockey caught his mount,

Branford on Greystoke Pillar, to his intense mortification, failed to do so and Some Surprise eventually finished the course alone. Not until he went back to hurdling did Greystoke Pillar manage to win a race, and Queen Elizabeth disposed of him at the end of the season.

In the middle of December, Walwyn managed to win a novice chase with the moderate Just Lit, and a week later at the Boxing Day meeting at Kempton, Present Arms and Tammuz, both, sadly, bad-legged horses, appeared for Queen Elizabeth over hurdles. Present Arms unfortunately broke down again in his novice hurdle and never recovered his form. Tammuz, Bill Smith up, having been nearly a year on the sidelines, was an impressive winner of the Boxing Day Handicap Hurdle, proving much too good for Winter's High Hat horse Bladon, who was to run up a series of hurdling victories later in the season. Tammuz, in fact, was making his second appearance since his lay-off. Smith had ridden him for the first time in public in a handicap hurdle at Sandown a month before in yielding going which did not suit him. 'Tammuz wanted good ground,' recalled Bill Smith. 'He was a good jumper but he was inclined to cock his ears and to be too nonchalant when in front and, as an indirect result, he was apt to flatten his hurdles. You had to hold him up and arrive at the right time. At Sandown, he was going very well two furlongs out but, when I went to pick him up, nothing much happened, and I realised that in future I must start my run earlier.

'At Kempton on Boxing Day, he came round the bend into the straight in the lead with his ears cocked, doing nothing. I realised that I had come too soon and he proceeded to hit the last two hurdles hard, but in spite of that I won in a canter. Then we started thinking seriously about the Schweppes Trophy at Newbury at the beginning of February.' The Schweppes Gold Trophy had been run over two miles for the first time in 1963 as the most valuable handicap hurdle of the National Hunt season and four of the first five runnings had been won by hurdlers saddled by Ryan Price. It was one of the few valuable races of the jumping season Walwyn had not yet won and he had entered several horses in different ownership for the 1975 running of the race, including Tammuz. The race was to be run at Newbury on February 8, six weeks after Boxing Day, and Walwyn advised Queen Elizabeth that Tammuz would need another race beforehand so it was agreed to take him to Wincanton in mid-January to carry a four pounds' penalty in the Jamboree Handicap Hurdle.

Tammuz won his race at Wincanton but he was not nearly so impressive as he had been at Kempton. Smith had to ride him hard to get into a challenging position two hurdles from home and, though he sprinted away after jumping the last hurdle, the stable lost confidence in his Schweppes prospects. Walwyn, however, decided to continue with his plans and he had four runners in the Newbury race—Tammuz, ridden by Smith, the course winner Ghost Writer, ridden by Branford, Zellamann, ridden by K. Stone and Pitpan, ridden by S. Jobar. There was a field nearly thirty strong, headed by Lord Howard de Walden's Lanzarote, who had won the Champion Hurdle the previous year. Lanzarote started favourite, Ryan Price's Maddenstown and Turnell's Bird's Nest were joint second favourites, whilst Tammuz was an 18-1 outsider.

Let Bill Smith, relaxing in his Hampshire home, tell the story of the race. 'I walked the course the evening before the race and decided that the best ground in the straight was up the stand rails. There was a soft patch near the water jump, and we made up our minds to come up the stands' side. Before the start, two horses charged the tapes and got rid of their riders. We all got off and walked round and some horses got very "gee-ed up" as a result of the delay before the start. Happily, Tammuz was totally relaxed, as he always was at home. When the race started, the leaders set a furious gallop, Tammuz for the first time having to extend himself to the full to keep in the race. There were several fallers at the second flight of hurdles including the well-fancied Bird's Nest. Coming into the straight, Tammuz was back on the bridle again and, as planned, I came wide round the final bend over to the stand rails. I improved my position steadily in the straight and jumping the second last, I was moving up to the leaders who included Roaring Wind, Legal Tender and Tip The Wink.

'I went to the front between the last two hurdles. We flattened the last, as Tammuz was apt to do when out in front, but got away with it. In the run-in, I always felt I was just holding the challenge of Legal Tender, who came again. I had to give Tammuz a couple of smacks with the whip but he was very genuine and pulled out a bit more.' Queen Elizabeth's horse won officially by half a length from Legal Tender with the light weight Primerello third and Tip The Wink fourth. The first eight horses finished within eight lengths of Tammuz which gives a good idea of the excitement of the race.

As Tammuz was led in, someone called for three cheers for Queen Elizabeth. I cannot definitely remember another racing occasion on which this has happened in Britain, although I think Sir Winston Churchill may have once been similarly honoured, but it did happen at Newbury that February day before an immense crowd, who were clearly full of joy that Her Majesty should have won. Walwyn, used to training big winners, said simply, 'I have never had a bigger thrill in my training life than winning the Schweppes for Queen Elizabeth.'

The victory of Tammuz was certainly a training triumph for Walwyn. As Bill Smith put it: 'Though Tammuz is a tough horse and enjoys jumping, it was a miracle that the guv'nor got him on the racecourse fit to win this very competitive race. He had been fired and split-tendoned, but the guv'nor is very clever with horses' legs. He takes such terrific care and shows one hundred per cent consideration for his horses.'

After most of the big winners at Saxon House, Walwyn likes to give a

OPPOSITE PAGE:

100   Tammuz (W. Smith) flattens the final flight on his way to winning Newbury's Schweppes Gold Trophy Hurdle on 8 February 1975. Legal Tender (R. G. Hughes), half-hidden by Tammuz, was second.

101   BOTTOM: Queen Elizabeth receiving the trophy from Mrs Donald Methven, wife of the deputy chairman of Cadbury Schweppes.

party for his staff and their wives at the near-by Malt Shovel Inn. 'We had a great party after the victory of Tammuz,' said Henry Forrester, now head lad to Walwyn, with a quarter of a century of service behind him. 'All the staff and their wives came and we had drinks, snacks, music and a sing song—a tremendous evening, and we very much appreciated the Queen Mother's thought in sending us signed photographs of Tammuz to remind us of the great day.'

Three weeks later, on 1 March 1975, at the next Newbury meeting, Game Spirit was back on his favourite course, trying to carry top weight in the Geoffrey Gilbey Memorial Chase, named after a racing journalist who wrote with verve for many years. Since finishing fourth in the Mackeson Gold Cup, Game Spirit had twice run disappointingly. In a handicap at Ascot in December, he had been pulled up after laming himself, and then a month later at Wincanton he had jumped without confidence in a match against the American, Soothsayer. Game Spirit had shown his dislike of Wincanton a year before and no doubt he remembered.

Favourite for the Geoffrey Gilbey Chase was Even Up, running in the colours of Mr Noel Whitcombe, founder and president of the *Daily Mirror* Punters' Club, whose members took a keen interest in Even Up's fortunes. On this occasion Even Up, a good steeplechaser, blundered at the third fence and got rid of his rider. This eased the path of Game Spirit, who gained his first success of the season from King Kong, owned by Mrs B. Moresby and formerly trained at Fairlawne, but now in the stable of Richard Head.

'I remember the race well,' said Bill Smith. 'John Francome had ridden the first two winners and was hoping to complete a hat-trick on King Kong, who led two fences from home. Game Spirit always led with his near fore and had a tendency to jump to his left. Newbury really suited him. I remember David Mould saying to me, "You will love Game Spirit at Newbury. He will start happy and relaxed and if you give him a pat in the race, you will get the same response as showing the whip to another horse". When I asked Game Spirit to win his race going to the last, he changed gear, went by King Kong without ado and cantered in.'

After the race, Walwyn announced that Game Spirit would next go for the Cheltenham Piper Champagne Gold Cup and that Queen Elizabeth would have two other runners at the National Hunt meeting—Isle of Man in the Arkle Challenge Trophy Chase of two miles and Sunyboy in the Sun Alliance Novices Hurdle of two-and-a-half miles. There was torrential rain, however, at the beginning of Cheltenham week and no racing was possible on the Tuesday—normally the first day of the National Hunt meeting. Eight races were run on the Wednesday and only five races on the Thursday—normally the third and last day. As the going was very heavy on Gold Cup day, it was decided not to start Game Spirit, as he

would have had little chance in such conditions.

    Isle of Man, however, was started in the Arkle Challenge Trophy. Following his spectacular victories over two miles in his first two novice chases at Sandown and at Ascot in November, Isle of Man had been started in the two-and-a-half mile Hopeful Chase run at Newbury towards the end of November 1974 but had been all out to defeat the six-year-old Pengrail and had been nowhere near so impressive. Queen Elizabeth's chaser seemed to be lacking in stamina and this was confirmed on New Year's Day at Cheltenham when Isle of Man was outstayed and beaten at level weights by Tamalin in the Worthington E Novices' Chase over two-and-a-half miles. The race was run in soft going and Tamalin, rated at the time the best novice chaser in the north, definitely stayed on the better up the Cheltenham hill.

    Walwyn had given Isle of Man a ten weeks' rest from racing before the Arkle Trophy. 'He was absolutely at his best that day,' recalled Bill Smith. 'There were four front runners in the field and after the second fence, Isle of Man took up the running and was soon hacking in front, well clear. He already jumped like a seasoned handicapper and I felt at the time that he was the best novice that I had ever ridden. It was desperate ground that day and two fences after the water he stood off a trifle too far, his hind legs slipped from under him and that was that. I cannot say that he would have

102   Isle of Man (W. Smith) leading Henry Tuffnut (R. Champion) in the Arkle Challenge Trophy at Cheltenham on 12 March 1975.

won under such conditions but he was going like a winner at the time, and he wanted soft ground.'

The following day, Sunyboy was one of a field of twenty for the Sun Alliance Novices' Hurdle in very heavy ground. Sunyboy had twice been beaten in two-mile hurdles since his success in the Reynoldstown Pattern Hurdle and it seemed certain that two-and-a-half miles in heavy ground up the Cheltenham hill would give his stamina a real chance. Smith set out to make the best use of his stamina and kicked for home at the top of the hill, taking up the running. Sunyboy kept galloping on at the same pace, was about fifth jumping the last hurdle but fought back in the long run-in and finally finished second to the Irish-trained Davy Lad, who won by three lengths. 'Sunyboy was one hundred per cent genuine,' said Smith. 'He used to finish exhausted because he used to try so hard. He had to have soft ground and a trip.'

When April came, the going was still soft and on Easter Tuesday, Queen Elizabeth made her first visit to Chepstow to see her Schweppes winner Tammuz appear in the Welsh Champion Hurdle and Sunyboy in the Raglan Novices Hurdle of two-and-a-half miles. Sunyboy was fully equal to giving weight and a beating to all his opponents. Tammuz had to take on Lanzarote at level weights instead of receiving twenty pounds from him as in the Schweppes, and the seven-year-old also had to meet Tree Tangle and Mr Straight, who had been third and fourth in the Champion Hurdle the previous month behind the winner Comedy of Errors. Tammuz was too good for Tree Tangle and Mr Straight but Lanzarote beat him. Two hurdles from home there was not much between the two and Walwyn thought that they were going equally well but Tammuz's near fore went again at the second last.

It was decided to try a tendon transplant operation on Tammuz as a last resort. He had nearly two years off but he never again came back to form. The operation was not really a success. With a horse in the top class, however, it was well worth persevering for a long time.

At Ascot ten days later in the second week of April, Game Spirit, having missed Cheltenham because of the desperate ground, reappeared as a fresh horse in the Sardan Handicap Chase over his right distance of two-and-a-half miles. Also in the field were the gallant Crisp, now a twelve-year-old and past his prime after breaking down, and Bruslee, who had beaten Game Spirit and others in the Mackeson Gold Cup in the autumn. These two Game Spirit met at level weights, but he had to give six pounds to Mr H. J. Joel's Summerville, who had just beaten Bula in the Welsh Champion Chase and had previously won the Mildmay of Flete Challenge Cup at Cheltenham. Crisp was still equal to making much of the running but he was feeling his years and Game Spirit, though ill-suited by the yielding going and a right-handed course, was still equal to giving weight and a beating to the favourite Summerville. As at Newbury in his

previous race six weeks before, he jumped exceptionally well. During the day, Smith also won another long-distance novice hurdle on Sunyboy to land another double for Queen Elizabeth.

Not until May was there firm going that spring. Then Colonius reappeared after a seven months' absence from the course. Walwyn started him in a novices' chase at Worcester as well as his stable companion Menehall, who had just won a novices' chase at Warwick. Smith chose to ride Menehall, who started a hot favourite and Branford was on the front-running impetuous Colonius, who was no ride for a timid soul. Both Smith and Branford were to have crashing falls on Colonius but fortunately not on this occasion. 'Colonius was pig-ignorant,' recalled Branford. 'If you got over the first three fences, you could almost guarantee that you would get round. What you had to try to do was to run the steam out of him early on. He wanted no work at home. We used to train him mostly on the roads. When trying to school him, he was apt to get out of control! Although he gave me some bad falls, I think I got the hang of him in the end.'

On this Worcester occasion on the ground he liked, Colonius led to three fences out, was then collared and ran on well to hold the challenge of Smith and Menehall by a head. A week later at Stratford-on-Avon in another novice chase Colonius, Branford up, made every yard of the running to win his third race of the season. Seeking a spring hat-trick at

103 The head-strong Colonius (A. Branford), the winner, leading Scatterbrain (D. Sunderland) in the Bewdley Chase at Worcester on 10 May 1975.

Stratford-on-Avon a fortnight later, Colonius was too impetuous. Branford had a crashing fall and broke some bones. Walwyn then felt Colonius had done enough for the time being. He had been Queen Elizabeth's first winner of the season in the second half of September and her twentieth and last winner eight months later in the middle of May. Her Majesty was approaching her 300th winner.

As the start of the new National Hunt season of 1975–76 approached, the Queen was preparing for Queen Elizabeth's seventy-fifth birthday on August 4. 'Queen Elizabeth has almost become a symbol of all that Britain wants to stand for, something safe, sane, stable and as everlasting as the Tower of London,' wrote one of her admirers. Five days after Her Majesty's birthday, Colonius appeared for the first time in the new season at Worcester and did not cover himself with glory, but whilst the firm going lasted during the autumn he won a couple of races at Fontwell.

Jim Fairgrieve had found a promising young horse in Lauderdale called Burning Bush, who went into training with the Olivers. Burning Bush won a novices' hurdle at Ayr in December, ridden by the Yorkshireman Colin Tinkler who, for the first time had finished high in the jockeys' table in the previous season. Unfortunately, Burning Bush broke down badly towards the end of the season when it looked as if he might do well in

104   Colonius (A. Branford) somehow survived this ghastly mistake at the open ditch at Worcester on 9 August 1975, and completed the course finishing fourth to Osbaldeston.

novice chases. Burning Bush's success at Ayr in December was Queen Elizabeth's 298th winner. Queen Elizabeth had not been able to see either Earl's Castle or Burning Bush in action on the course and felt in future that her horses should be trained near London, and not in faraway Scotland. At Newbury in February, Game Spirit on his favourite course brought Queen Elizabeth's score to 299, carrying top weight successfully in the Thatcham Handicap Chase. It was hoped that Isle of Man would be Her Majesty's 300th winner in the Newbury Spring Handicap Chase the next day but he was just beaten by Helen Mildmay-White's Uncle Bing.

Next week Queen Elizabeth came to Ascot to see Sunyboy run in the three-mile Fernbank Hurdle. He had been rather disappointing in his previous races earlier in the season on ground which did not suit him, and it was feared that the going at Ascot would be firmer than he liked. As a result, Prince Eleigh, trained in the West Country, was thought by many to be the probable winner. To the delight of the crowd, however, Sunyboy, ridden by Smith, gradually wore down Prince Eleigh, and in the end won decisively. Queen Elizabeth was particularly delighted that her 300th winner should come at Ascot and that she had postponed a couple of private engagements to come down to see Sunyboy run. On such occasions television, however well presented, is definitely a poor second to the racecourse itself.

105 Sunyboy (W. Smith) on his way to victory in the Fernbank Hurdle on 18 February 1976, Queen Elizabeth's 300th winner under N.H. rules.

106 Isle of Man (W. Smith) on his way to victory in the Magna Carta Chase at Windsor on 25 February 1976. C. Goldsworthy on Chance A Look is following.

Later in the afternoon, Walwyn and Smith were invited up to celebrate the occasion with Sunyboy's owner. 'It was one of Ascot's greatest moments,' reported a racing scribe. 'The Queen Mother, steeplechasing's first lady, rose from her seat in the Royal Box, and clapped with pleasure as Sunyboy swept by to victory. A cheer lit up a cold grey afternoon.' At Windsor a week later, Isle of Man added to the score—his first victory of a season in which he did not have the soft ground he liked. At the National Hunt meeting at Cheltenham, Game Spirit ran in the National Hunt Two Mile Champion Chase in preference to the Piper Champagne Cheltenham Gold Cup. Three fences from home he looked to be going like a winner but made mistakes at the next two fences and lost his chance. The winner was his old rival Skymas, whom he met at level weights. On old form, Game Spirit should certainly have beaten Skymas at these weights, but it was one of the few occasions in his racing life that he blundered badly twice and paid the penalty. Game Spirit rallied towards the end of the race and ran on up the hill to finish second.

When the going firmed up in April, Colonius was in action again, winning at Towcester and winning at Worcester in record time although it was only a match. He ended up by giving Smith two horrible falls at Ludlow and at Fontwell in May, by which time the ground was unpleasantly hard. Poor Branford was on the sidelines, and his race-riding was at an end, due to a smashed wrist and arm.

When the new 1976–77 season started, Queen Elizabeth only had six horses in training—her smallest number for twenty years. Sunyboy, with leg trouble threatening, had been sold and had gone to stud. Game Spirit, Isle of Man and Colonius were still on the war path. Little Colman was still in training but just failing to meet with success. Queen's College, a half-brother to Isle of Man and company by the Sandringham 'teaser' College Green, and Desert Wind, a half-brother by Dear Gazelle to the brilliant Black Magic, were the young horses yet to prove themselves.

Isle of Man had come from Fairlawne in charge of a Kentish lad Peter Standen who was the only Fairlawne man to stay on at Saxon House. He was looking after Isle of Man on Cazalet's death and he did not want to be parted. He had already looked after Chaou II, Zaloba and two other horses of Queen Elizabeth's at Fairlawne, and now at Saxon House he had Colonius to do as well as Isle of Man.

Colonius, as usual, was in action first in the new season. Standen and Tommy Turvey, ex-flyweight boxer and Walwyn's experienced travelling head lad, took him to run at Worcester three days after Queen Elizabeth's birthday on August 4. Turvey had served his time as an apprentice with Vernell Hobbs at Park Farm, Lambourn, had gone back to Ireland to ride work for Paddy Beary, had done stud work at Lord Glentoran's New Abbey stud near The Curragh, and had come back to Lambourn in 1954, working for a few months for Keith Piggott before joining Walwyn in 1955.

Turvey, slim and short and who still looks as if he could go to scale as a flyweight, has had few horses who have really alarmed him in the fifty years he has worked with horses. Colonius is one of them, and Colonius at Saxon House used to answer to the name of 'Mouse', because he was so completely un-mouse-like in all his ways! 'We took him to Ascot to run as a five-year-old in a hurdle race in his first season here,' recalled Turvey, 'and Ron Barry rode him and he had a fairly hard race. It happened to be the last race of the day, and "Mouse", who was a worrier, got very overwrought after it. Not knowing the horse well then, we loaded him up fairly quickly after the race, without giving him much time to unwind, and made for home. Before we realised what was happening, Colonius had nearly climbed over the top partition of the horse box into the driver's seat! We stopped, let down the ramp of the box and somehow managed to pull Colonius out—mainly by the tail, with some strong shoulder work by "Big Pete" Standen. If the horse had not been fairly dazed, I don't know what would have happened. It was really frightening.

'After this experience, Colonius always rode in the back of the horse box so imagine our consternation on the way to Worcester with Colonius as Queen Elizabeth's first runner of the 1976–77 season, when a tyre of the horse box burst on the motorway. Neither Standen nor I much fancied getting Colonius out of the horse box onto the motorway whilst we changed the tyre. We felt he would probably go berserk, but the police came to our rescue. Hearing that one of Queen Elizabeth's horses was inside the horse box and a very difficult customer, they closed two lanes of the motorway whilst the tyre was changed, and we got away with it. What is more, when we got him to Worcester, the happenings on the motorway had not taken too much out of "Mouse", and he won his race.'

Colonius, Bill Smith up, having defeated two opponents at Worcester on the Saturday on the hard ground he liked, stayed on at Worcester over the weekend and defeated a single opponent in another two-mile chase on the Monday. Turvey and Standen gave 'Mouse' plenty of time to unwind after the race before they set out for Lambourn on the return journey in the horse box! At the beginning of September, three weeks later, Bill Smith, Turvey, Standen and 'Mouse' went down to Newton Abbot to win the Viscountess Petersham Trophy—Queen Elizabeth's first victory at Newton Abbot. Less than three weeks later at Plumpton, Colonius gained his fourth victory of the season in the South Downs Chase. This Plumpton victory was far from bloodless, for he beat Mighty Marine, another hard ground specialist, fair and square after Mighty Marine had made the running for the greater part of the race. Mighty Marine had won seven races off the reel before Colonius humbled him. It was perhaps his best performance.

Queen Elizabeth returned from a five-day official visit to France towards the end of October and the day after her return went down to Sandown and saw a brilliant display of jumping by Isle of Man when winning the Pirbright Handicap Chase under top weight. Bill Smith reported to Queen Elizabeth afterwards: 'I made all the running and was never off the bridle. Like Game Spirit, he is one hundred per cent genuine and always a very good horse indeed when he is fresh.' Fulke Walwyn put it succinctly in five words: 'He jumped his rivals silly.' Later in the afternoon, Isle of Man's half-brother Queen's College appeared for the first time in the new season in Division II of the Waterloo Novices' Hurdle. He started favourite in a big field and ran well to finish third, but he was not going to prove as good as his three winning half-brothers.

A week later, with the soft ground he liked, Isle of Man was in action

107 Colonius (W. Smith) winning the South Downs Chase at Plumpton on 20 September 1976.

again in the Buckinghamshire Chase at Windsor where he had a tough opponent to face in Spanish Tan, who had shown good form in Ireland the previous season and had just beaten the spectacular American chaser Tingle Creek on his favourite Sandown course. 'Isle of Man made all the running again,' recalled Bill Smith, 'but he is really better suited by a left-handed track, because he is inclined to go left-handed when in trouble and the last part of the Windsor figure of eight course is right-handed. He blundered badly at the third last after the intersection of the courses, he got too close to the last two fences, and in a desperate finish with Spanish Tan we only got home by inches.'

Standen—'Big Pete' to the other lads as he was the heaviest stableman in the Walwyn team—had so far that season taken Queen Elizabeth's two chasers Colonius and Isle of Man six times to the races and had always led them away from the winners' enclosure in triumph. That season he was also travelling a novice chaser of Walwyn's called Never Rock, who proceeded to win his first three races. 'That must be a record,' said Walwyn as Never Rock completed his hat-trick. And, to the best of my knowledge, no one disputed Walwyn's claim on behalf of his heaviest lad.

Meanwhile, whilst the half-brothers Colonius and Isle of Man were doing their Royal owner proud during the autumn of 1976, Game Spirit was also preparing to do battle. He had come out like a giant refreshed to run exceptionally well in his first race of the 1973 season as a seven-year-old, again as an eight-year-old in 1974 and again as a nine-year-old in 1975. He had been second in the Mackeson Gold Cup in the first year, just beaten by the brilliant Pendil in the Hermitage Chase at Newbury in the second year and the winner of the Hermitage Chase in the third year. Now, in 1976, Queen Elizabeth and Walwyn planned to start him off with another tilt at the Hermitage Chase. Walwyn, Mould, Branford, Smith and his Lincolnshire lad, Peter Payne, were just five people who knew from personal experience that Game Spirit loved Newbury and was a better horse there than anywhere else.

The only thing was that Fred Winter, training on Walwyn's doorstep at Lambourn, thought that the Hermitage Chase at Newbury would also be an appropriate race for the brilliant Bula. Winter had taken Bula up to Market Rasen in Lincolnshire near Peter Payne's old home for his first race of the new season and he had won in a canter. The American horse Soothsayer, second to Ten Up in the 1975 Piper Champagne Cheltenham Gold Cup, was also an intended runner in the race. It was a difficult decision for Queen Elizabeth and Walwyn to take whether to tackle an ex-Champion hurdler, full of speed at the start of a new season. Soothsayer had been on the sidelines after running in the Colonial Cup in America nearly a year before and so was almost certainly in need of a race. Game Spirit was due to receive four pounds from Bula and Bula was apt to make mistakes and had not shone at Newbury before as he had done at Cheltenham. Queen Elizabeth decided on a fighting policy.

There were four runners in the 1976 Hermitage Chase—Bula, now an eleven-year-old, ridden by the reigning champion jockey John Francome, giving four pounds to the other three runners, Game Spirit, Soothsayer, and Sir John Thomson's Lean Forward, a useful handicap chaser and a half-brother to the Cheltenham Gold Cup winner Fort Leney but on form not with the same ability as the other three stars. It was mixed racing that day at Newbury but the meeting of Bula and Game Spirit made the flat racing seem tame stuff.

As the four runners came into the straight with four fences to jump, it was already, in effect, a match between Game Spirit and Bula with Game Spirit definitely jumping the better. There was little between the two over the last four fences, but Game Spirit jumped the last superbly and that, I think, turned the scales, for he won all out by one length. Bula had made mistakes, as he was apt to do over fences, and Game Spirit had not, so Game Spirit deservedly gained the day. It was Game Spirit's ninth victory at Newbury and his twenty-first for Queen Elizabeth, and, in the view of Peter Payne, his devoted lad, it was his best.

108 Queen Elizabeth
with Game Spirit, Bill
Smith, Fulke Walwyn and
Peter Payne in the
unsaddling enclosure at
Newbury after the 1976
Hermitage Chase,
23 October 1976.

'I told Bill Smith that I felt the only way to beat Bula was to get him
hard at it and take him on all the way,' said Walwyn after the race, 'so that is
what Smith did and, in my view, he rode a brilliant race.' Queen Elizabeth
had come south from Scotland ten days before and saw Game Spirit and
Bula stealing the show. Reporting to Queen Elizabeth after the race, Bill
Smith, neat of figure and of a similar build to David Mould, modestly gave
all praise to Game Spirit. 'I was out to dictate the pace,' he said, 'and I got
first run on Bula going to the second last, and Game Spirit then beat Bula
for foot. Game Spirit flew the second last and the last superbly in his desire
to win, and we just got home.'

Without flinching, Game Spirit had given his all to win the Newbury
race and he was given plenty of time to get over it. He was to have made
his third attempt to win the Mackeson Gold Cup at Cheltenham in
November but the course was not fit to race on owing to a drought and the
meeting did not take place. He did not reappear until over two months
later at the Boxing Day meeting at Kempton in the Kenton Chase in which
he met his old rival Pendil and Spanish Tan, whom Isle of Man had just
beaten at Windsor. Pendil had had leg trouble and had been off the course
for nearly two years and Game Spirit was expected to win, but he ran
inexplicably badly and finished a bad last. Walwyn was mystified and
asked for a dope test and had his heart tested but the dope test was
negative and the vet could find nothing wrong with the horse. Bill Smith
at the time put it down to the ground which was rather loose and greasy
and on which Game Spirit did not jump with confidence.

Queen Elizabeth also hoped to see Isle of Man win his third race off the reel that day but the going was not soft enough to suit Isle of Man and he was beaten on merit by Mr John Rogerson's Early Spring, to whom he was giving a stone, and to the disappointment of Queen Elizabeth, in spite of soft ground, Early Spring beat Isle of Man again a fortnight later at Sandown.

At Newbury in mid-February, however, the going really came right for Isle of Man in the Newbury Spring Chase in which he carried top weight. 'I had to give over a stone that day to Dulwich, a well bred horse by Tamerlane, who took a lot of beating on his day,' recalled Smith. 'Most people thought Dulwich would win, but Isle of Man out-jumped him and beat him fair and square. It was Isle of Man at his best.' Isle of Man's success in this Newbury race was a Red Letter Day for 'Big Pete' Standen, for it was the twenty-fifth winner he had turned out for Queen Elizabeth—Zaloba and Chaou II for three races at Fairlawne, and Isle of Man and Colonius for twenty-two races between them at Saxon House. It is thought that no other stableman has had so high a total of Royal winners, and Queen Elizabeth sent Standen a special letter with a signed photograph to mark the occasion.

Nearly a month after Isle of Man's Newbury victory, Queen Elizabeth decided on Walwyn's suggestion to bring Game Spirit back to his favourite course for his next race and to attempt to win the Geoffrey Gilbey Chase for the second time. He had carried 11 st 8 lbs to victory in this race in 1975. Now, two years later, he had 12 st 4 lbs to shoulder in yielding going—a tough assignment. In fact, in the race he started to lose his good position with over half a mile to go and was clearly beaten at the bottom end of the course. He eventually finished a tired fifth of the field of eight, and went out of sight with the rest of the field behind the stand beyond the winning post. No one in the stands, which included his devoted owner and trainer, ever saw him alive again. Bill Smith, after pulling up, was just about to leave the course and bring him back to be unsaddled when Andy Turnell, who was beside Game Spirit at the time, saw him stagger sideways and shouted to Bill Smith to jump off, and a moment later down poor Game Spirit went.

It so happened that Geoffrey Brain, a leading veterinary surgeon, was on the spot, about to listen to another horse's wind, and he immediately hurried across to Game Spirit, but the horse was dead when he went down. Walwyn was quickly on the spot. He arranged for a post mortem which was carried out at the Department of Pathology at Bristol University. It showed a massive haemorrhage of the lungs and there were also signs of minor haemorrhages from the past, indicating that Game Spirit had probably burst minor internal blood vessels in previous races. With hindsight, it seems probable that when Game Spirit suddenly 'died' in Biddlecombe's hands in the 1974 Cheltenham Gold Cup after appearing to be on the bit, this was the unseen cause, and likewise that when Game

109 Game Spirit (W. Smith) jumping the water in the Geoffrey Gilbey Memorial Chase at Newbury on 5 March 1977—his last race.

Spirit ran very badly in a match against Soothsayer at Wincanton, something similar happened.

In sending the pathological report to Walwyn, Brain wrote: 'It is strange that the haemorrhage is over such a wide area of tissue and involves so many of the smaller pulmonary blood vessels rather than the main pulmonary artery. Obviously it must have affected Game Spirit during his race. How he finished so gamely amazes me. He certainly lived up to his name to his last breath—a very courageous horse. My sympathy and regret that you have lost him.'

Peter Payne, who had joined Captain 'Ossie' Bell as a thirteen-year-old apprentice at Lambourn in 1942, and had been with Walwyn since 1954, was, like everyone else, completely taken by surprise by Game Spirit's collapse. 'Game Spirit was never off his food and never had a day's illness,' recalled Payne. 'If he had been off his food, we would have suspected something. In my view, he had everything a racehorse should have, well-mannered and no vice to his name. The only trouble that he gave me was that he was very ticklish. He did not like me dressing him over. He only let me do his mane and tail.' Payne was hoping one day that Game Spirit would go for the Grand National. He had taken three Walwyn horses to Aintree—Armorial, Lord Jim and Royal Ruse and he was hoping that Game Spirit would be the fourth, but it was not to be.

The news was broken to Queen Elizabeth, who later asked to see Bill Smith. He reported to her that he had had no feeling during the race that anything was seriously wrong with Game Spirit, although he had been disappointed when he had dropped back five fences from home. 'Queen

Elizabeth was very sad,' said Smith later. 'Her Majesty told me that Game Spirit was to have gone as a hack for the Queen when his racing days were over. Game Spirit had a charming character and he would have been a marvellous hack.' His bare record showed that he had finished in the first three in all but thirteen of his forty-seven races.

Game Spirit's death was given out over the loudspeakers at Newbury. Jack Logan, writing in *The Sporting Life*, expressed well what racing people felt about Game Spirit and his owner. 'I happened to be listening in at the racecourse betting shop at Newbury on Saturday,' wrote Jack Logan, 'when the voice of the Exchange Telegraph Company announced that the Queen Mother's Game Spirit had died. By and large we are a cynical and money-grubbing lot who gather there between races to hear commentaries, and we would usually have resented the interruption. But this was different. We were in truth shocked by the news. Game Spirit was a well-loved horse. And if there is a shorter cut to a bloody nose in Tattersalls than to criticise the Queen Mother in any way, I do not know it. That she had lost a horse she loved was cause enough for grief in common.

'What is this secret of the Queen Mother's spell? Primarily I think that she treats everybody as the same. Whoever her escorts, she always has a smile and a word for stablemen. And the look she gives her horses reflects a love for them which runs parallel with her love for humanity. Such people need no Public Relations officers, for no image maker could improve upon the reality they represent. As we stood shocked and silent, the thought went through my mind that if only her example were more widely followed, there would be new joy in a sport which needs more than anything else to reflect in all its ways her concern for people and horses, her grace in victory and defeat and, above all, her sense of being with and not above us.'

In the passing of Game Spirit, Queen Elizabeth had lost her favourite, but horses like humans cannot go on for ever. With Game Spirit gone, Isle of Man was Queen Elizabeth's only runner at the National Hunt meeting at Cheltenham ten days later. Isle of Man had had the soft ground he wanted during most of the season and had either been first or second in his five races before going to Cheltenham to run in the National Hunt Two-Mile Champion Chase, for which Game Spirit's old rival Bula was favourite. Isle of Man made much of the running but he weakened disappointingly two fences from home and finished third to Skymas and Grangewood Girl. Poor Bula, a year older than Game Spirit, had a nasty fall, damaged a shoulder badly and had to be put down later. Two brave horses had disappeared from the racing scene within ten days of each other. 'Isle of Man had the soft going he liked,' recalled Bill Smith, 'but he never seemed to show his best form at Cheltenham.'

Fulke Walwyn likes to take runners down the motorway to Chepstow, which is within easy reach of Lambourn trainers and, in Walwyn's case, close to his old home near Raglan. On Easter Tuesday, he took Isle of Man down to carry top weight in a two-mile handicap chase and Queen's College and Desert Wind to run in the two divisions of the Raglan Hurdle over two-and-a-half miles. The ground was not soft enough to suit Isle of Man, and Dulwich, on his home course, turned Newbury tables on him decisively. Desert Wind also ran disappointingly but Queen's College deservedly gained his first success in his division of the Raglan Hurdle—Queen Elizabeth's ninth and last winner of the season, of which the three home-bred half-brothers, Colonius, Isle of Man and Queen's College, had won eight. Bill Smith's victory on Queen's College was his 300th success since becoming a professional jockey.

When Queen Elizabeth came down to Saxon House before the start of the 1977–78 season, she had eight horses in training. Two more of her own breeding had come into training—Upton Grey and Colonial Lad, the latter being a full brother to Colonello and Colman and the last foal sired by the gallant Colonist II, who was twenty-seven years old when he sired him. Colonial Lad's dam Mandella had been the only mare Colonist II had got in foal in 1972. Colonial Lad looked to have much more scope than Colman, but he had not as much speed and he just failed to make the grade under National Hunt rules, although he came near to winning once or twice. Upton Grey was by the versatile Whistler horse Rugantino, a winner on the flat, over hurdles and over fences, Upton Grey being the second foal of Queen Elizabeth's Colonist II mare Colonia. He was not to win in his first season at Saxon House but he was to do so in his second.

Queen Elizabeth found 'Big Pete' Standen still looking after Colonius and Isle of Man, but Colonius failed to repeat his succession of victories of the previous season in the early autumn, and only won one of his four races, jumping without confidence. A front runner without confidence is a bad risk and 'Mouse' ran his last race for Queen Elizabeth at Wincanton in October as a nine-year-old, leaving the racing scene as the winner of fourteen races over the six previous seasons. He was to go hunting.

Standen was able to tell Queen Elizabeth that his favourite, Isle of Man, was becoming easier to handle. In the off season in a paddock near the Standens' house, Jason Standen, aged four, had on one occasion successfully led Isle of Man from the paddock to the yard. Standen thought it might be something to do with the fact that Mrs Standen was apt to feed Polos to the horses in the paddock near their house and she had noticed that when Isle of Man sighted the Polos he would not allow any other horse to come near! She told Queen Elizabeth about this one day and Queen Elizabeth replied that she was not at all surprised as she remembered that Isle of Man was particularly greedy when she fed the horses at Sandringham!

110 Isle of Man (W. Smith) leading Count Kinure (J. Francome) at the last fence before winning Ascot's Dunkirk Chase on 26 October 1977.

Queen Elizabeth went racing for the first time in the 1977–78 season at the end of September when she supported the Perth Hunt meeting in aid of the Queen's Silver Jubilee appeal and was delighted to see one of the hurdle races won by a mare owned by Mrs W. H. Crawford, mother of Susan Crawford who had painted a picture of the Queen on her hurdler Worcran, which she had much admired.

A month later at Ascot, Queen Elizabeth saw Isle of Man, Bill Smith up, make every yard of the running to win the Dunkirk Chase under top weight. Like Game Spirit, he seemed to be at his best as a fresh horse first time out in a new season. It was hoped that he would take part in the first running of the Game Spirit Chase at the February meeting at Newbury in memory of Queen Elizabeth's chaser but the meeting could not take place owing to frost.

At Newbury at the beginning of March, Queen Elizabeth brought off her only double of the season, both ridden under difficulty, because of injury, by Bill Smith. Two of her young horses Queen's College and Desert Wind were her winners, Queen's College just winning a division of the three-mile Burford Novices' Chase and Desert Wind the two-mile Snelsmore Handicap Chase. 'Bill Smith at Newbury today turned up stiff and sore with a chipped bone in one arm and a mass of bruises on the other,' reported John Oaksey in *The Daily Telegraph*. 'He went home feeling better, having twice been greeted in the winner's enclosure by Queen Elizabeth through the victories of Queen's College and Desert Wind. Nelson Bay tried to make all the running in his division of the

Burford Chase but hit the last two fences and Queen's College was the only one with enough energy left to take advantage. Queen's College caught Nelson Boy almost on the line after Smith had had to use his right arm with the chipped elbow.

'At the second fence of the Snelsmore Chase, Smith hit his damaged elbow on his own knee, so it was just as well that Desert Wind began to hang to his left as he and Firesilk fought out the finish, Desert Wind being magnificently served left-handed by Smith.' Desert Wind looked a good prospect for the future, winning his third race of the season at Hereford in May, but, as bad luck would have it, Desert Wind came down heavily on a road, damaging his knees badly. He was never to come sound again, and eventually had to be put down.

During the year, Queen Elizabeth was the guest of honour at a small luncheon given by the trustees of the Injured Jockeys Fund—Edward Courage, John Barstow, Bob McCreery, John Oaksey, Mrs Lester Piggott, Brough Scott and Fred Winter. Her Majesty had agreed to become patron of the Fund during her first season at Saxon House. Having seen nearly all her principal jockeys suffering from bad falls at one time or another—Dick Francis, Arthur Freeman, Gene Kelly, David Mould, Bill Rees, Terry Biddlecombe and Bill Smith amongst them— Queen Elizabeth had been acutely aware of the problems of injured jockeys from her early days of ownership at Fairlawne.

When two of the leading jump jockeys of the day—Tim Brookshaw and Paddy Farrell—were partly paralysed by ghastly falls in the 1963–64 season, Clifford Nicholson and Edward Courage, at the time two of the leading owners in National Hunt racing, launched an appeal on their behalf, which Queen Elizabeth supported. Started a week after Farrell had broken his back in a fall in the 1964 Grand National, nearly £50,000 was subscribed within a month, and Brookshaw and Farrell then generously requested that some of the money subscribed should go to other injured steeplechase jockeys. As a result, the Injured National Hunt Jockeys Fund was established in May 1964 under the chairmanship of Clifford Nicholson, by whom Farrell was retained at the time of his fall. Nicholson, Edward Courage, the future Lord Oaksey, Wing Commander Peter Vaux from Yorkshire and Fred Winter were the five original trustees, John Barstow, a London solicitor, acting as secretary. The purpose was to give assistance to any steeplechase jockey or his family if a jockey was hurt or killed in the course of his profession. Similarly in 1971 the Injured Jockeys Fund was formed to cater for jockeys under both codes and to take the place of the original fund.

Christmas cards have been the principal source of income of the fund since the first appeal and this has been organised by a band of volunteers based on Knebworth in Hertfordshire under the guidance of Barbara Bateson, wife of a London solicitor. Stirred by the enterprise, Queen

Elizabeth took the trouble in the fund's early days to go to visit Barbara Bateson and the hut in her garden which at the time was the hub of the Christmas card distribution. Shortly before she agreed to become patron of the Injured Jockeys Fund, Queen Elizabeth had gone north to watch the Whitbread Gold Cup which was run at Newcastle during the rebuilding of the stands at Sandown. She had returned south much saddened by the fatal injuries sustained by Doug Barrott in a fall early in the race and was impressed at the same time by the importance of the fund.

Queen Elizabeth had six horses of her own breeding at Saxon House at the beginning of the 1978–79 season—the half-brothers Isle of Man and Queen's College, both proven performers, Upton Grey and Colonial Lad from the previous season, and the newcomers Roman Jack and Black Bear. Roman Jack was a first foal by David Jack out of Roman Meeting, the mare Edward Courage had given Queen Elizabeth as a birthday present; Black Bear was a gelding by March Past out of Mascara, the mare John Oxx had trained in Ireland for Queen Elizabeth to win as a four-year-old. Unfortunately neither Roman Jack nor Black Bear made the grade, pointing once again to the fact that only one racehorse in four wins a race of any sort. Fortunately other members of the Royal Family are now keen on hunting and eventing, so there are other uses at hand for those who do not make the grade as racehorses. The Prince of Wales has been down to Saxon House and schooled some of his grandmother's horses, and Princess Anne has been down on more than one occasion, too.

With the home-breds rather disappointing for a change, the hope of the side was Special Cargo, bought on Queen Elizabeth's behalf as a five-year-old at the Doncaster Bloodstock Sales in 1978, having won a two-mile flat race at Naas three months before. Walwyn was hopeful that Special Cargo and Upton Grey would win the two divisions of the Speen Novices Hurdle at the Newbury November meeting of 1978. Upton Grey was equal to the occasion and Special Cargo ran with promise to finish second.

At Newbury in February, Isle of Man finished third in the Game Spirit Chase, which Queen Elizabeth naturally hoped to win. Dropped in class, Isle of Man went to Worcester in March, found the soft ground he liked, and ridden as usual by Bill Smith, jumped really well, led from pillar to post, and just held on to win under top weight. At Chepstow on Easter Monday, Walwyn found another opportunity for Isle of Man in a two-mile chase, and he just succeeded in making practically all the running, giving two stone to the runner-up. Upton Grey won two novice hurdles and Special Cargo three, with Smith always on board.

The disappointment of the season was Queen's College who had a blank year. It was hoped that he would win the *Horse and Hound* Grand Military Gold Cup at Sandown, and Major Christopher Price, one of the best soldier riders amongst his contemporaries, was engaged to ride. Price had already won the race in 1977 on Double Bridal. Queen's College jumped well, but he was outpaced in the final half mile by the Cheltenham Gold Cup winner Ten Up, as was to be expected, and Queen's College finished second. Queen Elizabeth's chaser was placed in five of his six races without winning. There was no doubt that Game Spirit was being very much missed.

On 4 February 1979, England's oldest trainer Miss Norah Wilmot, to whom Queen Elizabeth had sent Devon Loch and other horses to be stabled and exercised whilst under treatment from Sir Charles Strong, celebrated her ninetieth birthday with a party in the Ascot grandstand. It was given for her by an owner-breeder, Mr N. R. H. Graham and his wife, who formerly assisted Miss Wilmot. Queen Elizabeth arrived before lunch to wish Norah Wilmot a happy birthday and to meet her staff, relations and many racing friends. When Norah Wilmot retired at the end of the 1979 season and went into hospital in failing health, Queen Elizabeth, with her kind heart, made a personal journey down to Berkshire to see her and to cheer her up.

For the new season of 1979–80, the Queen leased to Queen Elizabeth her useful middle-distance horses Rhyme Royal and Cranbourne Tower to run over hurdles. To the delight of the holiday crowd, Rhyme Royal won the valuable sponsored G. J. Novices Hurdle at Kempton on Boxing Day — Queen Elizabeth's last winner of the 1970s and her 328th in all. It was Rhyme Royal's second appearance over hurdles. At Sandown, he made rather a disappointing hurdling début when Bill Smith tried to get him to settle. At Kempton, he was allowed to stride along from the start and set such a strong pace that at half way he had his opponents strung out in a long line behind him and he won in the end virtually unchallenged. Bill Smith, reporting to Queen Elizabeth after the race, said: 'Rhyme Royal didn't jump well at Sandown when I tried to get him to settle. He was much happier today, bowling along in front, and I think the sharp Kempton course suited him well. At one stage he was jumping a bit to the left through greenness, but he ran on really well in the straight to win his race.' By Sir Victor Sassoon's Derby winner Crepello out of the good race mare Lyrical, who was owned and bred by Mrs George Lambton, Rhyme Royal, a dark chestnut, is full of good looks. He is perhaps on the small side to make a top class hurdler, but certainly knows how to gallop.

The G. J. Novices Hurdle hid the names of the sponsors Mr and Mrs George Jackson who won the 1978 Piper Champagne Cheltenham Gold Cup with Midnight Court. Their horses are trained by Fred Winter and run in the name of Olive Jackson. George Jackson had chosen a most attractive bronze of a mare and foal as the trophy for the winning owner, which gave Queen Elizabeth particular pleasure to receive. She had much admired it. George Jackson, through his sponsoring company, had arranged that the Injured Jockeys Fund would benefit by £10 for each

111 Cranbourne Tower (K. Mooney) winning at Windsor on 26 January 1980—Queen Elizabeth's first winner of the 1980s.

runner in his race. As there were sixteen runners, the fund benefited by £160—an innovation in the conditions of the race which also appealed to Her Majesty.

Queen Elizabeth's first winner of the 1980s was Cranbourne Tower, like Rhyme Royal bred by the Queen at Sandringham on classic lines. Cranbourne Tower is by Mr H. J. Joel's Derby winner Royal Palace out of the Hethersett mare Heathfield, who has also bred two good winners in Ascot Heath and Fife and Drum, and a useful racemare in Crofting. Cranbourne Tower ran well in a handicap at Royal Ascot 1979 for the Queen, and is of a better class than most recruits to hurdling.

Looking back over Queen Elizabeth's thirty years as an owner of steeplechasers, one thinks in the first ten years particularly of the 1949 victory of her first horse Monaveen in the first running of the Queen Elizabeth Chase at Hurst Park, of Manicou's victory a year later in the King George VI Chase at Kempton Park, of Devon Loch's tragic collapse in the 1956 Grand National with the race in his pocket, and of Double Star's victory in the Tote Investors Cup at Newbury against some of the best novices of the season.

In the 1960s, I think of Queen Elizabeth's memorable Lingfield treble at the December meeting of 1961 with three of her favourites—Double Star, Laffy and The Rip, of Laffy's victory in the Ulster Harp National, of the conquering run of Makaldar as a novice hurdler in the 1963–64 season, of Worcran's narrow defeat in the Champion Hurdle of 1964 and of Queen Elizabeth's exciting treble at Folkestone soon after Gay Record had won her her 100th race. I think, too, of The Rip's defeat of Frenchman's Cove at Kempton in 1965 and of Silver Dome's dramatic victory in the Becher Chase at Aintree in the same season. At the end of 1969, Queen Elizabeth had her 200th winner with Master Daniel in a humble novices' hurdle at Worcester.

In the 1970s, there was the close third of Escalus in the 1970 Champion Hurdle after a string of hurdling successes earlier in the season. I think, also, of Black Magic's defeat of Crisp in a marvellous duel at Sandown in 1971 and of Inch Arran's fluent victory in the Topham Trophy at Aintree in 1973—Cazalet's 250th and last winner for Queen Elizabeth. In Saxon House days, I remember vividly the duel between Pendil and Game Spirit at Newbury, the victory of Tammuz in the 1975 Schweppes Gold Trophy at Newbury and Game Spirit's defeat of Bula in the 1976 Hermitage Chase at Newbury—Game Spirit's twenty-first and last victory for Queen Elizabeth.

There are other races and other horses I should perhaps have mentioned—Antiar's gallant victory in the Spa Hurdle at the National Hunt meeting at Cheltenham in 1965, Chaou II's success in the Whitelaw Challenge Cup in 1972—his sixteenth and last but one victory for Queen Elizabeth—and the marvellous jumping of the front-running Isle of Man in recent years.

What are Queen Elizabeth's racing prospects in the 1980s? Apart from Rhyme Royal and Cranbourne Tower, she has six horses in training with Walwyn—the half-brothers Isle of Man and Queen's College who are probably near the end of their racing days, two promising horses in Special Cargo and Upton Grey who have proved their usefulness and two young horses in the five-year-old Brown Bowler and the four-year-old Russhill.

With William Hastings-Bass at Newmarket are the four-year-old filly Manushi by the stayer Crozier out of Roman Meeting, her three-year-old half-brother Hadrian's Wall by the Eclipse Stakes winner Scottish Rifle out of Roman Meeting, and Upton Grey's half sister Joliette, a two-year-old of character by the top class miler Jimmy Reppin out of Colonia. There are a couple of young horses being brought on by Major Eldred Wilson at Harpley Dams and a couple of two-year-olds with Mrs C. H. Bennion, widow of a well-known farmer and permit holder of Bircham Newton not far from Harpley Dams. There are a couple of yearlings at Windsor and one at the Queen's Polhampton Lodge Stud near Kingsclere in Hampshire.

Queen Elizabeth has four brood mares based on Sandringham. The grey Colonia is now the eldest. She traces to a mare of Sidney McGregor's breeding, and to the same family traces the unraced mare Heather Deep, who is by the Queen's Eclipse Stakes winner Canisbay out of Nicola, the dam of Charlot. Roman Meeting, as a twelve-year-old, is now Queen Elizabeth's second oldest mare. Her daughter Manushi is due to come into the stud after her hurdling days are over. Mandella, the dam of Colonello, dropped down dead in a paddock in 1979 at the age of twenty-two, six weeks after producing a Barolo filly foal. Mandella's unraced daughter Barbella has now taken her place in the stud.

Three years ago Mr and Mrs John Hislop decided to give Queen Elizabeth as a birthday present a free nomination to their gallant racehorse Brigadier Gerard. Roman Meeting was the mare chosen to visit Brigadier Gerard in 1978 and in March 1979 Roman Meeting gave birth to an outstanding colt foal at Wolferton under the expert eye of Pat Ryan, the stud groom. In Ryan's view the Brigadier Gerard-Roman Meeting foal was the best foal seen at Wolferton throughout the 1979 season, a view confirmed by Michael Oswald.

Perhaps this yearling of 1980, now at Polhampton, is Queen Elizabeth's big hope for the future. Who knows? In horse breeding so much can so easily go wrong, but whatever happens Queen Elizabeth will continue to enjoy her racing and will continue to show kindness and consideration to all sorts of people, whether it be some of the aged and infirm of Ascot who, from a special vantage point, watch the Royal Procession form up, or

112   Queen Elizabeth's promising Brigadier Gerard-Roman Meeting colt as a five months old foal in August 1979.

hunting friends enjoying their sport on one of her discards, or a stableman or a jockey or a horse-breeder, valuing a personal letter of praise or thanks.

With Queen Elizabeth's eightieth birthday, I am reminded of a story told by Princess Marie Louise about Queen Elizabeth on her wedding to the future King George VI in 1923. Princess Marie Louise recalled that at the wedding reception she turned to Queen Elizabeth's mother, the Countess of Strathmore, and said, 'How lovely Elizabeth looks.' Lady Strathmore's face lit up as she replied, 'Elizabeth not only looks lovely, she is lovely. I do not believe she has ever had an ugly thought or said an ugly thing in all her life.'

Since that April day fifty-seven years ago, many ugly things have happened in the world and the Second World War left many scars. The most Christian of people must have had ugly thoughts as they lost those they loved and Queen Elizabeth, under such conditions and seeing so much devastation and suffering in bombed Britain, cannot have been without such thoughts. Nevertheless, as far as steeplechasing is concerned, racing people know that Queen Elizabeth for the last thirty years has shown herself caring and considerate and also highly appreciative of courage and skill and good work done. All racing people hope that Lady Strathmore's 'Lovely Person' will remain a friend to and a champion of steeplechasing for many more years to come.

ENDPIECE   Queen Elizabeth talking to Isle of Man's lad, Pete Standen, at Windsor.

APPENDIX 1

Queen Elizabeth's Winning Steeplechasers and Hurdlers up to the end of the 1979–80 season.

Horse (year of birth)	Breeding	Number of victories
Antiar (1958)	b.g. Antares—V. Day	5
Arch Point (1960)	b.g. Archive–Sol Point	6
Augustine (1957)	ch.g. Aureole—Young Entry	1
Ballykine II (1959)	ch.g. Roi de Navarre II—Flowery Path	6
Bel Ambre (1961)	gr.g. Amber X—Belle Gitane	3
Black Magic (1964)	b.g. Black Tarquin—Ballyrory	7
Burning Bush (1970)	b.g. Lower Boy—Wishbone II	1
Castle Yard (1963)	b.g. St Paddy—Spanish Court	3
Chaou II (1963)	gr.g. Marino—Djanet	17
Charlot (1963)	br.g. Doutelle—Nicola	5
Colman (1971)	ch.g. Colonist II—Mandella	1
Colonello (1968)	b.g. Colonist II—Mandella	2
Colonius (1969)	ch.g. Colonist II—Queen of the Isle	14
Colonsay Isle (1964)	gr.g. Colonist II—Queen of the Sea	2
†Cranbourne Tower (1976)	b.c. Royal Palace—Heathfield	1
Dargent (1956)	b.g. Domaha—Silverina	1
Desert Wind (1972)	b.g. Dear Gazelle—Ballyrory	3
Devon Loch (1946)	br.g. Devonian—Coolaleen	6
Double Star (1952)	br.g. Arctic Star—Bright Star	17
Earl's Castle (1969)	b.g. Rubor—Castle Inn	3
Escalus (1965)	b.g. Lord of Verona—Singing Hinny	9
Game Spirit (1966)	ch.g. Game Rights—Castile	21
Gay Record (1952)	b.g. Archive—Merryland	9
Greystoke Pillar (1968)	ch.g. Straight Cut—Residence	6
Hibiscus (1962)	b.g. Tangle—Gay Flower	2
Inch Arran (1964)	gr.g. Colonist II—Queen of the Isle	14
Inquisitive Pete (1952)	ch.g. Grand Inquisitor—Duchess of Pedulas	2
Irish Rover (1960)	ch.g. Star Signal or Vulgan—Random Inn	7
†Isle of Man (1967)	b.g. Manicou—Queen of the Isle	14
Jaipur (1956)	br.g. Bois Roussel—Ynys	3
Just Lit (1967)	br.g. Eborneezer—Hill Flame	1
Kelso Brig (1968)	b.g. New Brig—Coin Box	1
King of the Isle (1951)	ch.g. King Hal—G.B.R.	2
King's Point (1949)	ch.g. Queen's Eyot—Steel Girl	2
Laffy (1956)	b.g. Rigolo—Vatelinde	12

† in training during the 1979–1980 season.

Horse (year of birth)	Breeding	Number of victories
Lochmore (1961)	b.g. Mustang—Loch May	2
Makaldar (1960)	ch.g. Makalu—La Madouna	15
Manicou (1945)	b.h. Last Post—Mylae	3
Master Daniel (1965)	b.g. Night Life—Avanti	5
M'as-tu-vu (1946)	br.g. Pampeiro—Malle Poste	6
Mel (1959)	ch.g. Manicou—Sweeter and Sweeter	3
Monaveen (1941)	b.g. Landscape Hill—Great Double	4
Newbrough (1964)	b.g. New Brig—Smile	3
Oedipe (1958)	br.g. Foxlight—Ondee de Fleurs	4
Out of Town (1954)	b.g. Owenstown—Dismissal	7
Present Arms (1969)	ch.g. Relko—Amicable	1
†Queen's College (1971)	br.g. College Green—Queen of the Isle	2
Retz (1963)	b.g. Franc Luron—Redite	3
†Rhyme Royal (1975)	ch.g. Crepello—Lyrical	1
Silver Dome (1954)	ch.g. Domaha—Silverina	7
Sparkling Knight (1952)	b.g. Cameron—Sparkling Gold	3
†Special Cargo (1973)	b.g. Dairialatan—Little Tot	3
Steel Drum (1965)	b.g. Pandofell—Tommie	1
Stubbs (1964)	ch.g. Preciptic—Bay Fairy	3
Sunyboy (1970)	b.h. Mourne—Fair Bid	5
Super Fox (1957)	b.g. Supertello—Foxy Jane	8
Tammuz (1968)	b.g. Tamerlane—Highlight	4
The Rip (1955)	b.g. Manicou—Easy Virtue	13
Three No Trumps (1959)	b.g. Richard Louis—Gay Romance	1
†Upton Grey (1974)	gr.g. Rugantino—Colonia	2
Wild West (1951)	ch.g. Mustang—Blissful	1
Woodman (1962)	br.g. Woodcut—Kirghiz	5
Worcran (1958)	ch.g. Worden II—Craneuse	2
Young Rajah (1955)	gr.g. Rajah II—Belle Bailey	1
Zaloba (1962)	b.g. Zarathustra—Alesia	3
		330

APPENDIX 2

Winning National Hunt jockeys
up to the end of the 1979–1980 season

D. Mould	106	E. F. Kelly	5	B. Fletcher	1
W. Rees	51	D. V. Dick	4	N. Gaselee	1
W. Smith	49	B. Marshall	4	C. Goldsworthy	1
R. Dennard	38	H. Beasley	3	J. Lehane	1
A. Freeman	22	R. Barry	2	R. McCreery	1
R. Francis	10	D. Nicholson	2	K. Mooney	1
A. Branford	9	W. Powell	2	G. W. Robinson	1
T. Biddlecombe	7	C. Chapman	1	M. Scudamore	1
A. Grantham	5	D. Evatt	1	C. Tinkler	1

APPENDIX 3

Queen Elizabeth's Yearly Record of Winners under National Hunt Rules August 1949–May 1980

Season	Horse	Number of Races Won	Total	Season	Horse	Number of Races Won	Total
1949–50	Monaveen	4	4	1962–63	Double Star	1	
1950–51	Manicou	3	3		Gay Record	1	
1951–52	—	—	—		Silver Dome	1	
1952–53	—	—	—		Super Fox	2	5
1953–54	M'as-tu-vu	2	2	1963–64	Gay Record	1	
1954–55	Devon Loch	2			Laffy	2	
	M'as-tu-vu	2	4		Makaldar	6	
1955–56	Devon Loch	2			Out of Town	2	
	M'as-tu-vu	2	4		The Rip	1	
1956–57	Devon Loch	2			Silver Dome	2	
	Double Star	3			Super Fox	4	18
	King's Point	1	6	1964–65	Antiar	3	
1957–58	Double Star	3			Arch Point	4	
	King of the Isle	1			Ballykine	1	
	King's Point	1			Gay Record	2	
	Wild West	1	6		Laffy	4	
1958–59	Double Star	4			Makaldar	3	
	Out of Town	2			Mel	3	
	Sparkling Knight	3	9		Silver Dome	1	
1959–60	Double Star	2			Super Fox	2	
	Inquisitive Pete	1			The Rip	2	
	King of the Isle	1	4		Worcran	2	27
1960–61	Double Star	1		1965–66	Bel Ambre	2	
	Gay Record	1			Irish Rover	4	
	Inquisitive Pete	1			Laffy	1	
	Jaipur	2			Lochmore	2	
	Silver Dome	1			Makaldar	2	
	The Rip	4	10		Oedipe	1	12
1961–62	Augustine	1		1966–67	Arch Point	2	
	Dargent	1			Ballykine	4	
	Double Star	3			Chaou II	2	
	Gay Record	3			Charlot	2	
	Jaipur	1			Gay Record	1	
	Laffy	4			Hibiscus	1	
1961–62	Out of Town	3			Irish Rover	3	
	The Rip	5			Laffy	1	
	Silver Dome	2			Makaldar	2	
	Young Rajah	1	24		Oedipe	2	

Season	Horse	Number of Races Won	Total	Season	Horse	Number of Races Won	Total
	Retz	1		1972–73	Chaou II	2	
	The Rip	1	22		Colonello	1	
1967–68	Bel Ambre	1			Colonius	1	
	Chaou II	3			Game Spirit	5	
	Charlot	2			Greystoke Pillar	1	
	Makaldar	1			Inch Arran	3	
	Woodman	3	10		Kelso Brig	1	14
1968–69	Antiar	2		1973–74	Colonello	1	
	Ballykine	1			Earl's Castle	2	
	Chaou II	5			Game Spirit	4	
	Charlot	1			Greystoke Pillar	2	
	Escalus	4			Inch Arran	1	
	Newbrough	2			Isle of Man	3	
	Oedipe	1			Tammuz	1	14
	Retz	1		1974–75	Colman	1	
	Stubbs	2			Colonius	3	
	Three No Trumps	1			Earl's Castle	1	
	Woodman	2	22		Game Spirit	2	
1969–70	Black Magic	1			Greystoke Pillar	1	
	Castle Yard	2			Isle of Man	3	
	Chaou II	3			Just Lit	1	
	Escalus	5			Present Arms	1	
	Hibiscus	1			Sunyboy	4	
	Inch Arran	2			Tammuz	3	20
	Makaldar	1		1975–76	Burning Bush	1	
	Master Daniel	3			Colonius	5	
	Steel Drum	1			Game Spirit	3	
	Stubbs	1			Isle of Man	1	
	Zaloba	2	22		Sunyboy	1	11
1970–71	Black Magic	5		1976–77	Colonius	4	
	Castle Yard	1			Game Spirit	1	
	Chaou II	2			Isle of Man	3	
	Colonsay Isle	2			Queen's College	1	9
	Game Spirit	2		1977–78	Colonius	1	
	Inch Arran	6			Desert Wind	3	
	Master Daniel	2			Isle of Man	1	
	Newbrough	1			Queen's College	1	6
	Retz	1		1978–79	Isle of Man	2	
	Zaloba	1	23		Special Cargo	3	
1971–72	Black Magic	1			Upton Grey	2	7
	Game Spirit	4		1979–80	Cranbourne Tower	1	
	Greystoke Pillar	2			Isle of Man	1	
	Inch Arran	2	9		Rhyme Royal	1	3

330

APPENDIX 4

Principal Races Won

(including certain other races mentioned in the text)

Antiar (1958)	11 March 1965	Spa Hurdle, Cheltenham
	19 March 1965	Beech Open Chase, Sandown
	1 May 1965	Wentworth Chase, Ascot
	26 February 1969	Magna Carta Chase, Windsor
Arch Point (1960)	4 November 1964	Marden Hurdle, Folkestone (Folkestone Treble Day)
Black Magic (1964)	16 January 1971	Mar Lodge Chase, Ascot
	6 February 1971	Scilly Isles Chase, Sandown
	6 November 1971	Sandown Park Pattern Chase, Sandown
Chaou II (1963)	6 April 1967	Lancashire Hurdle, Aintree
	28 February 1968	Magna Carta Chase, Windsor
	26 October 1968	Sports Medicine Chase, Newbury
	8 April 1970	Royal Porcelain Chase, Worcester
	11 November 1970	Royal Lodge Chase, Windsor
	30 January 1971	Walter Hyde Chase, Kempton
	22 November 1972	Whitelaw Challenge Cup, Fontwell
	1 December 1972	Ewell Chase, Sandown (run at Kempton)
Charlot (1963)	5 November 1966	Toll House Hurdle, Sandown
	3 March 1967	March Hare Hurdle, Newbury
	8 March 1968	Eastleigh Hurdle, Newbury
Colonius (1969)	10 May 1976	Hanbury Chase, Worcester (broke 2-mile time record for course)
	3 September 1976	Viscountess Petersham Trophy Chase, Devon & Exeter (run at Newton Abbot)
Desert Wind (1972)	3 March 1978	Snelsmore Chase, Newbury
Devon Loch (1946)	5 February 1955	New Century Chase, Hurst Park
	18 March 1955	Beech Open Chase, Sandown
	25 November 1955	Blindley Heath Chase, Lingfield
	14 December 1955	Sandown Chase, Sandown
	(24 March 1956	Grand National, Aintree: collapsed 50 yards from post with race apparently won)
	13 December 1956	Ewell Chase, Sandown

Double Star (1952)	15 December 1956	Maze Hurdle, Hurst Park
	30 November 1957	Tote Investors Cup, Newbury
	24 October 1958	Evenlode Chase, Newbury
	6 December 1958	Ashdown Chase, Lingfield
	8 January 1959	Star and Garter Chase, Hurst Park
	13 February 1960	Gainsborough Chase, Sandown
	3 December 1960	Ashdown Chase, Lingfield
	9 December 1961	Ashdown Chase, Lingfield (Lingfield Treble Day)
	27 January 1962	Hidden Mystery Chase, Lingfield
	9 March 1963	Paddington Chase, Newbury
Escalus (1965)	9 November 1968	Toll House Hurdle, Sandown
	8 November 1969	Ackermann Skeaping Trophy, Sandown
	13 December 1969	Gold Bond Hurdle, Sandown
	20 December 1969	Copper Horse Hurdle, Ascot
	(18 March 1970	3rd to Persian War and Major Rose in Champion Hurdle, Cheltenham)
Game Spirit (1966)	12 March 1971	Lilac Hurdle, Sandown
	11 March 1972	Beech Open Chase, Sandown
	20 January 1973	Royal Windsor Chase, Windsor
	19 March 1973	Whitbread Fremlins Elephant Chase, Folkestone
	24 March 1973	Kencot Chase, Newbury
	(10 November 1973	2nd to Skymas in Mackeson Gold Cup, Cheltenham)
	23 November 1973	Clanfield Chase, Newbury
	31 January 1974	Wincanton Challenge Cup, Wincanton
	20 February 1974	Fairlawne Chase, Windsor
	(14 March 1974	3rd to Captain Christy and The Dikler in Cheltenham Gold Cup)
	(26 October 1974	2nd to Pendil in Hermitage Chase, Newbury)
	1 March 1975	Geoffrey Gilbey Memorial Chase, Newbury
	10 April 1975	Sardan Chase, Ascot
	25 October 1975	Hermitage Chase, Newbury
	14 April 1975	Sardan Chase, Ascot
	23 October 1976	Hermitage Chase, Newbury
Gay Record (1952)	17 November 1961	Withington Stayers' Chase, Sandown
	3 February 1962	Herne the Hunter Chase, Windsor
	9 November 1963	Walton Green Chase, Sandown
	20 October 1964	Sevenoaks Chase, Folkestone (Queen Elizabeth's 200th victory)
	4 November 1964	Canterbury Chase, Folkestone (Folkestone Treble Day)
Inch Arran (1964)	30 November 1970	Round Oak Chase, Windsor
	19 December 1970	Dunkirk Chase, Ascot
	4 November 1971	Winterbourne Chase, Newbury (broke time record for course)

	28 October 1972	B.P. Chase, Aintree (broke time record for course)
	27 December 1972	Christmas Chase, Kempton
	29 March 1973	Topham Trophy, Aintree (broke time record for course)
	17 April 1974	Gratwicke Blagrave Memorial Cup, Cheltenham
Irish Rover (1960)	17 December 1966	Henry VIII Chase, Sandown
Isle of Man (1967)	26 December 1973	Yule Tide Hurdle, Kempton
	4 January 1974	Metropolitan Hurdle, Sandown
	1 November 1974	November Chase, Sandown
	15 November 1974	Hurst Park Chase, Ascot
	29 October 1976	Pirbright Chase, Sandown
	6 November 1976	Buckingham Chase, Windsor
	12 February 1977	Newbury Spring Chase, Newbury
	26 October 1977	Dunkirk Chase, Ascot
King of the Isle (1951)	23 January 1960	Staines Hurdle, Kempton
Laffy (1956)	9 December 1961	Oxted Chase, Lingfield (Lingfield Treble Day)
	17 February 1962	New Century Chase, Hurst Park
	6 April 1962	Ulster Harp National, Downpatrick
	22 February 1964	Manifesto Chase, Lingfield
	(21 March 1964	Grand National, Aintree: fell)
	24 October 1964	Capital and Counties Chase, Newbury
	27 February 1965	Manifesto Chase, Lingfield
Makaldar (1960)	9 November 1963	Toll House Hurdle, Sandown
	11 January 1964	Village Hurdle, Sandown
	7 March 1964	Victor Ludorum Hurdle, Haydock
	19 February 1965	Stroud Green Hurdle, Newbury
	13 November 1965	Mackeson Hurdle, Cheltenham
	29 October 1966	T.W.W. Hurdle, Cheltenham
	3 March 1967	Eastleigh Hurdle, Newbury
	(15 March 1967	2nd to Saucy Kit in Champion Hurdle, Cheltenham)
	18 November 1967	Black and White Gold Cup Chase, Ascot
	3 January 1970	Londesborough Chase, Sandown
Manicou (1945)	24 November 1950	Wimbledon Chase, Kempton
	14 December 1950	Ewell Chase, Sandown
	26 December 1950	King George VI Chase, Kempton
Master Daniel (1965)	3 December 1969	Hindlip Hurdle, Worcester (Queen Elizabeth's 200th victory)
M'as-tu-vu (1946)	5 December 1953	Blindley Heath Chase, Lingfield
	16 March 1955	Sussex Chase, Lingfield
	(26 March 1955	Grand National, Aintree: fell)
	14 March 1956	Sussex Chase, Lingfield
	(24 March 1956	Grand National, Aintree: fell)
Monaveen (1941)	10 October 1949	Chichester Chase, Fontwell (the first winner of many)
	26 November 1949	Walton Green Chase, Sandown
	31 December 1949	Queen Elizabeth Chase, Hurst Park

	11 February 1950	George Williamson Chase, Hurst Park
	(25 March 1950	finished 5th in Grand National, Aintree)
Oedipe (1958)	29 January 1966	Royal Windsor Centenary Chase, Windsor
	29 October 1966	Pratt & Co. Chase, Cheltenham
	1 March 1967	Runnymede Chase, Windsor
Out of Town (1954)	8 December 1961	Blindley Heath Chase, Lingfield
	25 September 1963	Whitelaw Gold Cup, Folkestone
Rhyme Royal (1975)	26 December 1979	G. J. Hurdle, Kempton
Silver Dome (1954)	14 January 1961	Londesborough Chase, Sandown
	9 November 1962	Littleworth Chase, Sandown
	(2 November 1963	2nd to Team Spirit in Grand Sefton Chase, Aintree)
	29 October 1964	Becher Chase, Aintree
Sunyboy (1970)	25 November 1974	Reynoldstown Pattern Hurdle, Wolverhampton
	10 April 1975	Sardan Hurdle, Ascot
	18 February 1976	Fernbank Hurdle, Ascot (Queen Elizabeth's 300th victory)
Super Fox (1957)	4 November 1964	Chilham Chase, Folkestone (Folkestone Treble Day)
Tammuz (1968)	4 January 1974	Metropolitan Hurdle, Sandown
	27 December 1974	Boxing Day Hurdle, Kempton
	16 January 1975	Jamboree Hurdle, Wincanton
	8 February 1975	Schweppes Gold Trophy, Newbury
The Rip (1955)	17 October 1960	Mayflower Hurdle, Hurst Park
	24 April 1961	Fremlins Elephant Chase, Folkestone
	18 October 1961	Grand Sefton Trial Chase, Hurst Park
	23 November 1961	Cottage Rake Chase, Kempton
	9 December 1961	Eridge Chase, Lingfield (Lingfield Treble Day)
	(15 March 1962	Cheltenham Gold Cup: unplaced)
	5 February 1965	Walter Hyde Chase, Kempton
	13 March 1965	Coventry Chase, Kempton
	(27 March 1965	finished 7th in Grand National, Aintree)
	31 October 1966	Newhaven Chase, Plumpton
Worcran (1958)	23 February 1965	Elmdon Hurdle, Birmingham
	(10 March 1965	3rd to Kirriemuir and Spartan General in Champion Hurdle, Cheltenham)
	7 May 1965	Melody Man Trophy, Taunton
Zaloba (1962)	25 January 1971	Robertsbridge Hurdle, Folkestone (a dead-heat)

General Index

Italic indicates illustration

Index of Horses

Principle steeplechasers and hurdlers only, with Queen Elizabeth's own horses in CAPITALS. *Italic* indicates illustrations.